Best Before

Despite record sales and an ever-growing global industry, the simple fact is that videogames are disappearing.

Most obviously, the physical deterioration of discs, cartridges, consoles and controllers means that the data and devices will crumble to dust, and eventually will be lost forever. However, there is more to the disappearance of videogames than plastic corrosion and bit rot. *Best Before* examines how the videogames industry's retail, publishing, technology design, advertising and marketing practices actively produce obsolescence, wearing out and retiring old games to make way for the always new, just out of reach, 'coming soon' title and 'next generation' platform.

Set against the context of material deterioration and the discursive production of obsolescence, *Best Before* examines the conceptual and practical challenges faced within the nascent field of game preservation. Understanding videogames as rich, complex and mutable texts and experiences that are supported and sustained by cultures of gameplay and fandom, *Best Before* considers how – and even whether – we might preserve and present games for future generations.

James Newman is Professor of Digital Media and Director of the Media Futures Research Centre at Bath Spa University. He is the author of numerous books on videogames and gaming cultures including *Videogames* (2004) and *Playing with Videogames* (2008). James is a co-founder of the National Videogame Archive, which is a partnership with the National Media Museum, and is a co-producer of the GameCity international videogames festival.

Best Before

Videogames, Supersession and Obsolescence

James Newman

LONDON AND NEW YORK

First published 2012
by Routledge
2 Park Square, Milton Park, Abingdon, Oxon OX14 4RN

Simultaneously published in the USA and Canada
by Routledge
711 Third Avenue, New York, NY 10017

Routledge is an imprint of the Taylor & Francis Group, an informa business

© 2012 James Newman

British Library Cataloguing in Publication Data
A catalogue record for this book is available from the British Library

Library of Congress Cataloging in Publication Data
Newman, James (James A.)
Best before: videogames, supersession and obsolescence / by James Newman.
p. cm.
Includes bibliographical references and index.
1. Video games. 2. Video games--Social aspects. 3. Video games industry.
4. Video games--Marketing. I. Title.
GV1469.3.N46 2012
794.8--dc23
2011049083

ISBN: 978-0-415-57791-5 (hbk)
ISBN: 978-0-415-57792-2 (pbk)
ISBN: 978-0-203-14426-8 (ebk)

Typeset in Bembo
by Taylor & Francis Books

MIX
Paper from
responsible sources
FSC
www.fsc.org   FSC® C004839

Printed and bound in Great Britain by the MPG Books Group

Contents

Acknowledgements

One thing I have learned from writing and working on collaborative projects is that among the trickiest parts of the process is thanking people. For every name remembered and mentioned, at least one other should have been. It is, I have come to realise, something of a thankless task. And so, in the certain knowledge that I will inadvertently omit the contribution of somebody important, I would like to offer my sincerest gratitude to some of the people who helped guide the book into its current form. In particular, my thanks go to Rebecca Feasey, Lucy Newman, Neil Russell and Tim Simpson for reading through the manuscript in draft form, working through my often esoteric approach to spelling, and offering me valuable feedback, commentary and ideas; Eileen Srebernik, Natalie Foster and Andrew Watts at Routledge for their help and support in bringing the book to fruition; the anonymous readers of the original proposal for their generous and supportive comments and feedback; and to Christopher Locke, whose 'Modern Fossil' you see pictured on the cover of this book and whose work was a key source of inspiration that led me to embark on research into game history and preservation in the first place.

Special thanks must also go to GameCity festival director, National Videogame Archive co-founder and pillar of the UK games establishment, Iain Simons, with whom I discussed and developed most of the ideas in this book. As I've come to expect, Iain's suggestions were utterly invaluable even if a large number of them related to the musical stage show of the book that he is convinced we should take to Broadway.

My genuinely heartfelt thanks go to the packaging designers of whichever brand of croissants I was staring at when the words 'Best Before' leapt out at me and immediately solved the year-long problem of what to title a book about old games and obsolescence.

Finally, this book is for the developers, players and fans of all the games I have played, not played, enjoyed and not enjoyed, finished and not finished; all the games that are still around and all those that have been lost; all the games that have not yet been made and which, hopefully, might not yet be lost.

Abbreviations

CPU	central processing unit
CRT	cathode ray tube
DiGRA	Digital Games Research Association
DLC	downloadable content
DRM	digital rights management
EA	Electronic Arts
ESA	Entertainment Software Association
GDP	gross domestic product
HVSC	High Voltage SID Collection
ICHEG	International Center for the History of Electronic Games
IGDA	International Game Developers Association
I/O	input/output
IP	intellectual property
LCD	liquid crystal display
LED	light-emitting diode
MAME	Multiple Arcade Machine Emulator
MMO	massively multiplayer online game
NES	Nintendo Entertainment System
OoT	*Ocarina of Time*
PSN	PlayStation Network
PVW	Preserving Virtual Worlds
RF	radio frequency
SIG	special interest group
SNES	Super Nintendo Entertainment System
VCR	video-cassette recorder
VCS	Atari Video Computer System
WTF	what the fuck? [expression of incredulity]
XBLA	Xbox Live Arcade

1

VIDEOGAMES ARE DISAPPEARING

No really, they are

Disappearing? Surely there can be little about the contemporary videogames marketplace or the state and status of videogaming as a mainstream cultural practice undertaken and enjoyed by millions of people across the world that can lead us to think that videogames might be disappearing. Even if we believe Peter Vesterbacka, whose company, Rovio, is responsible for *Angry Birds* and the now infamous assertion of 2011 that 'console games are dying', this only describes a shift in the preferred platform and context for play rather than signalling any decline in the popularity of gameplay itself (Ha 2011). In fact, partly because of the addition of platforms such as Apple's iOS devices, all indications point to the fact that the games market is growing apace with new titles, new platforms and new opportunities to play revealing themselves with each passing year.

Retailers' shelves heave under the weight of new and soon-to-be-released titles, whether these be the annual (re)iteration of *FIFA* or *Madden*, the somewhat less regular instalments of *Mario Kart*, *Halo* or *Street Fighter*, or new titles like *Child of Eden* or *Heavy Rain*. Thinking ahead, the sheer number of titles available for pre-order alone must reassure us of the longevity of videogames as a medium. At the time of writing in late 2011, Nintendo have just launched their 3DS handheld console that boasts glasses-free 3D and Augmented Reality gaming, while the successor to the Wii, the Wii U, has been seen and played publicly for the first time at 2011's E3 trade show. For its part, Sony has spent much of 2011 drip-feeding information, technical specifications and teaser trailer videos of games for its forthcoming handheld console, the PlayStation Vita (codenamed 'Next Generation Portable' or 'NGP').

The speed with which new platforms and delivery mechanisms can establish themselves and proliferate is little short of astonishing and speaks of the apparently insatiable desire for new gaming experiences. The iTunes App Store is a case in point, with analyses of the range of available titles suggesting that gaming is not only far and away the most populous genre of app, but that the iTunes App Store game catalogue significantly outweighs those of the previous few decades' worth of consoles such as the Nintendo Entertainment System (NES), MegaDrive, Xbox *et al.* combined (see Gaywood 2010, for instance). Such is the significance of gameplay as a mainstream practice that Apple, a company historically, if not notoriously, cool about gaming (see Gilbert 2005), now routinely touts the graphical performance of games such as *Infinity Blade* and *Real Racing HD*. *Infinity Blade* (then known as *Project Sword*) was demonstrated on-stage during the official launch of the iPhone 4 at the Apple Worldwide Developer Conference in 2010. 'It's on a phone', opined Steve Jobs with mock incredulity as he encouraged the audience to marvel at the potency of the audiovisual demonstration they had just glimpsed (Jobs 2010). By 2011, Tim Cook introduced Apple's latest revision to the iPod touch as 'the most popular portable game player in the world' (Cook 2011).

The sheer number of available games, 'coming soon' titles, new and in-development platforms must allay any fears that videogames are a passing fad or the equivalent of the digital roller-skate or virtual hula hoop. If we want to be assured not merely that there is a future for gaming but that the future of videogames is truly innovative, exciting – perhaps even unimaginably so, as what was once the stuff of science fiction becomes retail product – then the rows of pre-order boxes for the raft of 'coming soon' games as well as new hardware platforms make a materially persuasive case.

To underscore the situation, developers, publishers and industry trade organisations miss no opportunity to proudly boast of the size of their national and global sales figures and the rapidity of their growth. Satoru Iwata, president of Nintendo, recently announced that over 50 million Wii and 100 million DS consoles had been sold worldwide while, according to the Entertainment Software Association, 'On average, nine games were sold every second of every day of 2007' (Iwata 2009). Platforms and distribution systems that just a few years ago were non-existent now deliver games in astronomical numbers. By way of example, *Doodle Jump* recorded its 10 millionth download from the iTunes App Store in early 2011, while downloads of Rovio's *Angry Birds* healthily exceed half a billion across all platforms at the time of writing, with new versions planned for consoles, handhelds and mobile devices (the *Angry Birds Rio* tie-in posted 10 million downloads in its first 10 days of release; Crossley 2011). In the wake of these demonstrable success stories, it is small wonder that governments promote their national videogame industries' contribution to the creative sector. In the UK, games development is proclaimed as 'one of our most important creative industries' (Woodward 2006), while the National Endowment for Science Technology and the Arts' skills audit proudly boasts that, 'At over £2 billion in global sales, the UK's video games sector is bigger than either its film or music industries' (Livingstone and Hope 2011: 4). Projections from Pricewaterhouse Coopers suggest that the future is equally rosy: 'the sector will grow at an average annual rate of 10.6 per cent between 2010 and 2014 – faster than film, music and TV' (Livingstone and Hope 2011: 20). In the US, the ESA (Entertainment Software Association) is not shy in noting the size of the games sector's contribution: 'In 2009, the entertainment software industry's value added to the U.S. Gross Domestic Product (GDP) was $4.9 billion', or the rate and sustainability of its growth against the prevailing economic trends: 'From 2005 to 2009, the entertainment software industry's annual growth rate exceeded 10 percent. Over the same period, the entire U.S. economy grew at a rate of less than two percent' (ESA 2011a; see also Siwek 2007, 2010).

And yet, for all this apparently manifest growth, innovation and diversification, the simple fact remains that videogames are disappearing.

Perhaps I should be a little clearer about what I mean by 'disappearing'. My point here is not about industry growth, the quality of games or any yearning for what is sometimes referred to as a 'golden age' of gaming (Day 1998; Kent 2001; Whittaker 2004). I do not mean to suggest that we are headed for the kind of self-destructive market crash that was experienced (primarily in the US) in the early 1980s in which consumers temporarily turned their backs on what was seen as a marketplace super-saturated by quickly made, low-quality, cash-in products (see Taylor 1982; Cohen 1984; Kent 2001; also Consalvo 2006). It is worth remembering that, even in the aftermath of a crash of catastrophic proportions, which saw prices slashed and infamously drove Atari to bury in the desert its inventory of literally thousands of unsaleable cartridges rather than store it in warehouses, such was its negative equity (McQuiddy 1983; Guins 2009; Montfort and Bogost 2009), 'videogames' did not disappear. If history teaches us anything about videogames as a medium, as an enter-tainment form, it is that they are remarkably durable. If we look at this macro level, then certainly videogames appear to be enjoying a level of cultural acceptance and penetration that they have long sought. Not only does the marketplace appear to be in rude health, but also an increasing number of university curricula are dedicated to delivering the next generation of games developers and critics for the 'next generation' of videogames.

However, if we delve a little deeper, a more disturbing picture emerges. If we consider individual games rather than the health of a medium, we start to see vul-nerability. If we turn our attentions to the games that already exist rather than taking solace in the multitude yet to come, we begin to see a somewhat unexpected fragi-lity. If we consider 'old' games, the games that were once 'coming soon' and that had their moment at the cutting edge, taking centre stage at retail, being advertised on television, online and in print, but which are now outdated, superseded, and unsup-ported by their publishers and developers, we often find surprisingly little, and what we do find are sometimes only unreliable traces of existence.

Mario is missing

To illustrate some of these points, it is instructive to recount an apparently simple task I set my game studies students. It involves one of gaming's most well-recognised characters: Super Mario. Many will recognise him as a plumber, with some knowing that he was originally a carpenter. Aficionados will know that before he was 'Super', before even he was 'Mario', the character was known only by his rather more literal and gameplay-centric 'Jumpman' soubriquet when he appeared in Nintendo's 1981 *Donkey Kong* (though exactly when in 1981 is a topic of some discussion; see Patterson 2011). *Donkey Kong* is revered in the canon of videogames not only because it introduced the character that would later become Mario, who would become Nintendo's corporate mascot and a globally recognised cultural icon (see Sheff 1993), but also because the title was one of the first and most influential 'platform games' (a genre that was part of the mainstay of 1980s and 1990s gameplay; see Curran 2004; Loguidice and Barton 2009). Let us not forget also that this was the first *meisterwerk* of designer Shigeru Miyamoto, the legendary 'father of modern video games' and 'the "Steven Spielberg" of the gaming world' (BAFTA 2010). With that on board, and recognising that what we are dealing with is one of the truly seminal titles in video-gaming's history, it should be easy enough to find out about it and locate a copy to play through. Or so one might think.

Where to start? If I know my students, *Wikipedia* will be the first port of call for many. Once we've navigated the disambiguation of *Donkey Kong* the character versus the game, we find some useful, if potentially confusing, information. There are literally dozens of ports, conversions, translations and clones of the game. As such, *Donkey Kong* appears on myriad platforms and systems. However, we know that *Donkey Kong* was originally an arcade, or Coin-Op, game so this should be our starting point as the ports and translations are versions, remakes and remodels of this 'original' incarnation. And so we encounter our first problem. If we want to play this original version, we have to find a 30-year-old Coin-Op cabinet. Maybe champion *Donkey Kong* players like Billy Mitchell and Steve Wiebe (see Seth Gordon's 2007 *The King of Kong*) have them on hand, but the chances of finding a working cabinet are slim at best, let alone a 1981 *Donkey Kong* machine with its custom graphics and decals.

Cancelling the trip to the funfair at the end of the pier, we should perhaps widen the search to investigate some of the many console and home computer ports, conversions and clones. But which ones? Even a quick glance reveals that there are dozens and that, despite their name, they are in fact not all the same, with some having levels missing or omitting animation sequences found in the Coin-Op version (their omission is particularly important given that, as *Moby Games* (Donkey Kong n.d.) suggests, 'Donkey Kong is also notable for being one of the first complete narratives in video game form, told through simplistic cut scenes that advance the story'). Nonetheless, ColecoVision *Donkey Kong* looks promising. Helpfully, *Wikipedia*'s editors note that 'Coleco's version was a more accurate port than earlier games that had been done' (Donkey Kong (video game) n.d.). Unhelpfully, they do not explain what 'accuracy' means, or how or by whom it is measured, so it is difficult to judge whether this refers to the integrity of the technical conversion, the consistency of the graphics, sound or structure, or the feel of the gameplay. However, we can see that the ColecoVision console's technical specification does not match up to that of the Coin-Op hardware. Although they use the same central processing unit (CPU), albeit running at different clock speeds, the sound chip is different, the screen resolutions do not tally and the ColecoVision is capable of displaying just 16 colours compared with the Coin-Op's 256-colour palette. And then we have the controller. The Coin-Op had a chunky, microswitched joystick with a large ball to grip onto with the left hand, with a momentary-switched button falling under the right hand for making Jumpman jump. The ColecoVision controller's button layout is wholly different and there is no joystick at all. We should remember also that, like all of the different home computer and console conversions, ColecoVision *Donkey Kong* sets out its action for a display in landscape orientation rather than for the portrait orientation of the Coin-Op (presumably based on the reasonable assumption that most domestic television sets attached to consoles are not rotated through 90 degrees).

Surveying the other console and home computer conversions we find further and different variations. Many versions omit the intermissions that punctuate and drive the narrative frame, cut animation sequences or even strip away entire levels. Others modify the levels they do include, presenting different numbers of platforms and obstacles to traverse before rescuing the princess, thereby altering the gameplay dynamic and rhythm, and demanding new strategies and tactics. *In extremis*, Nintendo's own Game & Watch handheld *Donkey Kong* (DK-52) distills gameplay and audiovisual presentation to their absolute barest. DK-52 offers monochrome graphics via two built-in LCDs accompanied by little more than rudimentary blips for a soundtrack. Similarly, DK-52 is based exclusively around a radically stripped-down version of the Coin-Op's first level, which is played *ad infinitum* with only an increase in speed providing additional challenge (see Newman 2004 for more on Game & Watch gameplay design and structure). Perhaps DK-52 captures something of the essence of *Donkey Kong*'s gameplay, but only a novice player would mistake it for the Coin-Op even though both carry the Nintendo badge, even (or perhaps especially) in its audiovisually 'updated' and 'enhanced' guise as part of 1994's *Game & Watch Gallery* collection for GameBoy Advance.

Indeed, updates and enhancements add considerably to the complication and, as of 2006, Nintendo offers a version of NES *Donkey Kong* running under emulation and available via the Wii's 'Virtual Console' digital download service. Designed for use with the 'Classic Controller', which is a hybrid of various Nintendo console controllers, it necessarily deviates from the specificities of the NES pad. Indeed, as it is a conversion of the NES incarnation, replete with omissions and limitations (however well implemented on the Wii), the Virtual Console *Donkey Kong* is treated by many reviewers as necessarily flawed.

> Don't download it.
> Don't download it, because this isn't the true Donkey Kong. This Virtual Console release is of the NES version of the arcade classic, not the arcade classic itself. Whereas the coin-op original had four full levels of play, the NES conversion only has three – it's only 75% complete.
>
> (Thomas 2006)

Even this brief example raises a number of important points. The widespread practices of porting, converting, translating and re-releasing give rise to a proliferation of titles, each making different claims to originality, authenticity and definitiveness, and each contributing to the story of *Donkey Kong* as a ludic, technological and cultural artefact. Quite simply, the more you look, the more you find. Which of these games is *Donkey Kong*? Are they all *Donkey Kong*? Is it possible, or desirable, to identify a single entity or incarnation we can confidently demarcate as *Donkey Kong*? Certainly, all of these (con)versions quite legitimately bear the title *Donkey Kong* and we are not dealing with sequels, spinoffs or the products of an apparently cavalier attitude towards intellectual property (IP) infringement (*Monkey Kong*, *Donkey King*, etc.). Perhaps only the Coin-Op cabinet contains the real *Donkey Kong* and all other console, computer and handheld versions here are derivatives or 'manifestations' of the original 'work' (see McDonough *et al.* 2010, esp. pp 24–27 on the problems of deploying library and information services' bibliographical frameworks such as the International Federation of Library Associations and Institutions' 'Functional Requirements for Bibliographic Records', IFLA Study Group 1997, in relation to videogames). However, moving beyond issues of classification and documentation, how do we account for and deal with the myriad titles that clearly carry the mark of *Donkey Kong* but are, simultaneously, distinctive games in their own right? Each has its own control system, level design and its own particular take on the aesthetic, whether born of artistic intention, technical limitation or the ability to utilise the capacities of later generations of hardware and software such that the 'enhanced' remake purports to better embody the original vision than the original ever could. Each of these different versions is similar enough to be *Donkey Kong*, yet different enough not to be.

Of course, while selection and definition present real issues, they are but part of the problem. Regardless of whether we plump for the Coin-Op, a console, handheld or home computer version, we still have to locate a playable copy. Although we noted a plethora of opportunities to buy new games, or even to pre-order games still in development, purchasing games released 30 years ago is altogether more challenging. And let us not forget that even if we were able to track down the ColecoVision *Donkey Kong* cartridge, our quest does not, indeed cannot, end there. The cartridge will not play on any currently available videogame system, as no current platform offers ColecoVision compatibility. As we will see later in this book, it is hard enough, if not actually impossible, to run a PS2 game on a PS3 console, so what hope is there of resurrecting games designed for a console three decades out of production? Consequently, in order to play our ColecoVision cartridge we will need a ColecoVision console, thereby instantly adding to the complication of our attempt to play videogaming's past. It goes without saying that just having the console is not sufficient and, once we have assured ourselves that it still works, we need also to ensure that we have the correct audio–video leads to connect it to a modern television set or to convert its analogue RF (radio frequency) audio–video signal so it can be viewed and heard at all. Assuming our trawl eventually delivers the requisite hardware and software, and, absolutely crucially, that it all still works (working reliably and consistently would be even better), only then may we get our chance to start dodging barrels, climbing ladders and rescuing princesses as we play a (version of a) game of *Donkey Kong*.

As with many a good game, however, there is an alternative strategy to reach our goal. Rather than sleuth around trying to find antique hardware and software that might or might not reliably work, we could use an emulator. An emulator is a piece of software that enables applications originally designed to operate on a specific hardware platform to run on another, usually more recent system even if the two platforms have different architectures. In simple terms, a 'videogame emulator' can transform a generic PC into a virtual ColecoVision or, conceivably, into any other console, home computer or Coin-Op device. Emulation is an interesting, if problematic, proposition, and one that we shall investigate in the final chapter of this book in relation to formal practices of game preservation, exhibition and display. For now, however, we will concentrate on two issues.

First, as we have already seen in relation to the console and computer versions above, control interfaces such as joysticks, pads or other custom controllers are often integral to the experience of *playing* a videogame and while they are extraordinary technical achievements, emulators such as ColEm and Mugrat (ColecoVision) or MAME (Coin-Op) do not in themselves address the absence of the joystick and microswitched buttons or the bespoke Coleco joypad/keypad combination. Emulation (re)constructs games as software, typically eschewing the particularities and specificities of hardware and the interplay between hardware and software in favour of the remapping of bespoke controls onto generic devices such as qwerty keyboards, mice or multipurpose joypads. As such, while the game may be resurrected *prima facie*, and we may see *Donkey Kong*'s platforms, barrels and hear its characteristically lo-fi distorted waveforms, we immediately encounter questions about the integrity of the experience of game*play* – the 'Donkey Kongness' of *Donkey Kong*. Though emulation appears to give comparatively easy access to obsolete platforms and games, thereby sidestepping one practical and material impediment to gameplay, it raises further questions. Accordingly, in addition to asking whether the ColecoVision (con)version of *Donkey Kong* offers 'authenticity' in relation to the Coin-Op incarnation, it becomes essential to find ways of interrogating and rating the efficacy of this emulated implementation of the ColecoVision conversion.

Second, while an emulator enables the creation of a virtual console or Coin-Op cabinet, it does not typically supply copies of the games to play. This is not to say that games in forms and formats suitable for use with emulators are not widely, easily and, in many cases, freely available. Even the briefest search on certain filesharing networks or even the open web returns links to a multitude of packages, often neatly arranged as compressed collections of many hundreds, or even thousands, of titles. However, these 'ROMs' as they are colloquially known are invariably illegally produced ('ripped' from cartridges or discs) and their use exists in what is at best a legally problematic state (see Libby 2003; Conley *et al.* 2004). The videogame industry's position is rather more unequivocal, with Nintendo's corporate website stating that 'The introduction of emulators created to play illegally copied Nintendo software represents the greatest threat to date to the intellectual property rights of video game developers' (Nintendo Legal Information n.d.). Similarly, in its frequently asked questions list on piracy and copyright, the ESA, the US videogame industry's trade body, clearly recognises that the problem of accessing games that are no longer easily commercially available is a potential motivator for the use of ROMs and emulators, but remains firm:

> Isn't it OK to copy games that are no longer distributed in the stores or commercially exploited?
>
> No, the current availability of a game in stores is irrelevant to its copyright status. Copyrights do not enter the public domain just because the works or products they protect are no longer commercially exploited or widely available. Therefore, the copyrights of games are valid even if the games are not found on store shelves, and copying or distributing those games is a copyright infringement.
>
> *(ESA, 2011b)*

The worrisome fact, however, is that, irrespective of their legality or any more qualitative assessment of the 'authenticity' of the resultant emulated gameplay experience, particularly where the original made use of specialised interfaces with bespoke combinations of pads, sticks or buttons, grass-roots collections of ripped ROMs represent by far the easiest – and sometimes perhaps the only – way to access old videogames. As we shall see later in this book, the comparative inflexibility of the legal position has significant ramifications for formal game preservation, archiving and digital history and heritage projects (see Anderson 2011).

Ultimately, whether we search for original hardware and software or packages of ROMs to be run on more current platforms, and to some extent whether we are players, students set an exercise, or museum, archive and gallery professionals, the process of accessing and playing old games is far from straightforward. It is clearly not impossible to resurrect *Donkey Kong* in some form or other, but given how significant this game is to the history and development of what is now a multi-billion dollar global entertainment industry and how influential this game and its sequels and offshoots have been, I would contest that it is astonishingly difficult and the results surprisingly variable. Imagine if we picked an obscure title.

Without doubt, videogames are disappearing.

It gets worse

As the *Donkey Kong* example begins to illustrate, the 'disappearance' of videogames is a complex, multifaceted issue. On one level, it will be clear that this is a matter of remembering and forgetting. However, I do not wish to create the impression that old games simply fade away or slip from view as newer titles excite the imagination. Nor do I wish to endorse or support the apparently 'natural' processes by which old games and gaming technologies are replaced and superseded by their updated and upgraded successors. Rather, following the ideas of scholars like Watkins (1993) and Gitelman (2008), for instance, I wish to point to the ways in which technological obsolescence is produced, often in the service of commercial interest. My assertion here is that much of the work of the games industry, in its broadest sense, is diametrically opposed to the project of game history, heritage and preservation. Throughout this book, I will identify and explore a range of diverse but concerted practices that contribute to the systematic discarding of gaming's past as playable and accessible and which selectively (re)construct some 'old games' in ways that seem less motivated by a desire to celebrate, interrogate or understand historic design and development achievement, or to position and critique the contribution of games to a popular cultural heritage comprising practices of play, use and consumption, than they are inspired to drive forward the games industry and games markets along its teleological journey of continual innovation and reinvention. As Gooding and Terras note,

> The games industry itself has thus far shown little interest in preserving its own heritage, although a few companies do maintain archives of their own games for internal research (Hyman, 2004). Generally, though, the industry prefers to concentrate its resources on defending itself against piracy through aggressive patenting (Boyd, 2005) and legal actions (Barton, 2005).
>
> *(Gooding and Terras 2008: 23)*

I wish also to draw attention to the role of advertising, marketing and journalistic discourse and practice in the self-conscious creation of what Kline *et al.* (2003) have called digital gaming's 'perpetual innovation economy'. The processes of upgrade and technological development put the videogames industry into an almost constant state of flux as new platforms, games and even new ways of controlling, engaging and interacting with them appear. Certainly, the announcement of the 'next generation' of hardware and software contributes to the sense of excitement and dynamism of the videogame marketplace and is surely one of the reasons why politicians are so keen to promote the importance of gaming within the creative sector. However, for all this innovation and renewal, for all the talk, speculation and rumour about future iterations of games or revolutionary new gameplay systems, we should remember that the 'next generation' does not simply add to the pantheon of gaming possibility in an uncomplicated way. Rather, as we will see in this book, each new gaming system, each new game, takes part in a process that replaces that which came before it. Platforms are superseded and eventually rendered obsolete as games are no longer available for them, while the games themselves slip from view as they are superseded by newer, faster, 'better' versions that, for their part, can only be played on current generations of hardware. Where we see old games and platforms referred to at all, perhaps in marketing materials, in reviews of hardware and software or occasionally in exhibitions of game history, it is often in this comparative mode, as a baseline by which we are invited to judge the additional processing power or graphical resolution of the replacement.

The inevitability of this technological development has some far-reaching consequences. Most obviously, it assures us that the best is yet to come and, in doing so, fixes attention and focuses longing on a future not yet playable. On the day of 3DS's

European launch in March 2011, Nintendo's general manager David Yarnton talked of the 'revolutionary' system that finally 'marks the day that 3D entertainment goes truly mainstream'. Here, then, the potential 3DS consumer not only buys the DS's technologically superior replacement but also buys into a world that not so long ago was available only in the imaginings of science fiction authors, 'without the need for 3D glasses for the very first time' (Roberts 2011). More than this, the discourse of upgrade and innovation comprehensively frames videogames as technology. The consoles on which we play games are 'systems' that output 'graphics' and receive 'inputs' via 'peripherals' (and still there is debate as to why videogames are not considered art; see Faber 1998; Choquet 2002; Adams 2007; Clarke and Mitchell 2007; Denerstein 2007; Martin 2007; note also Ebert 2007). If we look to specialist consumer reviews of games in magazines or online, this technical language is not merely reproduced but becomes part of the frame of reference for judging titles. Where, in relation to film, we might find discussion of cinematography, *mise-en-scène*, musical soundtrack or even set design, as well as acting, writing and dialogue, videogame reviews typically culminate in reductive summary panels that distil and rate the game according to its 'graphics' and 'audio' (see Future Publishing's *NGamer* magazine) or that explicitly rate and rank each game's 'innovation' (e.g. Future Publishing's *GamesMaster*). The world of videogames is one dominated by discourses of possible technological futures and is one in which a yearning for the future not only outstrips an interest in the past but is at least partly contingent on eradicating its memory, save for where it is useful as part of a benchmarking exercise. As such, videogames are not so much disappearing but are being made to disappear, or at least are forgotten and remembered in very particular ways and for very particular purposes. Deuze's comments signal the extent to which this dynamic informs production and consumption:

> The market for technically advanced games further drives the market for advanced graphics cards and next-generation consoles as consumers must purchase the latest upgraded computers of new consoles to play games developed to meet the technological specification particular to the new technologies.
>
> *(Deuze 2007: 216)*

Much of this book is concerned with exposing and exploring the agendas and interests at play in this forgetting and remembering, selective memory and recall of games. Before this, I wish to briefly focus attention on a rather more concrete, and in some cases literally material, issue. It is essential not to overlook another important aspect of videogames' disappearance. We have begun to see that, considered as an industry, an entertainment form and as cultural practice, videogames and videogaming appear remarkably resilient in being able to weather global crashes and buck national and international economic trends. However, this overall buoyancy and strength is potentially misleading and might easily lull us into a false sense of security about the longevity and security of this form, as it conceals the true fragility and vulnerability of videogames. I noted above in the discussion of the search for *Donkey Kong* that locating original hardware and software presents the videogame collector and researcher with something of a problem. Where this becomes a real issue is when we start to factor in reliability. This is not a trivial matter and is certainly not intended as a comment on any inherent unreliability of the ColecoVision console, its controllers or cartridge design. Rather, what we encounter in the search for working hardware and software is a stark and quite uncomfortable reality. Quite simply, as nestor/The Institute for Museum Research remind us in the title of their report on digital media preservation, 'nothing lasts forever' (Rohde-Enslin and Allen 2009). What is more sobering still is that the lifetime of many of the material objects and data that comprise what we think of as 'videogames' might not even last very long.

> Digital media have a shockingly short life span due to the natural decay of the original materials and the rapid obsolescence of older media forms, as well as the failure and obsolescence of the hardware necessary to run them. Many digital games that are only a few decades old are already at-risk and require immediate preservation attention.
>
> *(Monnens 2009: 3)*

And thus, against a backdrop of obsolescence, business, design, advertising, marketing and journalistic practices that foreground innovation and upgrade while simultaneously writing out compatibility with redundant, superseded platforms and software or ending support, we find that there is physical and data degradation to deal with. We should perhaps not be too surprised by the revelation that consoles and discs deteriorate over time, and few but the most faithful or deluded can have expected these media and materials to last for all eternity. However, it is genuinely shocking to note the rapidity with which the processes of decay can set in. In fact, as we shall see, Monnens' threat-level assessment of a few decades may turn out to be something of an underestimate.

There are two related but distinct issues at work here. The first will be immediately familiar to many console and computer owners, and concerns the material degradation and deterioration of hardware. The second is probably considerably less familiar to those outside digital media preservation and conservation circles but its consequences are equally, if not even more, serious. 'Bit rot' refers to the decay of digital data which in part arises as physical storage media deteriorate, but is also a potential unwanted and unpredictable by-product of duplication and copying errors.

Falling apart

> WOODY: Tuesday night's plastic corrosion awareness meeting, was I think, a big success. We'd like to thank Mr. Spell for putting that on for us. Thank you Mr. Spell.
>
> MR. SPELL: [mechanically] You're. Welcome.
>
> *(Toy Story 1995)*

I am fortunate enough to be writing this book on a brand new computer. It is an 11-inch MacBook Air and it has been in my possession for just a couple of days. As Apple goes to great lengths to point out in its corporate marketing materials, it is light, thin and packed to the gills with new technologies, like the solid-state drive that eliminates the vulnerable moving parts of an 'old-fashioned' magnetic hard drive. The machine's casing is made of aluminium, which is light and strong, and the screen is so gleaming and glossy that I can almost see my face in it. It looks futuristic, but above all, it looks new. Next to this vision of the future-in-the-present sits one of the many older Macs that I cannot bring myself to discard. This one, a Mac Classic, dates from the 1980s, has a case made of plastic, a monochrome display and, in its day, cost more than my new Air. What is perhaps most striking about the Classic, however, is its colour. It is yellow. Not beige like other PCs, and certainly not the brushed aluminium of Apple's current product line of iMacs and MacBooks, but distinctly yellow – although not uniformly so. Unlike the Air with its 'unibody' design that sees the computer casing machined from a single block of aluminium, the Classic is assembled from various plastic panels and each of these is now a slightly different colour – some dark, some light – and on top, above the display, is a perfectly circular patch much lighter than the surrounding plastic where once sat a plastic *Gundam* toy on its perfectly circular base.

The unavoidable fact is that plastic is an unstable material. Recently, we have probably become more used to thinking about the problems of plastic's permanence, as waste materials threaten the environment, whether through oceanic 'garbage patches' or by making their way into the food chain (see Kaiser 2010; Leichter 2011). However, for our purposes here, it is the fragility and degradation of plastic rather than its longevity that is crucial. Over time, plastic degrades and deteriorates. The differential yellowing of the Mac Classic casing is visible evidence of the chemical change that plastics naturally undergo, and sits as an important reminder that, however much our present 'new' computing devices might seem to connect us with the future, they are destined to become – and look – old. This is not even a matter of aesthetic judgement or an evaluation of whether the Mac Classic is more or less dated as a piece of design or as an object. This is a matter of ageing. Importantly, this ageing process may not be entirely graceful, predictable or even controllable.

It will be no surprise to learn that the situation is not unique to Macintosh computers and is absolutely no different for gaming devices. Discolouration of cartridges and consoles is well documented and is particularly concerning for collectors, who see their cherished possessions literally changing over the years. Where once cartridges and consoles were grey, now they are yellow or brown and, like the Mac Classic, where their manufacture brings together panels or sections fabricated from different types or batches of plastics, we see differential discolouration, with the tops of consoles and the backs of cartridges ageing at different rates. Benj Edwards (2007) eloquently documents his frustrations with and investigations into the discolouration of his much-loved Super Nintendo Entertainment System (SNES) consoles. Discounting tobacco staining and other more obvious environmental effects (or the simple build-up of dirt), suspicion moves to exposure to UV light, though on dismantling the console, the discolouration is equally visible inside, thereby further complicating the issue. Scanning online forums, consultation and feedback from Nintendo raises the possibility that an interaction of safety additives to the plastics might be the cause.

> Thank you for contacting us. That's an interesting question! For the Super NES, this is a normal condition and no cause for alarm. Cleaning or handling the system will have minimal impact to change or revive the original color.
>
> The Super NES, as well as our other systems, are made with a plastic containing flame-retardant chemicals to meet safety guidelines. Over time, the plastic will age and discolor both because of these chemicals as well as from the normal heat generated from the product or exposure to light. Because of the light color of the plastic of the SNES and NES, this discoloration is more easily seen than with other darker plastics such as on the N64 and the Nintendo GameCube.
>
> Thanks for your email!
>
> Nintendo of America Inc. Casey Ludwig
>
> *(cited in Edwards 2007)*

The irony of flame-retardants potentially being susceptible to the effects of heat is surely not lost, and whether these are truly the culprit remains inconclusive for Edwards as later analysis and further correspondence with Nintendo proves less decisively clear. Moreover, however significant maintaining the appearance of console and cartridges might be to collectors and archivists, there are yet more serious consequences to consider than discolouration. As Brenda Keneghan, polymer scientist at London's Victoria and Albert Museum, notes, 'The main challenge is the relatively short life expectation of plastics in comparison to materials such as stone, metal and paper' (Mehta 2008). Research projects such as that operating from the Plart museum in Italy are similarly concerned with understanding and, potentially, intervening in the processes of 'progressive embrittlement' which render plastics and polymers increasingly fragile, so as to conserve objects and artefacts. Icon, the Institute of Conservation (Icon 2011), goes further still in pointing to the fact that, in time, the effects of chemical changes in the composition of plastics or, indeed, the influence and impact of other environmental factors such as UV light may not just alter the way materials look but may actually cause them to disintegrate altogether.

> Plastics are different – the exact make-up and 'recipe' of each type of material has a great deal of influence over how long it will survive or stay looking good. Plastics are difficult to stabilise once they have started to deteriorate and they can fall apart quickly. A conservator can carry out treatment to stabilise certain plastics and can make enclosures and storage environments to stabilise an item at the very least.
>
> *(Icon 2011)*

The decay of gaming hardware, then, is a serious and potentially difficult to manage issue. In its outline of the issues affecting game preservation practitioners, the Digital Game Archive (DiGA) gives a palpable sense of the seriousness of this erosion as well as the urgency of the situation: 'General opinion has it that the life-span of hardware is limited, mainly because of physical and chemical processes within the microchips. (Established scientists like Ed Rothenberg estimate 30 years)' (DiGA 2004). It is small wonder that, in addition to heritage, museum and conservation sector organisations and gaming projects such as DiGA, online forums spill over with the homegrown advice of fans about the best way to deal with malfunctioning and deteriorating hardware. Unreliable SNES/MegaDrive/GameBoy cartridges occupy the attentions of myriad collectors and enthusiasts and advice varies from blowing dust from the contacts (in fact, more likely to introduce imperfects and foreign bodies), through applying small amounts of surgical alcohol with a swab, through rather more abrasive methods such as using emery boards, to instructions on using the official, and no longer available, Nintendo cartridge cleaning kits (see Fleck 2005; RawmeatCowboy 2011). Other common complaints relate to the exhaustion of built-in cartridge battery backup. Many SNES-era and GameBoy cartridges included a small amount of battery-backed memory to store game progress, thereby enabling games to be played over multiple sessions without having to restart from the beginning every time. Of course, while it works, the system is not something that players need to concern themselves with, and, with no concern for a time when the battery would be effectively absent, developers and designers were free to create entirely new types of gameplay and even games genres (consider the impossibility of the role-playing game where all progress is reset with every power-off) that existed over multiple play sessions. Many years after their original release, cartridge backup batteries die and the gameplay saving functionality dies with it, potentially leaving the cartridge all but useless save to those players for whom 100+ hours of uninterrupted gameplay is an option.

Just as fansites dedicate many pages to exploring gameplay, so do they explore and explain ways of keeping temperamental or naturally life-limited systems in play. Given that the batteries were never designed as user-replaceable parts and, indeed, the cartridges were never intended to be opened at all (immediately voiding the warranty), this apparently simple and literally game-saving process of reinvigorating a GameBoy *Pokémon* cartridge is not a job for the faint-hearted, proclaiming the need for 'basic soldering skills' and an equipment list that includes adhesive tape, spacers in case the replacement battery is a different depth to the original, and a hemostat to grip the screw on the rear of the cartridge (see Master Kirby 2007). For those wanting to replace depleted batteries in SNES cartridges, the process also involves damaging the stickers and decals on the cartridge's front and rear panels to access screws, thereby defacing the material object in order to preserve or prolong its functionality (see the discussion at the *Digital Press* forums, e.g. gamenthusiast 2004). We might be tempted to think that cartridges represent a particular problem isolated to an era of computer and videogames and that the move to optical media like CD, DVD and Blu-ray or even online digital distribution might alleviate these issues. As we will go on to see, each of these storage and distribution media brings with it its own set of challenges, but we should absolutely not forget that cartridges remain a key part of contemporary gaming. Nintendo's DS platform, including the current (at the time of writing) 3DS console, retains the proprietary cartridge as its principal means of distribution, suggesting that there lies ahead at least another generation of blowing on contacts and gently swabbing with rubbing alcohol.

All of this presents a stark reminder that videogames truly are in danger of disappearing, not only in a figurative sense as we forget about the old in favour of the new, but quite literally as the physical objects, the 'stuff' of videogaming – the consoles, cartridges, discs, joypads, contacts, microchips, batteries and silicon – erode, decay and disintegrate. It is worth remembering as we look at the advertisements for new, coming soon, pre-release, pre-order games and consoles that they are ultimately new for only a fleeting moment, whereupon the very materials from which they are constructed begin to disintegrate.

> Mainstream depictions of computers in films and television class them along with cars and other consumer electronics: they are clean, new, and generally work well unless sabotaged. 'New technology' conjures up well-lit images of sleekly designed computers and monitors; bright colors, spotless, smooth surfaces, clear screens, and quick applications. This obtains even though the average condition of computers is closer to dust-covered CPUs and monitors, screens dotted with fingerprints, and keyboards darkened by use.
>
> (Sterne 2007: 21)

Early adopters of the Nintendo 3DS may find themselves among the most recent sympathisers with this position as some report that their bleeding-edge handhelds freeze, displaying error messages (in 2D) (see Alexander 2011b; Dutton 2011b; taku 2011), while UK tabloids have been quick to luridly claim that the console 'makes gamers dizzy & sick' (Hamilton 2011). While the prevalence of these technical and use issues is uncertain, the availability of Nintendo's helpline, just like the troubleshooting and health and safety sections that bookend every hardware or software manual, reminds us of the fragility of much new technology. Sterne's perceptive and corrective assessment of the imperfection and grubbiness of new technology in use raises one more important issue that moves us beyond simply considering the inevitable material decay and deterioration of new technology and the dichotomy of popular representations of new technology, and the rather more underwhelming and problematic material reality. Sterne draws our attention to the fact that these devices do not just wear out or disintegrate on their own but that they bear with them the visible signs of use. Fingerprints on displays, grease from hands gumming up keyboards and mice, all contribute to the reality of computing. Nowhere are the visible traces of human interaction with technology clearer to see than in the case of the iPad.

> Because the primary input method of the iPad is a single piece of multitouch glass, developers have incredible flexibility to design unique user interfaces. It's

hard to appreciate the variety of UIs though, since turning the screen off removes virtually all evidence of them. To spotlight these differences, I looked at the only fragments that remain from using an app: fingerprints.

(Kokkinidis 2010)

The nature of the interface gives rise to unique patterns of grime and filth. Games such as *Angry Birds*, *Fieldrunners* and *Fruit Ninja* are immediately recognisable even with the iPad turned off because their gameplay leaves behind a telltale trace of their touch interfaces – these are perhaps the most literal of 'digital' media. Dirty, grimy and, above all, like the humans that use them, and in doing so make them grimy and dirty, they have incontrovertibly finite lifespans.

Bit rot

We might think it bad enough that access to what we think of as even comparatively recent videogames and systems is hindered by the kinds of material deterioration, malfunctioning and eventual disappearance of consoles, the corrosion of contacts and microchip, and the depletion of battery-backed memory that we have seen. However, the threat to games extends yet further and we should remember that, on one level, videogames are code. For many of us, particularly those of us who are primarily players rather than developers, videogames might seem to be predominantly material objects. They are physical objects to purchase, interchangeable discs and cartridges to be handled, swapped and shared, while gameplay is typically an inherently visceral undertaking that involves grasping controllers, touching screens or aiming light guns at displays. However, videogames are also digital data. They are comprised of code that, in different formats and according to different conventions and technical restrictions, describes rulesets, outlines the physics models that govern the in-game behaviours of the objects whose contours and vectors are similarly mapped out; they are data that, when suitably interpreted, give rise to graphics and sound; they are code that defines and prescribes gameplay opportunity, that governs how the inputs and outputs of the system are interpreted and translated into 'gameplay'.

Thought of as series of zeros and ones, the videogame as 'data' is considerably more immaterial, which, in turn, might lead us to consider it either more or less permanent. In one sense, the endlessly recursive nature of digital media encourages us to foreground the mutability of data as it is reused, reworked and remixed. Simultaneously, the endless reproducibility of digital data and the apparent indistinguishability of the copy inculcates notions of permanence that are only heightened through the work of digitisation projects that transfer important documents and artefacts from the putatively vulnerable 'analogue' world of paper and parchment to the security of digital space. The British Library's digitisation strategy for 2008–11 notes that 'Through digitisation, we are creating a valuable and enduring resource for scholars and the public alike' (British Library Board 2008). Moreover, it is worth remembering that the language of CD and DVD 'duplication' moves beyond copying to evoke notions of identical clones turned out *en masse* (we will return to questions of 'duplication' with specific regard to videogames experience in the closing chapter of this book).

What soon becomes clear, however, is that digitisation brings with it its own set of challenges and that data is not quite as enduring as we might at first think. Why else would we need rigidly implemented 'data backup strategies' that promote the use of multiple formats across multiple locations to protect against accidental or malicious deletion or the unreliability of hardware and software (Van den Eynden et al. 2009)? For Rohde-Enslin and Allen (2009: 6), the very language of computing is responsible for creating an illusory sense of archival activity: 'We humans are not in fact "saving"; rather, we are instructing a computer software program to record information in the form of a file to a particular location on your computer's hard drive.' The point here concerns both the procedure of 'saving' actually being one that creates agglomerations of data in specific formats that may or may not be readable in the future and also that the data, as bits and bytes, zeros and ones, becomes 'saved' only when it resides on some form of storage medium, whether this means writing to a magnetic or flash drive, pressing onto an optical disc, or 'burning' onto an EPROM. The 'fixing' of these data in the material form of storage media marks one point from which degradation and decay can be traced because storage media, just like game consoles and controllers, have finite lifespans. Any of us who have experienced a hard drive crash or a music CD that consistently skips will have some first-hand insight into the problem of storage media deterioration.

For digital preservation practitioners, this decay over time of digital information and storage media is referred to variously as 'bit rot', 'data rot' or 'digital decay'. Much like the degradation of plastics that we saw earlier, there is an inevitability about the process of bit rot. As Monnens (2009: 3) notes, bit rot ensures that data will eventually become unreadable. The storage media will eventually erode to a point where the data they contain simply cannot be accurately read and extracted. While deterioration over time is a problem common to all storage media, whether analogue or digital, Dag Spicer, curator of the Computer History Museum in Silicon Valley, points out that the very nature of digital data may actually compound the problem:

> The problem, strangely enough, is not so bad on the older stuff, but quite bad on the more recent stuff. So we can read tapes here at the museum that are 50 years old … Even VHS tapes are holding out better; at least they keep playing if there's a problem with the tape. The real problem lies in newer formats. With a CD or a DVD, if there's an error, often it's non-recoverable, and you've just lost all your information.
>
> (Spicer interviewed in Pogue 2009)

As we can see, although media decay is a widespread problem, its nature and, in particular, the speed and severity of its onset, varies greatly from storage medium to storage medium. In relation to videogames, the Game Preservation Special Interest Group of the International Game Developers Association notes that

> Bit rot affects different storage formats at different rates depending on the format's durability. Magnetic storage and optical discs are especially subject to varying forms of digital decay. For the time being, masked ROM cartridges appear to be fairly durable while EPROMs are at greater risk.
>
> *(Monnens 2009: 3)*

The Software Preservation Society's work examining magnetic media suggests that the life of the 3.5" floppy disks on which numerous games (and other applications and data) of the 1980s and 1990s were and are stored may already be in an unreadable state: 'Our practical findings show that disks from 1985 are frequently found "rotten", and thus we would estimate around the 20-year mark is about right for 3.5" DD floppy disks' (Software Preservation Society 2009).

As Gilbert (1998/2003) notes, 'Testing by Imation/3M indicates that their CD media will last for over 100 years, although this figure should be viewed with at least a little skepticism. Research by Kodak also shows that CD-ROM media is estimated to last for over 100 years.' The accelerated testing of manufacturers is, as Rohde-Enslin and Allen (2009: 34) observe, somewhat selective and tends to focus on the influence of humidity and temperature, at the expense of considering the number of times media are read/written to, exposure to UV and other environmental and handling factors:

> In practice, the information vendors provide us about the estimated life expectancy of their storage media is based on in-house tests carried out under conditions defined by the firms in question. Results, perhaps needless to say, are interpreted according to in-house criteria.
>
> *(Rohde-Enslin and Allen 2009: 34)*

As an indication of their fragility, despite the claims of century-long archival lives, optical media such as CDs, and latterly Blu-rays, have been found to be susceptible to, among other things, 'bronzing' and 'CD rot'. While handling may be to blame in some instances (see Svensson 2004), some problems have been seen to arise as a consequence of manufacturing errors or even the unanticipated interaction of the optical disc's coatings and other materials, such as the printed booklet packed into the case. 'The problem was that the lacquer used to coat the discs was not resistant to the sulphur content of the paper in the booklets and inlays, which resulted in the corrosion of the aluminium layer of the disc' (Hyperion n.d.; see also Bishop 2004).

Ultimately, digital media preservation practitioners and researchers have begun to confront the fact that, in some senses, the storage media in use in today's computing environment are potentially some of the most vulnerable and least durable.

> Recording media for digital data are vulnerable to deterioration and catastrophic loss, and even under ideal conditions they are short lived relative to traditional hard copy format materials. Although we have been dealing with acid-based paper, fax paper, photo film and other fragile media for decades, the

risks posed by magnetic and optical media are qualitatively different. They are the first reusable media and they can deteriorate fairly rapidly, making the time frame for decisions and actions to prevent loss a matter of years, not decades.

(Gilbert 1998/2003)

Given the severity of data rot and the unpredictable nature of media decay, it perhaps comes as little surprise to find that the International Game Developers Association's (IGDA) Game Preservation Special Interest Group (SIG) considers bit rot to be 'The greatest threat to the longevity of digital games' (Monnens 2009: 3). If we factor in the need for contemporary devices to read the data from these old (and not so old), vulnerable storage media, and the challenges of locating and maintaining such hardware for replay or extraction purposes, we see the problem amplified.

Who cares?

Even at this early stage in our investigation, it will be clear that videogames are vulnerable to long-term, and perhaps even not-so-long-term, loss, and while Gooding and Terras (2008) rightly note that there has been little scholarly work conducted in this area, with Barwick *et al.* (2010) suggesting that there has been a lack of interest in games within preservation circles, a number of projects and initiatives do exist, albeit in sometimes nascent form. It is not the intention here to present an exhaustive survey of current or past academic or heritage sector work on gaming (for a fuller list of current projects see Lowood 2009a, and note also that the IGDA's Game Preservation SIG maintains a list of current preservation projects on its wiki). Rather, the concern of this section is to draw attention to some of the contexts in which the care and preservation of games are beginning to develop, as well as to start the process of identifying and evaluating some of the different approaches. We will return to interrogating the efficacy of particular strategies and techniques in more detail in the concluding chapter of this book, but here it is useful to give a sense of the various ways in which game preservation is conceived of as a problem and, accordingly, where the foci of attention lie for different practitioners.

While the discipline of digital curation is comparatively young (see Higgins 2011), over the past few years, we have seen the emergence of what we might collectively call 'game preservation' efforts spread across the academic and heritage sectors. Recent articles in scholarly journals such as the *International Journal of Digital Curation* have begun the process of surveying extant work (e.g. Gooding and Terras 2008) as well as outlining and evaluating particular game preservation strategies (e.g.McDonough and Olendorf 2011; Newman 2011; Guttenbrunner *et al.* 2010; Swalwell 2007, 2009). These focused investigations of game preservation issues and challenges must be set against a backdrop of special issues of broader cultural studies publications that follow the work of scholars such as Marvin (1988), Gitelman and Pingree (2003), Chun and Keenan (2006), Acland (2007a) and Gitelman (2008) in turning readers' attention to discussions of 'old' and 'new' media. *M/C Journal*'s 'Obsolete' issue (see Wilson and Jacobs's 2009 editorial) and *Transformations*' collection on 'Slow Media'

(Ashton and Newman 2010; Karppi 2011; McFarlane 2011; Rauch 2011; Skågeby 2011), for instance, both directly and tangentially raise questions of special significance to game preservation, in some cases because articles specifically address the medium, and in others because wider themes of obsolescence and technological 'progress' chime with practices, processes and discourses that we see in operation in the games sector and to which we will turn our attentions throughout this book. However, although we can identify a handful of scholarly works on game preservation, it is notable that little of this research is published within journals of game studies per se (though note Barwick et al.'s 2010 survey of extant game preservation projects in *Games and Culture*). This is not to say that games history is not a focus for game studies researchers and scholars, as Parikka and Suominen's (2006) attempt to look behind the marketing hyperbole of mobile gaming attests, but it does perhaps suggest that preservation is far from the centre of the research agenda in game studies. As an indication of the formalisation of 'game preservation' as a research area, while serving as an eloquent reminder of its nascent state and comparatively minor position within the wider context of videogame research, it was not until 2009 that the Digital Games Research Association (DiGRA) hosted its first panel session dedicated to the subject (see Barwick et al. 2009; Lowood et al. 2009; Newman and Woolley 2009; Pinchbeck et al. 2009).

In addition to this scholarly work, other projects such as the IGDA Game Preservation SIG's 'Digital Game Canon' (Lowood et al. 2007) have been instrumental in beginning the process of communicating with wider audiences the issues of game preservation and the immediacy and potency of problems such as material and media decay. The Digital Game Canon identified ten titles, ranging from 1962's *Spacewar!* through *Super Mario Bros.* (1985) to *Warcraft I–III* (1994–2003), that should be preserved for posterity. Whether or not these titles truly represent the 'most important video games of all time' (Montfort 2007) is, clearly, debatable (McCalmont 2010; Mensah 2010; Totilo 2010). We shall return to consider, among other things, the implications of preserving *Super Mario Bros.* as well as the complexity of defining what we mean by *Super Mario Bros.* at all, given the huge variety of versions of that game that exist, not to mention the variety of ways in which it has been modified through hacking and creative play. However, regardless of the practical and conceptual questions that the Digital Game Canon raises, there can be little doubt that at least part of the project's importance can be measured in the amount of publicity generated and in its contribution to reframing the popular understanding of videogames' cultural and historical significance (e.g. Chaplin's 2007 coverage of the Digital Game Canon in the *New York Times* entitled 'Is That Just Some Game? No, It's a Cultural Artifact').

At the same time, a number of museums, galleries and archives have emerged that are dedicated to or largely interested in videogames, their long-term preservation and issues of access. Sterling's (2011) presentation of Carbone and Giordano's (2011) work highlights some of the international exhibitions and projects:

> The exhibition 'Museogames – Une histoire au rejouer' at Musée des Arts et Métiers de Paris; the Computerspielemuseum in Berlin; the U.T. Videogame

Archive promoted by the Dolph Briscoe Center for American History and the University of Texas in Austin; the International Center of Electronic Games in the Strong's National Museum of Play in Rochester, New York; and the European Community Projects CASPAR and KEEP (Keeping Emulation Environments Portable), a network dedicated to the preservation of numerical content.

(Giordano translated in Sterling 2011)

According to J.P. Dyson, director of the International Center for the History of Electronic Games (ICHEG) at the Strong National Museum of Play, as of 2009–10, the project has processed 'close to 20,000 game artifacts and 100,000 game-related artifacts in the last 18 months', as well as engaging in considerable restoration and the creation of documentation (McDonough *et al.* 2010: 58). Germany's Computerspiele Museum is another important initiative dedicated to the collection and exhibition of hardware software and ephemera. Founded in 1997, the museum was the world's first permanent exhibition on digital interactive entertainment culture and now holds Europe's largest collection of entertainment software and hardware. Not all is quite so positive, however, with projects such as the Musée du Jeu Vidéo in Paris lasting just a short time before closure. National situations and protocols vary considerably with some museums, galleries and libraries actively modifying and extending their collecting and exhibition policies to accommodate videogames. In Germany, games submitted for age-rating approval are routinely deposited for archiving so that their initial release data can be catalogued and the physical media preserved, while in France, the Bibliothèque Nationale de France holds titles published in France with 'several thousand video games available for consultation' (BNF 2011).

The UK situation sees a number of projects attending to computing and, often tangentially, to gaming. The National Museum of Computing at Bletchley Park holds collections of computing hardware, for instance, as does the Science Museum and The Museum of Science and Industry while more specifically related to videogames, the National Media Museum's National Videogame Archive expands on the museum's existing new media collections to tackle the specific challenges of gaming cultures. UK Exhibitions such as the Barbican's *Game On* (and latterly *Game On 2.0*), which has toured the world over the last decade (see also King 2002), *Into the Pixel* (which showcases videogame art) and Urbis' *Videogame Nation* all speak of a public appetite to engage with the histories of videogames and a willingness to encounter and consider them in cultural and heritage contexts and outside the arcade. In the collection and exhibition work of these museums and galleries, we note an interest in material as well as virtual cultures of games, as well as a desire to make available, not just preserve, games, gameplay and ephemera.

These questions of access raise critical questions about the importance and long-term availability of original hardware and software versus emulations and simulations that might stand in their place as effective facsimiles. The idea that a preserved game might need to be played presents a series of challenges that relate to the authenticity of experience and force the consideration of the contexts in which play takes place, whether these be the physical surroundings of a gallery or the hushed reverence of an archive reading (ludus?) room, or the location of this playing within the wider field of gameplay and the demands on players' *a priori* knowledge of gaming convention and form. At present, many of the exhibitions that present playable games effectively, and deftly, sidestep many of these questions by essentially (re)constructing arcades in their gallery spaces. The National Media Museum's *Games Lounge* and the *Game On* touring exhibition are cases in point. The exhibitions draw heavily on 1980s coin-op arcade games that were self-consciously designed to explain themselves through attract sequences that lay out the boundaries and parameters of their play while offering only comparatively short play sessions of just a few minutes (motivated by their original purpose to maximise throughput and generate more revenue through the coin box). Where home console and PC titles such as those comprising the *Final Fantasy* and *Metal Gear Solid* series present introductory movie sequences that last considerably longer than entire play sessions of *Pac-Man* from insert coin to game over, and where gameplay in role-playing games, platform games and even driving and sports games is intended to be portioned out over many hours of individual, cumulative sessions, we immediately note the incompatibility of the gallery-as-arcade model.

While media decay and bit rot are self-evidently central issues, game preservation involves more than storing or securing code, and demand for access, whether this be in the form of public exhibition or to aid future scholarly study, introduces questions of interpretation and experiential authenticity that challenge preservation practitioners and game studies scholars alike as they search for appropriate techniques that are sensitive to the mores of games as playable media in which performance and the complex interaction of hardware, software and human systems are key. Videogames are, after all, interactive media and the delivery, and the maintenance of the integrity, of this interactivity presents a significant challenge for game preservation practitioners. Games are, at once, like and unlike other forms of digital media. They are both computer hardware and software systems and they are environments within which to play and perform.

At least part of the intent of this book is to contribute to the discussion of this second point and consider some of the presuppositions about what games are and how they could and should be apprehended in the future. The position ultimately expounded is one that is grounded in an appreciation of games and, in particular, of the significance and contours of play as a configurative act, and will be both familiar and potentially controversial for those versed in game studies scholarship.

Preserving virtual worlds

To date, perhaps the most significant and challenging project in the field of videogame preservation is Preserving Virtual Worlds (hereafter PVW; McDonough *et al.* 2010). PVW is a collaborative research project undertaken by the Rochester Institute of Technology, Stanford University, the University of Maryland, the

University of Illinois at Urbana-Champaign and Linden Lab, conducted as part of Preserving Creative America, an initiative of the National Digital Information Infrastructure and Preservation Program at the Library of Congress. We might see the very existence of such an initiative, particularly one whose funding comes from no less an institution than the Library of Congress, as an important step towards the legitimisation of videogame preservation activity. However, in reality, many of the findings contained within the PVW final report are as troubling as they are reassuring. The authors raise many questions about the state of extant preservation work in relation to the specificities of gameplay. Most telling, however, and adding to the keenly felt sense of urgency, is the discussion of threats arising from commercial contexts within which the games that might be the object of our preservation activity exist.

> Most virtual worlds are also buffeted by the inexorable pressures of the marketplace. During the two-year span of our project, no fewer than seventeen virtual world properties winked out of existence, with varying degrees of bang and whimper ... Even when profit-motive is not a consideration and a virtual world is built and maintained out of something like love, it remains vulnerable to the patience, attention span, resources, disposable income, and of course ultimately the inescapable mortality of its founders.
>
> *(McDonough* et al. *2010: 9)*

If we were to have any remaining doubt as to the fact that videogames are, literally, disappearing, then here is proof positive. Not only might games be under threat from material and digital decay as their data, storage media, interfaces and systems inevitably and rapidly deteriorate, but they are vanishing as the commercial pressures of the marketplace conspire to make them unviable. It is not merely that we must act to arrest the 'natural' death of these games but that their demise is being 'artificially' accelerated in the service of commercial and competitive advantage. From a commercial standpoint, this is quite understandable, of course, and there is no particular reason to assume that a developer or publisher should or could maintain their game in perpetuity, but perhaps we might be surprised to learn just how quickly games turn from their moment in the spotlight to obsolete and, in some cases such as those noted above, completely inoperable and unplayable.

To be clear, this is not simply a matter of niche or marginal games that are unable to find a sustainable user base. Nor are they the products of small companies who have to redeploy resources to support new projects. Though each of these situations would be equally problematic in terms of preservation, they might be recognisable as the rational, even reluctant, acts of resource-starved companies operating in a highly competitive marketplace. However, among the list of 'virtual worlds that died during the grant' (McDonough *et al.* 2010: 134–39) are titles such as *EA Land* (aka *The Sims Online*), Beautiful Game Studio's *Championship Manager Online*, Google's *Lively*, Sony Online Entertainment's *The Matrix Online* and Sega's *Phantasy Star Online*. Indeed, it is worth noting that not all of these virtual worlds have disappeared simply because they were unsuccessful. As the PVW report notes, Disney's *Virtual Magic Kingdom* (2005–9) was 'Created for 50th Ann[iversary] and promotion ended long after originally planned.' As such, although it ultimately lasted for considerably longer than initially anticipated, it was, from the outset, conceived as a time-limited game that would inevitably disappear as its servers were deactivated and redeployed. These are not isolated examples. The 2011 announcement of the cessation of videogame publisher THQ's deal with Lucasfilm had significant ramifications for developers and players alike.

> Due to forces beyond my control, it turns out that Thursday, March 31 will be the last day fans can get their hands on Star Wars Arcade: Falcon Gunner for iPhone and iPod Touch. Ever.
>
> *(Shabtai 2011)*

In fact, and possibly as a result of the widespread coverage that the potential disappearance of this high-profile game received, it was given a reprieve and remains available. However, the episode is a stark reminder of the variety of factors that contribute to the vulnerability of games, particularly those like *Falcon Gunner* that exist in such an immaterial state and whose distribution rests in the hands of third-party networks. We will return to questions of online games and, in particular, online access to games through activation codes, for instance, later in this book, but for now it is worth adding into the mix not only the idea of self-consciously limited shelf-lives but also the fundamental 'elsewhereness' of server-based games whose data reside on and whose gameplay is activated via machines, systems and services over which even the keenest collector or archivist could have no access or control. If keeping running a ColecoVision console or replacing the batteries in a GameBoy cartridge seems a challenge, at least these items may be in the possession of the player. Once Disney's remote servers are decommissioned, the very possibility of future gameplay is immediately and decisively extinguished (see McDonough and Olendorf's 2011 discussion of the 'failures' in attempting to archive *Second Life* that arise from both ephemerality and complex ownership and intellectual property rights).

The fragility of games reliant on network and server access was shown in sharp relief when the early 2011 hacking and subsequent outage of the Sony PlayStation Network (PSN) and Sony Online Entertainment network services left many titles such as Valve's *Portal 2* unplayable or severely limited as online play was unavailable for many weeks. Moreover, the absence of online copyright protection and authentication systems rendered some other titles completely unusable even without their online play. Indeed, a number of titles, including Capcom's *Bionic Commando Rearmed 2* and the *Final Fight/Magic Sword* game pack, for instance, were rendered unplayable without an active connection to PSN for digital rights management (DRM) authentication (Crecente 2011). That *Bionic Commando* contains no online gameplay modes and requires a connection to the PlayStation Network only for its DRM raises a further complication, as even offline games may require the availability of fragile and potentially time-limited networked services operated – and closed down – by publishers (see Good 2011 for more on Bionic Commando's DRM, and Chapter 3 for a fuller discussion of the issues arising from the dependency on online authentication systems for offline play in relation to Electronic Arts' (EA) Online Pass and Capcom's *Super Street Fighter IV* DRM, for instance).

The reliance on digital distribution systems and on networks such as Apple's App Store, Sony's PSN, Valve's Steam and Microsoft's Xbox Live Arcade (XBLA) service is equally problematic. As Monnens (2009: 7) notes, 'If a title were to be delisted from XBLA, it would only be available on systems whose owners had purchased and downloaded the title', while Pigna's (2008) analysis makes it clear that, although it has not yet acted upon them, Microsoft has set parameters by which titles can be delisted from the XBLA service. In fact, the situation is potentially more problematic than this, depending on the network and system under scrutiny. For Monnens, 'Installation licenses and encryption key verification tools introduce further problems for preservation.' By limiting the number of times a game may be installed or by relying on remote servers for verifying the legitimacy of a particular copy and (dis)allowing it to be run, 'These practices ultimately tie copies of a game to a particular computer that is prone to failure and obsolescence rather than to a particular user, who has greater permanence' (Monnens 2009: 7). Purchases via Nintendo's Virtual Console, for instance, are locked to the specific Wii or 3DS unit on which the purchase was made, with no end-user ability to transfer purchases to a new system in the event of hardware replacement, failure or loss.

Issues like DRM, authentication and the heavy reliance on proprietary technologies within gaming systems should make it immediately clear that not only does the scope of the game preservation project demand collaboration across sectors, but also the kinds of access to materials that institutions of cultural memory such as museums and archives may wish to hold may be highly commercially sensitive. It comes as little surprise to find that the need to foster trust and to work in partnership with publishers and developers is a key message communicated in the PVW final report:

> This is not to say that game companies will necessarily be unwilling to share these materials, but there are obviously a number of factors working against making them available that libraries, archives or museums seeking to collect and preserve games must address. The most fundamental issue for any cultural memory organization attempting to collect this material is trust. Many software companies would view sharing something like source code as equivalent to handing over the crown jewels. Assurances that material will be 'dark' archived and made available only at some later date or under certain conditions are not of any real significance to a software company unless they already have trust in the individuals and the institution making the promises.
>
> *(McDonough* et al. *2010: 24)*

The position echoes that expounded by Henry Lowood in his introduction to the IGDA Game Preservation SIG's White Paper entitled *Before It's Too Late*, in which he directly addresses the producers and developers of the videogames that are seen to be under threat: 'if we fail to address the problems of game preservation, the games you are making will disappear, perhaps within a few decades' (Lowood 2009b: 1). While this sentiment is unquestionably laudable and the attempt to hail the development and publishing communities might well be considered essential, especially in light of the kinds of DRM and intellectual property rights issues we have seen above, the potentially painful truth is that a host of current industry practices actually exacerbate rather than solve the problems facing preservation practitioners. In fact, as we will see throughout this book, the issue cuts deeper than DRM implementation, authentication systems and the patenting of invention. Industry practices through development, publishing, advertising, marketing and retail all contribute to the creation of a peculiarly problematic context within which game preservation currently exists. As we shall see, industry and, to some extent, player attitudes towards games history and the value of old games are as much the problematic of game preservation as technical issues of long-term access and compatibility.

Fans as collectors

The recent discovery of game preservation by academics, museum and archive professionals will, no doubt, come as something of a surprise to a number of gamers and fans who have long engaged in extensive practices of collecting and, in some cases, cataloguing and archiving projects. As was the case in the previous chapter, it is not the intention here to present an exhaustive survey of every fan project, though, as we shall see, such an undertaking may well have merit in the broader context of game preservation even if it is a potentially Sisyphean task. Rather, here, the object is to account for some of the types and areas of work that gamers and fans attend to. The reason for this is twofold. First, it might be some slight reassurance to know that some work is and has been under way for a number of years, with some practices and projects existing in a state of maturity despite what is often a complete absence of formal, institutional or financial support. Second, and as a consequence, just as the contributors to the IGDA Game Preservation SIG's White Paper (Lowood 2009a) note the importance of industry collaboration, it is inconceivable that any formal game preservation endeavour should not involve partnership with constituencies of players. However, we should be mindful not to overstate the degree to which amateur, fan-led projects compensate for the comparative lack of academic and heritage sector preservation activity. Indeed, while partnership and knowledge exchange are fundamentally important, much of what we will see players and fans produce might just as easily be considered to be objects in need of archival attention as opposed to presenting solutions to the problems of game preservation.

Among the most visible of amateur archival projects is the High Voltage SID Collection (HVSC), and it presents a perfect example of the strengths of fan-driven game collecting, the extraordinary depth of knowledge possessed by amateur curators and the levels of dedication, care and attention that are lavished on these labours of love. As the project's 'About' page on its website declares,

> The High Voltage SID Collection (HVSC) is a freeware hobby project which organises Commodore 64 music (also known as SID music) into an archive for both musicians and fans alike. The work on the collection is done completely in the Team and contributors' spare time and is proudly one of the largest and most accurate computer music collections known.
>
> *(About HVSC n.d.)*

'Accuracy' is a key word here. The HVSC is considerably more than a simple collection, and while it strives for completeness, with over 39,500 discretely identifiable music files currently available for download, the team is meticulous in its processes of authentication and cataloguing. Detailed guidance about the ways in which SIDs should be ripped comes complete with a 17-page guide entitled 'Ripping for Dummies' (Steppe n.d.), which outlines the required assembly language commands as well as information on cycles and scanlines with algorithms to ensure correct complex interface adapter timer values for multispeed tunes at PAL (phase alternating line) timings. Coupled with the carefully documented structured database entries that form the STIL.txt file (SID Tune Information List) that provides composer credits and additional information about each of the pieces of music in the library, what we see in the HVSC is a painstakingly detailed project whose output speaks both of a dedication to the technology and of the creativity of SID composers, and manifestly demonstrates a desire to archive, catalogue and preserve rather than just collect.

This desire to catalogue and document is felt across a variety of projects, even those whose focus and potential uses occupy an altogether more problematic legal status than the HVSC. It may initially seem perverse to suggest, but in some senses the vast collections of illegally downloaded and shared ROMs that exist on filesharing networks in the outer reaches of the Usenet and that are increasingly available for download via websites on the open Internet share many of the same curatorial inclinations as the HVSC or, for that matter, any professional cataloguing or archiving project. We are well used to thinking of ROMs, the ripped data from game cartridges and discs, in terms of their illegality. Certainly, videogame publishers, developers and industry trade organisations go to great lengths to point to the criminality of illegal ROM creation and use, and we will return to considering the impact of ROMs on both the games industry and the ways in which (old) videogames are monetised and valued. Here, though, it is useful, if a little unusual, to consider ROM acquisition and, in particular, the distribution of (illegal) ROMs from a different perspective. Typically, collections of ROMs are far from haphazardly arranged and are, instead, organised and categorised with proprietary numbering systems and structured filenaming/metadata schemas that allow potential downloaders to identify critical information such as the platform, release territory, revision and technical/technological dependencies (e.g. expansion packs, console version, etc.).

If we examine websites such as worldofspectrum.org, whose creators, it should be noted, go to considerable lengths in attempting to secure the permission of rightsholders to distribute materials via their portal (see the revealing distribution permissions lists at World of Spectrum 2011a, 2011b), we find authenticated ROMs alongside copious documentation and documentary material, including scans of contemporaneous reviews, hints and strategy guides, as well as scans of covers, inlays and even the cassette cases themselves. Setting aside questions as to the legality of much ROM acquisition and distribution and the challenges of seeking IP permissions, what is striking about the cataloguing systems and documentation schemas we see in these projects is not merely the meticulousness of their design but also the widespread nature of their implementation across apparently unrelated sites and services. None of this should be read as an endorsement of the practice of illegally acquiring or distributing ROMs, of course, but it is suggestive of a couple of things. First, the need to document variations in ROM versions, whether these are the products of updates or of differences in territorial releases, reveals to us the complexity of defining 'the game' as an object of preservation. Any given title frequently exists in a range of different forms some of which may be markedly different from one another in their functionality, not to mention their intelligibility (in the case of language translation and localisations) or hardware and software compatibility. The game's fluidity and its multifaceted nature as an object of − or rather, series of objects for − preservation is far from trivial and is an issue to which we will return in the final chapter of this book, and assessing extant (con)versions, ports and patches as well as ascertaining the authenticity of specific ROM dumps presents a potentially mammoth challenge. Indeed, for some such as Giordano (see Sterling 2011), this 'extreme fragmentation' problematises, or perhaps even renders impossible, the whole project of game preservation. At the very least, the recognition of 'the game' as a segmented agglomeration of like and unlike, related and distant pieces, rather than a coherent object, draws attention to the complexity and 'instability' of the form.

Second, and perhaps a little more reassuring, the detail and rigour of archival efforts such as the HVSC and worldofspectrum.org as well as the cataloguing and organization of illegal ROM collections demonstrates the existence of a vast knowledge among fans and players. These databases and the knowledges they contain constitute an invaluable source that distinguishes and documents the variations between versions of games and, most significantly, their potential impact on the ability to play or the specific contours that these multiple versions of game and gameplay offer.

The collection and documentation of ROMs serves a variety of purposes, but most typically the acquired and collated materials are destined for playback under emulation. The development of videogame emulation software has become a staple of gaming culture and is dedicated to the virtual recreation of old systems and platforms using current iterations of hardware. Projects such as the hugely ambitious MAME (Multiple Arcade Machine Emulator) and its derivatives are among the most well-known of these amateur projects.

> When used in conjunction with images of the original arcade game's ROM and disk data, MAME attempts to reproduce that game as faithfully as possible on a more modern general-purpose computer. MAME can currently emulate

several thousand different classic arcade video games from the late 1970s through the modern era.

(Welcome to MAME ... n.d.)

As its name implies, *MAME* sets out to emulate old coin-op machines, though countless other emulation projects exist dedicated to single and multiple platforms, or even aspects/components of wider platforms such as the many SID chip emulators, such as SIDPlay, that forgo recreating the entirety of the Commodore 64 in favour of its sound chip alone. Similarly, the emulator codebase is, itself, frequently converted to enable it to be run on different general-purpose computers (e.g. DOS, Windows, Mac OS, Linux etc.). On top of the technical challenges associated with developing and maintaining these complex pieces of software, which effectively turn one hardware and operating system's platform into another, come questions of legality and intellectual property. In common with most amateur-developed emulation software, MAME's boilerplate outlines its focus and treads a fine line between the investigation and preservation of hardware and the operation of software.

> MAME is strictly a non-profit project. Its main purpose is to be a reference to the inner workings of the emulated arcade machines. This is done both for educational purposes and for preservation purposes, in order to prevent many historical games from disappearing forever once the hardware they run on stops working. Of course, in order to preserve the games and demonstrate that the emulated behavior matches the original, you must also be able to actually play the games. This is considered a nice side effect, and is not MAME's primary focus.
>
> *(About MAME n.d.)*

Regardless of whether making available otherwise impossible-to-play games represents their primary focus or is merely a nice side-effect, the fact remains that, for a host of reasons, emulators are presently at the very heart of preservation activity. As we shall learn in the following chapters, this is due in part to varying approaches to backwards compatibility (the ability of subsequent gaming hardware platforms to run the software of previous generations), which often leaves old games unplayable on currently available and supported systems. It is also due to the fact that many commercially re-released collections of 'classic' games are actually emulations rather than rewritten programs for current systems, and so, whether we know it or not, many of us play with emulated games on our consoles and mobile devices (indeed, some of Good Old Games' commercially republished PC titles make use of community-developed emulators such as DOSBox and ScummVM; see Au 2011 on Good Old Games' output).

For most game preservation practitioners and critics, emulation is considered to be the only currently viable long-term strategy. Although we will save our analysis of this last claim until the final chapter of this book, it is worth noting here that much of the most significant work that is undertaken in relation to videogame emulation is the product of amateur, not-for-profit, freeware project teams motivated by interest, passion and enthusiasm. As the PVW report notes, 'The community for emulation development, especially for video games, can be best characterized as a grass-roots movement led by a few dedicated programmers' (McDonough *et al.* 2010: 62). While in no way undermining the quality and quantity of this work, we should perhaps be mindful of the potentially precarious nature of this situation where tools so central depend so greatly on the energy and goodwill of 'grass-roots' projects and motivated individuals. As the findings of the PVW project's evaluation of emulators found, many potentially promising tools were eliminated at an early stage because they were in an indeterminate state of upkeep, thereby themselves becoming outdated and obsolete.

We should remember also that amateur collecting and curating is by no means limited to games and gameplay. Projects such as the Def Guide to Zzap!64 (n.d.) present scans and transcriptions of Newsfield Publishing's 1980s–90s Commodore 64 gaming magazine, while *Gamebox64* aims to be the 'complete resource for packaging related scans such as instructions, inlays, boxes, tapes, disks, cartridges and other miscellaneous items' (GameBox64 project homepage n.d.). Probing deeper still, initiatives such as Unseen 64 are concerned not with games that were once played but rather with games that never were played.

> Unseen 64 is an archive with articles, screens and videos for cancelled, beta & unseen videogames. Every change & cut creates a different gaming experience: we would like to save some documents of this evolution for curiosity, historic and artistic preservation.
>
> *(About Unseen 64 n.d.)*

Despite, or perhaps even because of, a rabid interest in games that are in development and coming soon, much is known about games before they are released and become playable. While non-disclosure agreements prohibit the communication of many details, nonetheless interviews, screenshots and even video showreels all deliver information and insight into what might be. Development schedules, budgets and technological shifts all conspire to ensure that some of these games, in fact, never come to be, and never make it beyond the development or technology demonstration stage. Projects such as Jeff Minter's *Unity*, a psychedelic, abstract 3D shooter developed for the Nintendo GameCube, is illustrative. Featuring on the cover of Future Publishing's well-respected *Edge* magazine (issue 120, February 2003) and enjoying a comprehensive 8-page preview, the game was officially cancelled towards the end of 2004 (Minter 2004). In explaining the announcement on his forum, Minter highlights the difficulty of producing inventive software to the schedules of hardware generations:

> in the past couple of years it's become clear that getting it all together into something that I'd be happy to call Unity and put my name to was going to take a lot of time and effort both from myself and the guys at Lionhead, and realistically it was becoming unlikely that it'd be finished in time for anyone to

want to publish it on Gamecube. The alternative would be a rush job and we simply didn't want to do that.

(Minter 2004)

Unseen 64 is far from unique with other projects attending to distant and more recent cancellations often in relation to specific platforms. *ColecoVision.dk* identifies countless games that were advertised for the system yet were never commercially released (ColecoVision Unreleased Games 2011), while *Games That Weren't* has expanded beyond its initial interest in unreleased, cancelled and alpha-stage C64 games to cover a range of formats. Lest we consider this simply an exercise in out-of-control fandom, Ruggill and McAllister remind us of the importance of the unreleased, the cancelled and the failed game:

> It is important for those committed to game preservation to recognize these stoppages, however, because stopping work on a game is often the first step in its complete disappearance: a well-funded game is canceled, the developer cut loose, the physical studio packed up and closed down, the hard drives stored, ruined, lost.
>
> *(Ruggill and McAllister 2009: 17)*

Moreover, in light of the sheer amount of effort that goes into engaging players, as potential purchasers, with games prior to their release (what Jones 2008 calls the 'pre-game' stage), we cannot be surprised to find such interest in projects that fail to come to fruition.

Just a whole bunch of stuff

Of course, in addition to the work we have noted above, we find numerous fans making use of eBay (famously described by William Gibson as 'just a whole bunch of *stuff*'; Gibson 2006: 21, originally 1999) or other auction sites and services to amass vast private collections of games, merchandising and marketing materials that bring them closer to the objects of their fandom. As Hillis *et al.* (2006: 2) observe in the opening of their collection of essays on eBay, 'Pleasure still comes from actually possessing the object, but also from closer association with the channels of desire urging its acquisition.' It is certainly the case that forms of discernment and the exercising of cultural capital may be seen at play here, particularly in recovering obsolete materials, games and systems, and bestowing upon them new meanings and value. Accordingly, much of what we see on eBay is concerned with the performance of identity just as it is with the acquisition of ephemera (see White 2006, for example), and certainly there are few better expressions of cultural capital than finding value where none was thought to be. However, not all collecting involves sifting through old media and reclaiming it as newly reinvigorated or creating 'memorable experiences'. Channels dedicated to the delivery of 'collectibles' are manifold with merchandising like action figures, clothing and trading cards often sold alongside and even in bundles with games. Manufacturing the sense of lack in the collection is critical, whether this is achieved through new series of collectible toys or unreleased game projects listing their target titles — known to exist but elusive. Not in the collection, but possibly collectible. As Frank Gasking notes on the *Games That Weren't 64* website, 'There are some big shocks always around the corner, and who knows … we may even find that bloody "Daffy Duck" game one day! … :-)' (Gasking 2010). The importance and appeal of the elusive chimes with Baudrillard's commentary in *The System of Collecting*:

> What makes a collection transcend mere accumulation is not only the fact of its being culturally complex, but the fact of its incompleteness, the fact that it lacks something. Lack always means lack of something unequivocally defined: one needs such and such an absent object.
>
> *(Baudrillard 1994: 23)*

Ultimately, then, we should not be greatly surprised that gamers are motivated to collect in these ways. As Jones (2008: 47) notes, 'fan culture — and especially game-fan culture — is collecting culture'. But there is more to Jones's point than the simple observation that fans collect or that markets and channels exist to facilitate and profit from these transactions. For Jones, gameplay and collecting are intrinsically linked. 'Games involve collecting, and collecting is itself a game.' However, for Desjardins (2006), it is a particular feature of eBay that the already ephemeral, the disposable items of merchandise, the collectibles that eBay's CEO Meg Whitman considers still to be 'the essence of community', are rendered even more fleeting (see Helft 2001). Thus, while objects are made available as 'visual spectacles', these presentations are strictly time limited. Sellers choose how long items will be made available for purchase 'and the collector-viewer-fan-buyer often purchases them through frenzied bidding in the last moments of their availability' (Desjardins 2006: 34). However, Jones offers a different reading. Considering Desjardins's position, which speaks of the potential temporal incompatibility of eBay and fan cultures, Jones notes,

> Desjardins considers traditional media fan cultures and concludes that 'the ephemeral temporal structure' of eBay bidding and its 'competitive' set of interactions and transactions work against some of the constituent elements of fan culture. I would suggest, however, that this is not the case if we consider game culture where timed and competitive 'interactions and transactions,' what might be called 'emergent collecting,' are the norm.
>
> *(Jones 2008: 56)*

Viewed in this way, the online auction's competitive, timed bidding resembles gambling, or 'gaming' and the auction site becomes an apparently infinite and renewable field of play for collectors/players. Certainly, the affective bonds that unite and structure what is typically referred to as eBay's community (see Desjardins 2006) remind us of the kinds of constituencies of gamers and fans that coalesce around shared interest in particular titles or series at fansites and projects like those above. Continuing the discussion of gaming/collecting, Jones explores Keita Takhashi's *Katamari Damacy* (a game, incidentally, never released in European territories and, as such, something of a collectible artefact in its own right, due to its cult status and scarcity). In Jones's analysis, it becomes manifestly clear that the gameplay in *Katamari Damacy* is oriented around the acquisition of objects – literally rolling them up and attaching them to the giant sticky ball (the titular 'katamari') that is under the player's control. In fact, collecting is inescapably central to *Katamari Damacy*'s gameplay. What at first appear to be random and frequently incongruous objects are not only added to an invisible inventory but are added to the increasingly massive ball of 'stuff' whose size is at once key to the completion of the level and a physical impediment as manoeuvrability is inhibited. *Katamari* is collecting-as-gameplay writ large, but it is far from a unique example.

The completion of inventories is a staple of gameplay as new items, objects and techniques augment characters' capabilities or stand as trophies and markers of past gaming successes. Fron *et al.* (2007: 1) note that 'The design and acquisition of virtual fashion is among the most popular activities in metaverse-type social worlds, such as Second Life and There.com', while Taylor (2003) has drawn attention to the ways in which costuming is woven into the fabric of numerous games. Examining MMOs ('massively multiplayer online games') such as *EverQuest*, Taylor notes that the complexity and quantity of in-game costumes accumulated in the player's inventory and displayed on their in-game characters stand as visible markers of gameplay success and prowess. Any player familiar with beat-em-ups like the *Street Fighter* or *Tekken* series will be more than *au fait* with alternative in-game costumes as rewards for successful gameplay challenges. As players progress through the game, the new levels of achievement and character development are visually reinforced and displayed through the acquisition of new armour or costume combinations. Given the strong connections between gameplay and collecting, the urge to acquire and amass 'outside' the game might be seen to be inevitable, or at least encouraged and legitimised.

However, it is worth noting that collecting objects so as to become more intimate with the object of fandom or closer to the channels of distribution is only a part of what characterises much of the amateur archiving and curatorial work. Unseen 64, for instance, does considerably more than list cancelled releases. In addition to collections of screenshots grabbed from websites and scanned from magazines, its original articles present the most rigorous analyses, which scour multiple sources, often in translation, triangulating sources and comparing various published screenshots. These investigations theorise and infer details about possible directions in which gameplay might have developed, or speculate on reasons for the cancellation of the project beyond those officially announced. In some cases, attentions centre on the differences between in-development and finally released versions of games. Unseen 64's analysis of *The Legend of Zelda* postulates levels missing from the *Ocarina of Time* series, based on fragments of translated text and screenshots of graphics depicting garments and items absent or removed from the published title. (See Newman 2008 for more on the creative, investigative work undertaken by fans in search of information on games released and unreleased.)

It is worth pausing momentarily to focus on the notion of creating, analysing and documenting information pertaining to unreleased games, as to some extent this endeavour comes to represent an important intersection between rapid obsolescence or disappearance and what we might term a 'slow media' approach. In common with other fan practices like the creation of fanart, and even the production of walk-throughs and strategy guides that we will explore in detail in later chapters, what we see here might be read as an act of defiance. In pausing on the unreleased products of an industry in perpetual motion, in documenting particular moments, creating and celebrating images, levels, graphics and sequences of gameplay, these amateur archi-vists, analysts and curators defy the logic of upgrade. We might also argue that these practices and projects go some way to addressing the problems of game preservation that we have begun to document, and we will certainly draw on the kinds of in-depth analyses and documents produced by these projects in our consideration of formal preservation strategies later in this book. However, it is equally likely that the kinds of documentary materials that are the products of these investigations and practices, whether they be analyses of unreleased beta versions of games, walkthrough texts or STIL.txt files, should, themselves, become the focus of preservation activity. These practices, after all, are intrinsic parts of gaming culture. If we extrapolate from Buckingham and Sefton-Green's (2003: 379) characterization of *Pokémon* as being 'something you do, not just something you read or watch or "consume"', and Jones's (2008: 45) 'Pokémon is a universe of meaning', we come to see the videogame not as a text or even a series of interconnected texts but rather as a broad cultural practice. In this light, these documents, these practices of fan culture are critical and vital elements of the preservation landscape of game culture existing both as objects and strategies.

Best before …

This is not a book about game preservation, per se. It is written from the perspective of a game studies scholar involved in game preservation and exhibition rather than by a heritage or digital media preservation practitioner. As such, the book does not attempt to review or offer new regimes for metadata ingest or document the tech-nical, specific properties of a list of canonical titles. However, this is a book whose analysis and findings on industry practices and the significance of play and playability have significant implications for the project of game preservation. In order to con-tribute to the discussion of how best to deal with the long-term preservation and, just as importantly, the long-term access to videogames, this book poses two key ques-tions. In fact, these questions are, themselves, drawn from the existing literature but are in danger, perhaps, of being overlooked as the urgency of the plight of video-games potentially pushes practitioners and theorists into particular courses of action based on assumptions about both what games are and how best future audiences might engage with them. The first question seeks to interrogate the reasons why we find ourselves in 2012 still at the beginnings of a concerted preservation effort that quite necessarily dedicates as much of its time to public and scholarly debates about whether games are even worth considering as cultural heritage at all as it does to discussing the merits or limitations of particular strategies. The idea that game preservation is overdue is probably the most common trope in extant scholarly writing, and the assertion sets the baseline for urgent action.

> We must understand the reasons for the current lack of computer game preservation in order to devise strategies for the future.
>
> *(Gooding and Terras 2008: 1)*

This is an absolutely critical question, and one that has perhaps tended to get lost as scholars and practitioners have taken up the reigns and urged immediate action. On one level, it is difficult to dispute for a second that we need to act 'before it's too late' (to quote the title of the IGDA Game Preservation SIG's White Paper, Lowood 2009a), particularly if we consider the rapidity of the material and digital deterioration we have seen in the opening of this book. Similarly, the need to work closely with industry partners in a distributed effort so as to tackle the range of technical issues that potentially shorten the life of games makes nothing but sense. Certainly, as Monnens elsewhere notes, 'The history of the game industry cannot be saved without support from its creators' (Monnens 2009: 6). However, as Gooding and Terras rightly suggest, we should think carefully about why so little has already been done, as this reveals some potential impediments to preservation activity that rival media decay in their seriousness but which remain largely undiagnosed, or at least unspoken.

A large part of what I am interested in exploring in the beginning of this book is the influence of a set of market conditions and business practices that make virtually impossible the kind of valuing and investment in gaming history and heritage that a concerted preservation effort requires as its foundation. The position here is that although they are often the most visible and certainly are the themes most typically foregrounded, data rot and the disappearance of both the immaterial code and the material objects of videogaming and DRM are not necessarily the most significant issues facing those interested in preserving and documenting the history and heritage of digital gameplay. These data preservation and material conservation questions are, without doubt, important and it is not the intention here to denigrate their importance or suggest that their significance is either illusory or overblown. However, the focus on material and digital patterns of deterioration tends to focus attention on game as either text or technology and, in doing so, potentially encourages the conception of the preservation effort as a series of technical, technological or conservational questions. I want to suggest that the project of videogame preservation may have as much to do with addressing attitudes to games as historical and cultural objects as it does with attempts to resurrect and resuscitate hardware, software, data and code. As Donahue (2009) notes in her discussion of the state of extant games preservation activity, 'industry disinterest [*sic*] is a key factor'. This important and insightful observation should signal a subtle but important shift in our analysis. The lack of interest in preserving games is quite different from a lack of involvement in the preservation effort and we would do well to probe a little deeper into what motivates this reluctance to preserve and archive an industry's past or perhaps even to view it as something worthy of preservation attention.

The brute fact is that videogames exist in commercial and cultural contexts which are designed to ensure that history and heritage fades from visibility and memory as much as the codebase of games fades from disks and cartridges. As Kline *et al.* (2003: 66–67) rightly note, it is an inevitable consequence of the creation of the 'perpetual innovation economy' of continual upgrade and technological (re)invention that we see in videogame markets the use of patents and other legal tools to protect and commercialise the industry's revolutions. As a consequence, it is, perhaps, natural that we focus our attentions on addressing or seeking to overturn the DRM or IP arrangements that restrict long- or even short-term access to playable games. However, this is to overlook, or at least take for granted, the idea of the perpetual inno-vation economy and to naturalise the processes of obsolescence, renewal and replacement that such a discourse cultivates. It is for this reason that a large part of this book is dedicated to documenting the multitude of ways in which videogame obso-lescence is produced through retail, publishing, journalistic, advertising and market-ing, and even game design practice. Importantly, this discussion draws attention to the influences and effects of these discourses on popular, academic and industry atti-tudes towards games, and in particular the trajectories of old and new games and the (im)possibility of valuing games as cultural heritage. If unchecked, the processes of systematic forgetting and selective recall of gaming history, and the ways in which old games are invoked as benchmarking yardsticks, may prove to be as potentially destructive, in fact self-destructive, as any other kind of degradation. We should remember also that none of this relates to the wider denigration and criticism of videogames that countless commentators have noted and which continues to drive attempts to valorise the form and gives rise to arguments about whether games con-stitute art or should be considered the equal of film, for instance. There is no need here to rehearse the arguments about the putative effects of videogames, whether these be behavioural, physiological or cultural, but we should be mindful that the broader context for calls to preserve videogames is one that frequently positions the medium as, at best, ambiguous and often unequivocally harmful (see Gunter 1998; Jones 2002; Newman and Oram 2006).

My second question deals more closely with the games themselves, and in parti-cular is concerned with understanding exactly what it could and should mean to preserve and present them in the future. As such, the final chapter of this book opens by posing some practical questions regarding our ability to define just what a video-game really is and, specifically, how it changes over time as it is updated and across territories as it is translated, or across platforms as it is converted or 'ported'. What we find is that the game is far from a static object or text but one that is frequently modified, sometimes by players, but often by developers and publishers and often in undocumented ways. Identifying 'authentic' originals is not only a challenge but may even be an impossibility, given the ongoing processes of upgrade, update and mod-ification that are part and parcel of the videogame world. This section of the book also probes more deeply into the ways in which players create and modify games through the act of play itself. For scholars like Sue Morris, videogames are ultimately co-creative media that are the products of work undertaken by developers and players who collaboratively bestow shape, form and meaning. The significance of play has far-reaching implications for any preservation activity and it would appear quite natural that ensuring that future generations of game scholars are able to play games should be a key objective. However, we have seen that original hardware and software are vulnerable to degradation over time, but we have also begun to note that there may be limitations to data migration and emulation as strategies for the stabilisation and exhibition of videogames precisely because of their uncertain inability to deliver authentic play (and aesthetic) experiences.

Put crudely, if the emulated incarnation of *Donkey Kong* does not look like the original (displaying graphical differences), does not sound like the original (having music and sound effects anomalies), is not controlled in the same way as the original (using a different hardware interface) and does not play like the original (with variations in the feel of the gameplay), then to what extent is it an appropriate archival or display resource? In the language of preservation, we might refer to these issues as defining the 'significant properties' of the original; those elements and aspects of the object to be archived that are so intrinsically important that they cannot be elided or unduly affected by the act of preservation or transformation. Clearly, there are technical aspects to defining specific properties, but the final report of the PVW project neatly asks us to think more broadly than this in posing the question, 'What makes Mario Mario?' (McDonough *et al.* 2010: 14). The definition of specific properties is often articulated in terms of technical requirements (e.g. frame rates, colour palettes, screen resolution etc.). But, as we know, videogames are far more than technology and we need to consider not only the technical environments necessary to reproduce them but also what qualitative specific properties they possess that are in danger of not making it intact through the transformative process of emulation.

> [W]e have little experience to date with users' desires and expectations regarding preserved software, or with their unstated criteria for what constitutes 'good enough' or 'better than good enough' preservation. In the language of the preservation community, we do not know what properties of games our users consider significant. Given that the preservation strategies we have evaluated with respect to computer games and interactive fiction all suffer from some degree of imperfection, a first major research question for the preservation community is 'what are the significant properties of digital games which we should seek to maintain and what are their relative degrees of importance?' Without this knowledge, we are poorly positioned to select an appropriate preservation strategy from the options available.
>
> *(McDonough* et al. *2010: 123–24)*

If it is not already apparent, I hope to show that because play is so absolutely central to understanding what a videogame 'is', it is inconceivable that we should embark upon preservation activity that does not place it front and centre. However, by examining the ways in which play configures and modifies the game in often unanticipated and sometimes unpredictable ways, I hope to show that current preservation techniques are potentially problematic and limited. Indeed, it is my assertion in this book that we may need to rethink the relationship between play and preservation. Present approaches to game preservation concentrate on making or keeping games playable in the long term. In doing this, they position play and playability as the key outcome of preservation practice. Given the centrality and transformativity of play, the efficacy of this strategy might seem incontestable. However, recognising the centrality and tranformativity of play might also lead us to an altogether different conclusion as to the purpose and objective of game preservation. If we consider that game and play are so intertwined and mutually dependent as to be essentially indivisible we arrive at what might seem like a counterintuitive position in which ensuring long-term playability need not be the principal aim of game preservation. Instead of designing strategies to preserve games so that they might be played in the future by generations of players unfamiliar with them, I want to suggest a preservation strategy focused on documenting games *in* and *at* play. What I am proposing is a shift from game preservation to game*play* preservation.

> Like Ozymandias' giant leg in the desert, the surviving software artifact will tell us nothing about what 'once dwelt in that annihilated place.' Future researchers will be sorely disappointed if we do nothing to ensure that historical documentation about virtual worlds, but created outside them, is preserved ...
>
> (*McDonough* et al. *2010: 49*)

It is clear that contextualising materials are crucial, and there can be little doubt that even the most ardent advocate of emulation would recognise the need for materials that account for the cultural, historical, economic, political as well as ludic contexts in which the game originally existed. Similarly, as Bogost (2007) notes, we should be mindful of the fact that archives and collections of videogames will serve the needs of numerous patrons with differing interests in games and gameplay. Like the National Videogame Archive, the ICHEG and the Strong National Museum of Play explicitly cater for two different audiences: the general public and patrons who visit the museum, as well as academics and scholars undertaking games and play research. As such, different strategies and foci will have more or less, or perhaps even little or no, relevance to specific audiences and stakeholders with some requiring access source code and others having absolutely no such interest in or use for such technicalities. Without doubt, different organizations and sites will accommodate variation and specificity in need and use. However, my argument here is that the issue is more serious and far-reaching than ensuring context. In fact, I want eventually to call into question current distinctions between the 'object' of preservation – its atomic unit – and the 'contextualising' materials that may enable future scholars, archive- and museum-goers to interpret or make sense of what they encounter. That the outcome of the PVW project's attempts to emulate some of its sample games reveals such variation not only between the emulation and the original but also between the output of different emulators suggests that we are some way from being able to assert that emulation truly is the only viable option. Let us not forget also that the subjects of these emulation efforts are typically games that, at a technical level at least, present a far less significant challenge than the comparative supercomputers that are the current generation of PCs, consoles and mobile devices. To be clear, I do not wish to suggest that emulation has no place in a game preservation effort, but I do hope to show that it is important to explore the potential for inaccuracies and approximations in emulated gameplay or audiovisual presentation and consider the consequences that these might have.

By considering some of the specificities and qualities of games from a player's perspective, I hope to demonstrate how in some cases even the smallest deviation in the replay of a game, whether this be in terms of interface, aesthetic or altogether more intangible qualities such the 'feel' of control and controllers, can have the most significant impact. However, as we shall see, far from being a problem around which to work, the potential limitations of emulation as a strategy for game preservation force us to engage with some fundamental questions about not only what is possible to preserve but also what is necessary and desirable to capture as we move forward. In some senses, the argument in this book follows a position outlined by Henry Lowood in some of his earlier work, in which he poses the simple but important question, 'How do we insure that future scholars will be able to play history with games?' (Lowood 2004: 3). In addressing this question, I certainly wish to align myself with the PVW position, which states that preservation is meaningless without access, but I also want to consider whether 'playing history with games' necessarily involves 'playing games'. It might seem faintly ridiculous to even posit such a question, given how important play is. However, at this stage in the project of game preservation, it is useful to interrogate the presuppositions and apparent truisms that underpin the activity. One such underlying assertion I wish to explore here is the necessity that games be preserved and presented in playable form. Emulation might well be the most pervasive strategy in current digital media preservation and its use is promoted by many commentators on game preservation (e.g. Guttenbrunner *et al.* 2008, 2010; McDonough *et al.* 2010; Monnens 2009). However, it is worth considering whether we are perhaps overly reliant on comparatively familiar approaches and whether there is a danger that we overlook some of the important qualities of games and gameplay, which are not readily accommodated by these approaches.

It is worth considering whether the availability of certain tools or their uses in other areas of digital preservation might be seen to be affecting our understanding of what game preservation could or should be. As Abraham Maslow famously noted, 'It is tempting, if the only tool you have is a hammer, to treat everything as if it were a nail' (Maslow 1966: 15). I realise that the position I am expounding here is somewhat provocative (if it does not seem downright ludicrous at this point), and if it does not seem heretical in the contexts of game studies, digital media preservation and beyond, then it must at least appear contradictory, given that I am also suggesting – and will continue to demonstrate – that play is absolutely central to any understanding and appreciation of videogames. Games are, in the words of Moulthrop (2004), 'configured' through the act of play often in unpredictable and unintended ways. Certainly, elsewhere in this book we will see examples of such 'superplay' and what the games industry itself likes to call emergent gameplay (possibly to create the illusion that its contours are more anticipated by designers and developers than they might in fact be).

There can be little doubt that play and games are intimately intertwined, and the study and preservation of the one without the other provides an incomplete or even distorted picture. However, I want to suggest that a belief in the centrality of play can lead, quite logically, to envisioning a future in which museums, archives, galleries or collections offer precisely no playable videogames. In fact, I wish to offer a way of thinking about game preservation from a gamer's point of view and suggest that placing playability as the goal of such activity might actually be a route to an incomplete or distorted picture. The key to this is distinguishing between activities that seek to make games 'playable' and those that seek to preserve, document and present the act of play. This position is informed by the assertion that play is not merely important, but rather it is *too* important to be considered separate from 'the game'. As such, just as it is important to document the complexities of narrative structure and the plasticity and mutability of games that we see through updates and versions, so too should the configurative and transformative impacts and influences of play be recorded and codified as part of the act of preservation. The position expounded in this book is that playability need not be the goal of game preservation. From the perspective of somebody involved in a project concerned with presenting games to specialist and general audiences in the context of a national media collection, the ultimate aim of 'game preservation' activity need not be to create contexts in which future patrons can play the games themselves. Rather, we might seek to document transformative and performative activity in the most thorough and imaginative ways possible. The final chapter of this book offers some more detailed analysis of the uses and limitations of emulation in the context of an alternative approach to game preservation based around the documentation of development, structures, forms and, importantly, gameplay as lived experience.

2

NEW GAMES

The production of obsolescence

It is often surprising, for both fans of videogames and non-acolytes alike, to learn that the history of the medium extends back as far as the 1960s (see Burnham 2003 for a thorough history of the early years of videogame development), and despite snappy (sub)titles like 'From Pong to Pokémon and beyond ... ' (Kent 2001), the bat and ball game comes almost a decade into gaming history. In fact, as Kent, Burnham and others note, while Steve Russell's 1962 *Spacewar!*, created in the university computer labs at MIT, is typically cited as the first videogame, experiments such as Willy Higginbotham's oscilloscope-based *Tennis for Two* potentially extend the history of electronic games back into the 1950s, while Egenfeldt-Nielsen *et al.*'s (2008) timeline manages to trace the antecedents of videogames back to 3500BC! Regardless of their identification of the exact point of origin, a few things are consistent across video-game histories. Almost all are oriented around a fairly uncontested chronology. Despite the comprehensiveness of their coverage back to classical civilisations, few timelines or histories account for the Soviet-era games collected at the Museum of Soviet Arcade Machines, for instance (see Zaitchik 2007; Connal 2010). Similarly, the plethora of often illegal copies of hardware and software, or even non-valorised games such as *Dora the Explorer* or the DS's seemingly infinite supply of horse-grooming titles like *My Horse and Me* and *Petz Pony Beauty Pageant*, are typically ignored in favour of *Doom* and *The Sims*, or more recent success stories such as *Grand Theft Auto* and *Halo*. As we shall see throughout this book, there is a palpable sense of 'progression' in gaming histories, which are invariably presented as chronologies that codify the movement not only from one decade to another but even from dominant genre or interface (Egenfeldt-Nielsen *et al.*'s chart demonstrates the (dis)appearance of 'text interfaces' and 'digitized film' in relation to adventure games, for instance; Egenfeldt-Nielsen *et al.* 2008: 52). What we detect in these and other chronologies, timelines and histories is not just a movement through time, not just progression, but rather a sense of 'progress' towards better, faster technology, if not better games. Indeed, the consistency of gaming histories and their focus on discourses of technical progress bear much in common with the broader historical narratives of computing and technology (e.g. Burnham 2003; DeMaria and Wilson 2002; Kent 2001).

In particular, we should note that, while it is incontestably moving forward, the trajectory of gaming history and technology enshrined in these narratives is far from continuous or smoothly progressive. Rather, the pattern is one that is over-whelmingly characterised by a series of 'ruptures' that demonstrably and inexorably alter the course thereafter (see Fox 2006). These 'generations', as they are known in gaming parlance, generally refer to versions of hardware and remind us of the sig-nificance of hardware platforms in delivering and ordering gameplay experience and the historical memory of it (see McDonough *et al.* 2010: 20), though we should note also the ability of particular games to operate in this similarly disruptive manner (see Lowood's 2006 discussion of 'The Doom Revolution', for instance). What is perhaps most interesting about the narrative of gaming is that, despite its use of this genealogical terminology, the notion of 'generations' is not primarily motivated by a desire to invoke lineage, the continuity of ages or the groundedness of contemporary gameplay in grand and venerable traditions of the past. Rather, what we see in nar-ratives of videogame history is a desire to maintain an inexorable sense of forward motion. It is worth noting that this is not simply a post-rationalised process, and we should note also that considerable discursive work continually takes place at the most fundamental levels. The naming conventions of gaming consoles is just one manifes-tation of this progressive urge and one place within which technology is 'spoken for' (Grint and Woolgar 1997: 32).

Whether it is because of the techno-suffix of the Nintendo 64 (N64) that alludes to the potency of the 64-bit CPU lurking inside the case or the GameBoy Advance that communicates in a rather more qualitative, prosaic way its superiority over the plain old GameBoy, we have become well used to the ways in which the nomen-clature of gaming hardware contributes to the keenly felt sense of technological progress. As a case in point, at the time of writing Sony has announced the existence and imminent release of the successor to the PSP (PlayStation Portable) handheld console, thereby obsolescing the now 'distinctly unimpressive' PSPgo.

> It's hard to believe now, but when the first shots of the PSPgo were leaked ahead of its official announcement, there was actually quite a bit of excitement around the device.
>
> *(Fahey 2011)*

Although unavailable at the time of writing, and inaccessible save for teaser videos and glowing endorsements from those apparently party to the specifications and capabilities of the device (see French 2011; Stuart 2011 though note the equally veracious claim that it is 'dead on arrival' Brightman 2011), the new console initially went under the unabashedly futuristic codename of 'Next Generation Portable'. The allusion to the next generation is as unsurprising as it is revealing, in signalling both the inevitability of future development and, perhaps as significantly, its mysterious, inscrutable, unknowable nature. However, it also takes part in the discursive narrative tradition of gaming development in signalling a break with the past rather than a continuity. The device's final production name, PlayStation Vita, which was announced at the E3 trade conference in June 2011, appears to reinstate the sense of familial continuity in reviving the PlayStation monicker, though the suffix still speaks of new life and perhaps even rebirth. Explaining the naming, Sony goes to great lengths to foreground the console's technological innovations and, above all, its revolutionary impact that 'offers new game play experiences never before seen on any device'.

> 'Vita,' which means 'Life' in Latin, was chosen as the most appropriate name for the next generation portable entertainment system as it enables a revolutionary combination of rich gaming and social connectivity within a real world context. SCE is aiming to transform every aspect of user's daily life into an entertainment experience.
>
> *(Sony Computer Entertainment 2011)*

According to deputy president of the Sony Corporation, Kaz Hirai, 'Vita means life, and we're confident that PlayStation Vita will be the first product that truly blurs those lines between PlayStation entertainment and your real life' (Purchese 2011). Vita, then, comes to speak both of the rebirth of the PlayStation system and the transformative effects of this revolutionary technology on all aspects of the life of the player.

In a similar vein, we would do well not to forget that, for all its apparent inclusiveness and the ways in which its motion controllers have been normalised as part of the lexicon of gaming, the Nintendo Wii carried its pre-production monicker of 'Revolution' (see Carless 2006) for so long that its use persists in some quarters even years after the final console's release. Of course, one thing that gamers know well is that revolutions are revolutionary for just a short time, and so, while the GameBoy Advance may once have represented a link between the present and the future, it is now unquestionably an object of the past, unavailable to buy at retail, and the subject of curious historical study. On the launch of Nintendo's 3DS handheld console in 2011, retrospectives abound: 'With the Nintendo 3DS shaping the future of handheld gaming, GamePro takes a look back at simpler times with the Game Boy Advance' (GamePro Staff 2011; Bailey 2011; Barnholt 2011; Bailey and Kemps 2011). As such, and echoing Kline *et al.*'s (2003) designation of the games industry as a 'perpetual innovation economy', Moore (2009) notes, 'The games industry relies on a rapid production and innovation cycle, one that actively enforces hardware obsolescence.' It is the contingency of future technology on the rendering out of date of present incarnations that is particularly noteworthy and, as Thompson *et al.* (2009) observe, in this 'narrative of technological novelty followed by ineluctable obsolescence' we find that gaming histories are influenced as much by these complex notions of renewal, remembering and forgetting as they are by equally problematic ideas of 'progress'.

Always already new

The contours of this discursive tradition should be familiar to scholars of 'new' media history. As Chun observes, in contrast with presently less favourable but potentially more inclusive terms such as 'multimedia', 'new media' is unaccommodating and 'portrayed other media as old or dead; it converged rather than multiplied; it did not efface itself in favor of a happy if redundant plurality' (Chun 2006: 1). Franzen's (2003) eloquent description of the trail of abandoned, superseded systems similarly draws our attentions to what he presents as an infatuation with the newness of new media. However, perhaps it is Lisa Gitelman (2008) who has best and most succinctly summarised the relentless turnover of technologies in the title of her study of the relationship between 'old' and 'new' media – *Always Already New* (and note also Gitelman and Pingree's 2003 ironically titled *New Media, 1740–1915*).

Such is the voracity and speed of renewal that the comparative nature of 'new' has shifted somewhat. As Sterne rightly notes, there has been a slippage in terminology which has seen a conflation of 'new with respect to other media' (i.e. analogue vs digital) and newness within a given medium (i.e. the 'state of the art' in design and function).

> For the better part of the nineteenth and twentieth centuries, 'new' media were primarily understood as 'new' with respect to other media: 'new' media forms replaced older media forms ... Yet computers and other digital media actually embody a different kind of newness: computers have reached a point where their 'newness' references other computers and not other media. That is why a magazine like *Wired* can call an operating system a 'revolution' with a straight face.
>
> *(Sterne 2007: 18)*

This recursivity might also explain the continued use of the term 'new' in relation to media that, in one sense, are demonstrably anything but, as we see in the case of computing and videogames alike. We must also be mindful of any temptation to consider these processes of technological obsolescence as 'natural'. As scholars such as Evan Watkins have noted, obsolescence is a category that is discursively produced in the service of particular goals and objectives. For Watkins, this is as much about creating obsolete people or groups who are unable to access the most up-to-date of technology as it is about the intrinsic nature of the technology itself. We will return to considering Watkins's perspective in the following chapter as we explore residuality and the persistence of 'old' games both as a strategy and as a necessity for different audiences. For now, we will follow the position of Thompson (1979) in noting that the categories of obsolescence, longevity and durability are socially constructed and frequently do not refer to the material qualities, functionality or utility of the things themselves, whether they be buildings, cars or videogames. In relation to videogames, much of what we see is related to and driven by commercial imperatives.

As Huh and Ackerman (2009) note, 'The ways in which computing devices are designed today are good resulting representations of planned obsolescence.' Obsolescence, then, is not simply a marketing discourse or a product of a sleight of hand in the naming of hardware or equipment. The rapidity of technological change and progress is sufficiently well known and even predictable that it has become enshrined in 'law'. Moore's Law, named after the Intel co-founder and originally proposed over 50 years ago (Moore 1965), has come to refer to the doubling in computing power that occurs every 18 months in the computer industry and its canonisation has come to symbolise the inexorability of technological development and progress. For game developers such as Epic's vice president Mark Rein, this means that the future of consoles can be glimpsed in the PC of today:

> Don't forget every game that's ultimately built is built on a PC. PCs are always going to be the tools through which all games get made … With the PC you can simulate the future – you can put enough hardware in a PC to show you what a future console will look like.
>
> *(Rein interviewed in Minkley 2011)*

Commenting on Epic's *Samaritan Unreal* demo (2011), created on current high-specification PC hardware to illustrate the putatively inevitable future of mainstream gaming systems, Epic president Michael Capps perfectly captures the sense of the ultimate inevitable availability of the presently unattainable. 'Very few if any consumers today would be able to run the demo, but with the rapid advancement of technology, it's not unlikely that we'll be playing something that looks like this before too long' (Capps interviewed in Kohler 2011). Similarly, Rein notes that its function was more than just a showcase:

> It was kind of our love letter to hardware manufacturers … The next-gen, we expect, will look like that. If you fast forward a year or two years that should be a fairly common gamer's spec … We hope the console manufactures [*sic*] look at that and go, jeez, if we aim for that in our next consoles we'll be competitive with what you'll be able to do on a PC in a year, year and half from now. A reasonably priced PC – obviously you can do it on an expensive PC already.
>
> *(Rein interviewed in Minkley 2011)*

As some commentators have noted, Moore's Law is, to some extent, a self-fulfilling prophecy, as it is used to help schedule and direct patterns of research and development as much as it documents them.

> The fact that it holds so well is an effect of the way actors (in industry, in science and in government) judge their own and each others' accomplishments with respect to what Moore's Law predicts. They direct their efforts towards achieving the predicted values.
>
> *(van Lente and Rip 1998: 206)*

As Sterne (2007) and others suggest, Moore's Law is far from an inconvenience to the computing industries and there is little desire to stabilise a situation that appears to drive innovation and sales in the marketplace. Longevity, or rather a lack of it, is built into the strategy for the product from the outset. Whether we see this in relation to General Motors' 1920s introduction of the yearly model change or more recent trends in the mobile phone marketplace that give rise to what Huang and Truong (2008) have called a 'disposable technology paradigm', we see business models normalising the process of rendering obsolete existing products and services and reducing the usage lifetime so that products and services are discarded long before they cease to function or before they cease to be potentially functionally useful. For Sterne (2007: 21), it is vital that we appreciate that technological obsolescence has shifted away from questions of 'genuine innovation, utility, and, to some degree, necessity'. As such, while we might see that obsolescence operates on what Slade (2006) and others have called a 'stylistic' level, in which less durable objects are 'made to break' and differ perhaps only marginally from those that they replace on their designated and designed-in 'death dates', they are nonetheless coded as revolutionary and new (Smart 2010: 85).

What is so striking about this situation is the realisation that however truly revolutionary or new we might really want to call them, the discursive space of advertising and marketing messages, for instance, within which new media like videogames are encountered and understood essentially founds them on their own eventual and inevitable designation as obsolete systems. As Dovey and Kennedy have noted, the games industry does a very effective job of selling a utopian dream of continual upgrade, although we should note that this concept has slightly different meanings in different parts of the games industry. The outdating of the old is an anticipated and predictable part of design practice: 'this is not a teleological dynamic, there is no end point in sight', they note, 'designers find themselves permanently looking for and exploring new capacities, falling enthusiastically upon each new generation' (Dovey and Kennedy 2006: 52–53). Upgrade may conjure images of a relatively stable core to which additions improve performance or augment capability. Certainly, we can identify any number of peripherals such as fishing rod controllers, dancemats and Wii Motion Plus devices. However, the idea of upgrading as adding components or peripherals is one that applies most specifically to the PC gaming. As the authors of PVW (McDonough *et al.* 2010: 111) note, 'But will it run *Crysis?*' has become a videogaming meme to rival 'All your base are belong to us' and refers specifically to the formidable technical requirements of Crytek's first person shooter, and more broadly to high or even outlandish technical demands. Accordingly, there exist vibrant markets for high-performance graphics cards and bespoke gaming PCs (e.g. from Alienware and Commodore Gaming) tuned for gameplay and motherboards supporting multiple graphics cards, high-bandwidth RAM and overclocked processors which may be individually replaced as new games push the technical requirements yet further. Indeed, 2011's *Crysis 2 Ultra Upgrade* pack expands on the bifurcation of its PC platform by offering differing features to systems equipped with DX9 versus the more recent DX11 multimedia, game programming and graphics APIs.

> When using the new 'Ultra' spec, DX9 platforms will benefit from real-time local reflections and contact shadows. The owners of DX11 platforms, in

addition, will be able to enjoy hardware tessellation (requires the installation of the 'DX11 Ultra Upgrade'), parallax occlusion mapping and several improvements for shadows, water, particles, depth of field and motion blur.

(Crytek UK 2011)

By contrast, upgrading in the console marketplace typically refers to the wholesale replacement of one system with another. The implications of this discarding of equipment are enormous, particularly when we consider the games console or platform as the direct means of accessing 'generations' of software along with PC and console peripherals, which, of course, each have their own biographies of obsolescence that may or may not be connected with the core system.

Videogames are rubbish

Before we proceed, we should consider the other impacts of stylistic and technological obsolescence, and once again Sterne is particularly insightful and forceful in his analysis of this as a 'spatial' problem:

> 'New' media technologies as we know them, and all of their counterparts, are defined by their own future decomposition. Obsolescence is a nice word for disposability and waste. Billions of computers, Internet hardware, cellphones, portable music devices, and countless other consumer electronics have already been trashed or await their turn. The entire edifice of new communication technology is a giant trash heap waiting to happen …
>
> *(Sterne 2007: 17)*

It behoves us to remember that the obsolescing of old videogames hardware and software, along with the rest of the detritus of old–new media equipment that Sterne lists, is not simply a conceptual issue that impacts on our ability to understand and appreciate history and context. It creates literal, material problems of waste. As scholars of trash and dereliction of materiality (e.g. Strasser 1999; Buchli and Lucas 2001; Neville and Villeneuve 2002; Edensor 2005; Grossman 2006) encourage us to appreciate, discarded consoles and joypads, mobile phones and computer monitors do not simply disappear. It is only comparatively recently that waste, or 'e-waste' as the by-products and debris of computing industries is typically known, has become an issue for scholars and policy makers. As Moore (2009) notes, 'each generation is accompanied by an immense international transportation of games hardware, software (in various storage formats) and peripherals'. The concerted effort to bring hardware and software to global markets for co-ordinated launches brings its own environmental impacts, but the true cost of obsolescence is to be found on Sterne's 'trash heaps'. The problem is not simply a spatial one, of course, and investigations into the e-waste reveal 'toxic chemicals and metals whose landfill, recycling and salvaging all produce distinct environmental and social problems' (Moore 2009). In recent years, organisations such as Greenpeace have begun to audit the impact and practices of consumer electronics companies and have found the games industry to be somewhat lagging in its attitudes, with Nintendo scoring particularly low in relation to its recycling procedures and the use and disposal of hazardous materials (see 'Guide to Greener Electronics – Nintendo, January', Greenpeace International 2010). One 'ugly reality' of the imperative to discard new media equipment such as videogames systems as they become coded as obsolete is

> mountains of old electronics piling up. Ground water in parts of China was so polluted by toxic chemicals that it was undrinkable. Children in Ghana, Pakistan, and India were enveloped in acrid fumes every day from burning the PVC insulation off wires to recover copper.
>
> *(Dowdall 2009)*

In addition to the environmental impact of this waste, the discussion of computer trash serves as another powerful reminder of the materiality of videogaming. Although it is tempting to focus on the immateriality, virtuality or 'demateriality' (after Slater 2000) of digital media, these issues force us to confront videogames on a physical plane. In late 2011, the inconvenient truth of e-waste was brought into sharp relief with Molleindustria's *Phone Story*. Released on the iTunes App Store, the game 'is an educational game about the dark side of your favorite smart phone. Follow your phone's journey around the world and fight the market forces in a spiral of planned obsolescence' (Molleindustria 2011a). Dealing with issues including the environmental and health impacts of the demand for minerals such as coltan, working conditions in Chinese manufacturing plants and cycles of planned obsolescence and the disposal of e-waste, Molleindustria (2011a) encourages players to 'Keep Phone Story on your device as a reminder of your impact'. The content of the game is worthy of consideration in terms its political and ethical position, while the choice to release on the iOS platform positions it in a complex network of meanings and practices. With Apple and its global production ecosystem at the heart of Molleindustria's criticism, the game exists as a self-referential critique of the platform – delivered on the platform. However, *Phone Story* is more than a digital *memento mori*. To fight what it describes as the exploitative and abusive practices of this product of global capitalism and consumer desire, Molleindustria takes advantage of the revenue model that underpins the iTunes App Store:

> 70% of the app store revenues go to the developers. We, Molleindustria, pledge to redirect this money to the organizations that are fighting corporate abuses. In addition, we ask festivals and art institutions that are interested in exhibiting the game to contribute to the cause instead of paying artist fees.
>
> *(Molleindustria 2011a)*

Of course, what is most notable about *Phone Story* is that its time on the iTunes App Store was short lived. Four days after it was approved for distribution via the Apple-curated distribution and retail network, it was removed. According to Molleindustria

(@molleindustria 2011), Apple's concerns related to violations of the 'App Store Review Guidelines' (Apple Inc. 2011). In its discussion of the details (accessed by clicking the 'Banned from the App Store' logo now adorning the *Phone Story* site), Molleindustria claims that the specific violations related to four sections of the Guidelines:

> Apple explained that the game is in violation of the following guidelines:
>
> 15.2   Apps that depict violence or abuse of children will be rejected
> 16.1   Apps that present excessively objectionable or crude content will be rejected
> 21.1   Apps that include the ability to make donations to recognized charitable organizations must be free
> 21.2   The collection of donations must be done via a web site in Safari or an SMS
>
> *(Molleindustria 2011b)*

Although contesting some of the claimed violations, Molleindustria remains unable to distribute *Phone Story* via the iTunes App Store and this leads to the consideration of alternative strategies:

> We are currently considering two steps:
>
> • Produce a new version of Phone Story that depicts the violence and abuse of children involved in the electronic manufacturing supply chain in a non-crude and non-objectionable way.
> • Release a version for the Android market and jailbroken ios devices.
>
> The users who managed to buy the app before it went offline are now owners of a rare collector edition piece.
>
> *(Molleindustria 2011b)*

Indeed, as Brown (2011) reports, the day after it was removed from the iTunes App Store, *Phone Story* was released on the Android App Store.

We shall return to issues arising from the fragility of online distribution networks and the resultant disappearance of games, but for now it is worth considering the issues *Phone Story* raises in relation to the materiality of new media. While in no way wishing to detract from the consideration of environmental impact, the mountains of discarded systems and software serve another important function. For preservation practitioners, the importance of materiality and the inherent limitations of software preservation approaches should be manifestly clear.

Crucial though it is as a global issue, the concentration on e-waste perhaps has a tendency to present 'new' and 'old', 'in use' and 'discarded', in binary opposition, and we will complicate the simplicity of this situation as our analysis of the lived experiences of gameplay unfolds throughout this book. For now, however, it is useful to follow Thompson *et al.* (2009) in ensuring that our understanding of the videogame industry's conceptualisation and invocation of its past in the process of encouraging interest and excitement in the next generation recognises the rather more nuanced position that we observe in operation:

You say you want a revolution

> Because obsolescence calls on the familiar in a pejorative sense – the obsolete thing has become too familiar (it now lacks novelty and surprise) – it is easy to overlook the necessity of familiarity (and thus obsolescence) to computer game development and play. After all, play demands familiarity as well as novelty; deeply complex and satisfying tasks – the kind the best play sets out and rewards generously – can only be accomplished with a level of mastery, of skill born of familiarity born of practice … Computer games must always be the same, only different, familiar enough to be recognisable as forms, but new enough to create wonder as ludica.
>
> (Thompson *et al.* 2009)

The revealing truth illuminated here is that, regardless of their naming strategies, revolution is precisely not what videogame developers are in the business of delivering. The videogame, thus, is required to appear both pioneering and familiar at once. For Acland (2007b), the move away from analyses that reproduce marketing discourses of rupture and breaks from the past is vital to any study of contemporary media. The preoccupation with technological change has seen 'new media' as a term 'evacuated of meaning' and has given rise to analysis that 'neglects the crucial role of continuity in historical processes [and] ignores the way the dynamics of culture bump along unevenly, dragging the familiar into new contexts' (Acland 2007b: xix).

Reflecting on the development of *Super Mario 64*, a game whose presentation in 3D is frequently seen as representing a 'paradigm shift' in game design (Loguidice and Barton 2009: 269), Ste Curran reveals the balancing act between the revolutionary and familiar faced by Shigeru Miyamoto:

> The game had to be as instinctive and tactile as it was in 2-D, allowing the player satisfaction in every single instant, as well as giving them excitement through the larger goal of exploration. 'I thought it was important to make the game so that players would feel fresh surprise and joy in such simple acts as moving Mario,' says the designer. 'But as well as that, I wanted the players to feel that they were playing with something really new and unprecedented.'
>
> *(Curran 2004: 50)*

Similarly, for all of its 'revolutions' in motion control, the Wii remains reassuringly a videogame console and its Wii remote is replete with a directional pad and buttons that have been the staple of all Nintendo videogame equipment from the Game & Watch handhelds of the 1980s onward. Indeed, speaking of the successor to the Wii (the Wii U, codenamed Project Café) prior to its launch or official announcement, Nintendo president Saturo Iwata noted that 'we have never abandoned the + Control Pad and buttons for our game systems because we think these functions are advantageous when creating highly reactive games' (Parfitt 2011a).

As such, while championing revolutions in console and controller design and heralding new types of gameplay and interaction, we see decades' worth of back-referencing and, in some senses, remarkably little change in some of the fundamental interaction design and interface layout decisions between the Wii family and Nintendo's handheld gaming systems of the 1980s. Indeed, it is worth remembering that, as Jones (2008: 127) notes, while expectations for the original Wii were shaped by high hopes, 'At the same time, the marketing has stressed simplicity, accessibility and a revolutionary *return* to the kind of simple fun long associated with the Nintendo brand.' The complexity of the Wii's marketing in offering a revolutionary return is more than a little redolent of Apple's recent strategies, particularly in relation to the iPod, and it is difficult not to notice the aesthetic similarities between the Wii and 'classic' iPod designs. Nonetheless, the cacophony of endorsements from development and publishing luminaries that greeted the Wii U console, and in particular the controller's official unveiling, unequivocally pointed in just one direction.

> 'This new controller really revolutionises the traditional pad.'
>
> Yves Guillemot, CEO, Ubisoft
>
> 'It has connectivity, advanced graphics and an engaging interface. This is exactly what it takes to shape the future.'
>
> Martin Tremblay, President, Warner Bros. Interactive Entertainment
>
> 'It's a phenomenal piece of technology. It's a platform that's really going to revolutionise what's happening in consoles.'
>
> Frank Gibeau, President, EA Games
>
> 'It means we can make games of the sort that we were never able to make before. It's not just more of the same, it really is opening up a whole new world of gameplay.'
>
> Warren Spector, Vice President & Creative Director, Junction Point, Disney Interactive Media Group
>
> *(Nintendo Network @ E3 2011)*

Yet, for all the talk of the future of gaming, the Wii U's controller, like the Wiimote before it, manifestly occupies a somewhat precarious position between innovation and familiarity, revolution and continuity. Nintendo's E3 announcement of the system treads a careful line between talk of the 'game-changing' nature of the system that at the same time draws on the legacy and success of the Wii. Wii U's touch-screen is a graphical indicator of its break with traditional game controllers, while its ABYX face buttons and 'shoulder triggers' are arranged and labelled in precisely the same way as those found on the SNES joypad from the 1990s. Nintendo's technical demonstrations operate in this liminal zone between past and present, revolution and evolution. As Boxer (2011) notes, the ability to use the controllers (Wiimotes) from the original Wii alongside the Wii U's touchscreen controller presents some intriguing gameplay possibilities, but above all the demos such as *Chase Mii* 'rammed home the message that part of the point of the new controller is about interplay with the familiar remote control'. What we see here is the actuality of familiarity and continuity wrapped in the hyperbole of innovation and revolution. Perhaps most strikingly, we should note the speed and ease with which the 'revolution' that was the Wiimote is rendered 'ordinary' and even mundane in the light of the new new technology.

Similarly, Mario remains an ever-present figure, not only featuring in 'next generation' titles like *Super Mario Galaxy* (literally from another world) but also in Wii versions and remakes of *Mario Kart, Smash Bros.* and the *New Super Mario Bros.* (which is inevitably featured front and centre in the launch line-up for the Wii U). Ashton similarly notes the ambivalence of the videogames industry's attitudes to its historical technologies and accomplishments:

> Past technologies are selectively remembered and recovered as part of the foundations for future success. This is a tension, that can be unpacked in a number of ways, across current industry transformations and strategies that potentially erase the past whilst simultaneously seeking to recover it as part of an evidence-base for future development.
>
> *(Ashton 2008)*

As such, while videogames might initially appear to be part of a relentlessly forward-marching industry, the reality of the situation is a balancing act that simultaneously invokes the revolution of innovation and reassuring familiarity of continuity of form and function. Old generations are not simply coded as obsolete but are selectively remembered and invoked as means by which the present may be assessed. In one sense, then, what was once cutting edge and new is recast as a benchmark by which subsequent development may be measured. Throughout the remainder of this chapter, we will explore the ways through which this dialogue between old and new, past and present, obsolete and forthcoming, takes place. Initially our analysis focuses on an examination of hardware systems and the literal writing out of old systems through both discursive practices and managed technological compatibility; it then moves to an investigation of the construction of the journalistic and retail practices that frame and structure ludic and technological desire, the apportioning of value, as well as the access to play.

The next generation

ANNOUNCER: Krusty The Clown is brought to you by the new Gamestation 256 … It's slightly faster! To the maaaax!

BART: 256? Oh and I'm stuck with this useless 252

[KICKS IT INTO AN OPEN FIRE]

GAMESTATION: Don't destroy me! I can still make you happy! To the maaaax!

(The Simpsons 2000)

As we have seen, the sight of Bart's 'old' Gamestation console causally tossed into the fire for not living up to the promise of the new '256' model speaks to both the excesses of a disposable consumer culture that generates literal mountains of waste and debris, and also to what Dovey and Kennedy (2006) refer to as the 'upgrade culture' that underpins the contemporary videogame business. What is so striking about the discarding is not merely that it is a wholesale offering, in reality less of an 'upgrade' than a straight replacement, but also that it is oriented exclusively around technology. There is nothing in the fictional advert to explain Bart's immediate volte-face or his derision for what has become 'the useless 252', save for the fact that the 256 is 'slightly faster', albeit to the max. We might well think that *The Simpsons* is simply operating at the level of pastiche here and that its portrayal of gaming culture borders on the grotesque, and while this might be the case to some extent, scrutiny of videogame manufacturer's promotional materials may give us pause.

> You don't really need to know how it works.
>   You don't need to know that the Cell Processor is one of the most advanced technologies you'll ever place in your living room. You don't really need to know about the RSX Reality Synthesizer, the advanced workhorse behind those high definition graphics. You don't even need to know about the seven vector processing chips designed to produce the smartest AI ever.
>   *(Sony Computer Entertainment Europe 2007)*

And yet we do know about these things because promotional and marketing materials like these produced by Sony to support its PS3 console make great play of these technical features, placing them front and centre in communications about console developments. As we saw earlier, Crytek's *Crysis 2 Ultra Upgrade* performs similar work in reassuring players of its cutting-edge credentials and, like Sony's discussion of the PS3, the impenetrability of the description of the visual processing effects and concepts on offer in the Ultra Upgrade becomes an important part of the message. As such, accompanying the slideshows of high-resolution images, journalistic and marketing discourse encourages players to bathe in the reflectivity of the gameworld – or, at least, lurk in the Variable Penumbra of its shadows. 'Don't know your parallax occlusion mapping from your custom shape based bokeh depth of field effects? Don't worry about it!' (McWhertor 2011).

This is far from a recent occurrence and we have grown well used to the putative technological prowess of the system being proudly emblazoned on the console casing itself, whether in the form of the huge gold '16-bit' logo conspicuously inscribed on the Sega MegaDrive or in the very name of the Nintendo 64. Indeed, Sony's previous console campaigns have performed very similar work, albeit in rather different manner. The PS2 'FunAnyone?' television and print advertising campaign is a case in point. According to Jonathan Mildenhall, joint managing director at agency TBWA, replacing the obscurity of the 'Third Place' UK launch campaign with its TV ad directed by David Lynch, 'Fun Anyone?', sought to 'broaden the brand proposition to a wider market by making the tone lighter but keeping the brand's cool image' (cited in Sweeney 2003). As Sweeney notes, the ad's strapline, 'I don't know how it works but it's good, isn't it?' draws on agency TBWA\London's research into non-players (see Wheeler 2003) and aims 'to demonstrate how easy the console is to use' and 'dispel the reasons people give for not being interested in gaming'. While we might read 'I don't know how it works, but it's good, isn't it?' as an assurance that no technical competencies are required to have fun, it positions the console as an inscrutable 'black box' in much the same way as the later PS3 campaign does.

The presentation of the platform as technology plays an extraordinarily important role in the discursive process of obsolescence. Certainly, Sony is absolutely correct, and on one level players absolutely do not need to know about the Cell Processor, the RSX Synthesizer, whether their console is 16-bit or 64-bit. However, as Donald Norman (1988) has pointed out, these 'liquid features' are crucially important in the marketing and coding of technologies as new, and, perhaps even more significantly, newer than those that they replace. What we see in Sony's PS3 promotional materials is not simply an assertion that the Cell and RSX technologies lurk within the console, impressive though they may be, or at least, impressive though they sound, whatever they actually do. Rather, what they encourage is a consideration of the way in which these technologies represent a quantum leap.

> The important thing to know is that the people designing PS3 games know – and the results are becoming more spectacular by the month. Really all you need to know is that everything required for the next decade of gaming is in this black box. With the PS3's strength only just being realised, you can only expect better, greater and stronger titles over the coming months.
>
> *(Sony Computer Entertainment Europe 2007)*

The conception of the console as a supercomputer comprising components so powerful as to be unfathomable by all but professional programmers and AI experts is both a paean to progress and also demands the consideration of the obsolesced technology that is replaced. As we see, whether they are in the accompanying promotional or instructional materials or staring back at us from the graphics on the casing, we do not have to look far for reminders of the white heat that burns inside this black box. The allusion to the black box is an equally important one here and carries associations of inscrutability, reliability and also a kind of techno-magic as it transforms abstract commands into something intelligible, even playable.

It is interesting to consider the way in which the presentation of platforms as technology operates in a strange kind of hinterland between the past, present and future. On one level, it feeds the kind of discourse of technological progression that, perhaps understandably, is reproduced in popular and scholarly literature on videogames. For instance, in their overview of console gaming, Guttenbrunner *et al.* (2010: 74) note that 'In the beginning of video game history the technology was limited to very simple graphics and sound', which, in retrospect, might seem to be self-evident, but which potentially overlooks, or at least understates, the fact that in their day these simple graphics and sound were the state of the art. If we follow the logic of technological progress, there will doubtless come a time when the PS3, Xbox 360 and their ilk will appear to offer limited graphics and sound too. However, Sony's bold claim that the PS3's technological superiority makes it 'Future Proof' (a phrase littered with some abandon throughout its promotional materials) negotiates an altogether more complex journey. Was the PS2 not future proof? Or perhaps the PS3 is future proofed only for the 'next decade of gaming'.

Backwards (in)compatibility

Once we begin to consider the business of videogame platforms, we might have some more confidence in Sony's ability to predict the longevity of PS3's lifespan. It is worth briefly considering how the current model of platforms arose in the games marketplace. In the earliest days of home videogames, games were delivered effectively 'hardwired' into dedicated systems. And so if a player wished to play *Pong* at home, they could purchase a *Pong* machine to attach to their television set. There was certainly ample choice and, in addition to Atari, a large number of companies produced *Pong* 'clones' or variations of the game that were, in turn, delivered on their own bespoke systems. We will see more of the variations between games and the processes of producing clones or conversions in the final chapter. For now, it is important to note that whether these early gaming systems were designed to deliver a single game or multiple games (or subtly different versions), each was 'built in' to the hardware.

Being tied to specific games meant that the hardware had a necessarily limited scope and could not be reinvented to deliver new gameplay or new game types. As such, when *Space Invaders*, or (more likely in the 1970s) football, hockey or a host of other 'sports games' that bore more than a passing resemblance to modified versions of ping-pong (see Burnham 2003) became the game of choice, the *Pong* machine might find itself relegated to the cupboard or loft, or, at best, would take its place alongside a growing collection of dedicated games machines. It would not be until the Fairchild Channel F in 1976 that the business model we are familiar with today would emerge. The Channel F introduced removable cartridges (Videocarts in Fairchild's parlance) on which games were delivered. By plugging in a cartridge, the console was effectively reprogrammed, allowing a single console to play host to a catalogue of games. While Fairchild was the first to market such a system it was Atari that capitalised on it and created commercial success with the VCS (aka Atari 2600) console in the late 1970s. For the first time, the VCS presented developers and players not simply with a videogame console but with a videogame 'platform'. For developers, the advantage of producing games for a stable, technically consistent and predictable target system reaps obvious rewards not least because it promises some degree of longevity in the marketplace, thereby offsetting some of the risk of financing lengthy game development processes. For players and consumers, the promise of the platform is found both in its commercial proposition and in its future promise. Once purchased, additional software in the form of cartridges, tapes, optical discs or downloads promises to transform the system into a host of new games perhaps spanning genres that do not yet exist. Simultaneously, the platform promises that the best games are yet to come. As the Sony PS3 literature implores, the platform is potent on arrival but only reveals its true strength through time as developers learn to harness, or perhaps tame, its raw power.

The promise of the platform sees it operating at the boundary of the future and present of gaming as it maps out the next generation from a position that renders obsolete the once-new. The flexibility and durability of platforms, certainly when compared with the built-in game systems of the pre-Fairchild marketplace, seems to offer much to consumers and developers alike. However, this presentation of the next generation is potentially troublesome and not a little scurrilous. The sleight of hand is perhaps a little harder to see when we consider examples from the here and now, but is potentially easier to detect when we look back further. Even at the level of considering them as technology, we would do well to remember the ease with which we fall into the trap of designating previous generations of games systems as limited in their capabilities, despite once similarly operating on this next-generation cusp. The ease with which we reproduce the discourse of technological progress in relation to videogames is certainly wrapped up in the designation of consoles and platforms as technology. The visibility of faster chips capable of generating greater fidelity in graphics and sound, richer AI, or even 3D where 2D was the standard, facilitates the comparison of the next generation with the present and, in the case of processor speeds or the polygon counts of graphics chips, literally if not meaningfully, allows for a quantification of technological progress. By dint of quantifiable inadequacies and made understandable and even inevitable by the implacability of Moore's Law, for instance, the present generation is rendered technologically impotent and obsolete. However, there is more to this process of obsolescence than technical one-upmanship and the trading in meaningful or liquid features. We must not overlook the fact that whatever we might think and whatever platform holders might claim, the longevity of a platform is at least partly dictated by the platform holder itself. Clearly, the market may intervene and some consoles may perform sufficiently badly at retail that their manufacture ceases before the intended time (the Sega Dreamcast is a famous example, but countless other consoles have come and gone over the decades). However, it is the planned obsolescence of platforms to which we turn our attentions here, the consequences of which are far reaching.

> When old media are replaced, there are no longer systems to support them, and they will not run on the latest software and hardware platforms. As a result, even if the medium on which a game's data is stored is able to last a hundred years, after only a fraction of that time, its data will be unreadable in the latest hardware and software environments.
>
> (Monnens 2009: 5)

The arrival of new systems means the loss of support for older platforms which, in turn, means that these machines eventually disappear as they are no longer manufactured, repaired, or exist under warranties or support contracts, which means that old games become literally unplayable. From a preservation and games history perspective, the consequences of this situation are with us now and, as we noted at the very beginning of this book, old games hardware and software is not now readily available. In 2011, Nintendo will gladly sell you any number of DS variants (in 2D, 3D, with large displays, smaller displays), but the GameBoy is unavailable. The GameBoy is obsolete; a previous generation of technologically superseded hardware. The clear message here is that GameBoy games have been similarly superseded. Perhaps, then, there is no need to play them, given the current generation of games available for the technologically superior DS platform? We can begin to see how the decisions to support or drop generations of hardware impact enormously on our conceptualisations about the value of old games. It is perhaps unsurprising given, Nintendo's effective silencing of GameBoy gameplay, that we should so readily wish to discuss the history of gaming as a movement from limited technology to the next generation. What is worse for our purposes here is that the lack of a platform's availability closes down the possibility of playing the games that were created for it. Just as the availability of the GameBoy as a platform made possible a generation of games through the release of a catalogue of cartridges over the years of its active life, with no GameBoy hardware, there are no GameBoy games.

Clearly, we are overplaying the hand here. GameBoys do not simply cease to exist in the wake of their technological betters. However, we have noted already that the half-life of consoles and cartridges is short and the physical media simply will not last forever. Surely, the world is not in danger of running out of GameBoy consoles today, but if we set our sights on preserving or documenting videogames for generations (in human terms) to come, then we must realise that the decision to cease production necessarily shortens the period wherein GameBoy games are accessible. Of course, even my concession here will not satisfy those familiar with backwards compatibility. Backwards compatibility refers to 'The strategy to let consumers use games of earlier systems on newer generation models [and] has been a successful commercial strategy since the third generation of video games' (Guttenbrunner 2007: 46). The existence of backwards compatibility systems would seem to undermine every aspect of the argument assembled in this section of the book and, worse still, it delivers the killer blow with cutting-edge technological aplomb – another marvel of the black box. At face value, backwards compatibility appears to ease the potentially uncomfortable transitions between the ruptures of new platforms and next generations. As Guttenbrunner (2007: 46) goes on to note, 'Sony's Playstation 3 is able to play games both from Sony Playstation 2 as well as Sony Playstation. Except that it isn't. Or rather it might be. It all rather depends on which version of the PS3 hardware you have. And which version of the firmware it is running. And which PS2 games you try to play. And which version of the games are actually pressed onto the discs that you own … ' In fact, Guttenbrunner recognises that there is variation in the implementation of backwards compatibility across different iterations of the PS3 console, noting that '[it] is backwards compatible to the PS2 and the original PlayStation. While this is done by hardware emulation in the first US and Japanese models it was switched to software emulation for cost reasons on the European model' (Guttenbrunner 2007: 27). Sony's European PS3 website does a good job of explaining the position:

PLAYSTATION 3 (60GB) System

Some PlayStation 2 or PlayStation format software titles may perform differently on this system than they do on PlayStation 2 or PlayStation systems, or may not perform properly on this system.

PLAYSTATION 3 (40GB) System

This model of the PLAYSTATION 3 system is designed to play PLAYSTATION 3 format software and has limited backward compatibility. This system is not compatible with, and will not play, PlayStation 2 format software. Some PlayStation format software may play on this system.

The vast number of PlayStation and PlayStation 2 games available in Europe (including upcoming titles) are being verified for play compatibility with PLAYSTATION 3.

The status of titles may improve as we continually update the PLAYSTATION 3 operating system software, including individual game software updates, so please be sure to visit this site often to check on the very latest PLAYSTATION 3 compatibility status for your PlayStation and PlayStation 2 games.

(Sony Computer Entertainment Europe 2008)

As an addendum to this advice, none of the currently available PS3 consoles in Europe supports any kind of backwards compatibility (see Sony Computer Entertainment America 2011 for detail of the similarly convoluted US backwards compatibility situation). Even for those consoles equipped with backwards compatibility, the picture is unclear (sometimes quite literally, with graphical aberrations as well as crashes and gameplay anomalies). As we see here, backwards compatibility is far from unproblematic and far from universally implemented. Lest we think that Sony is an edge case, Nintendo's approach to backwards compatibility with its handheld consoles is equally revealing. While the initial version of the GameBoy Advance offered backwards compatibility with original GameBoy cartridges, this was dropped for the release of the GameBoy micro, and all subsequent handhelds have offered no backwards compatibility with GameBoy games. Similarly, and following along the chain of progression, the original Nintendo DS offered GameBoy Advance backwards compatibility with a front-facing cartridge slot that accepted GBA carts. This was for single-player games only and did not support multiplayer linkup games, which required an additional (unsupported) GameBoy Advance Link Cable. This compatibility was retained for the DS Lite but removed for the DSi, DS XL and 3DS. It is small wonder that, as we saw previously, we are invited to 'Remember the Game Boy Advance' on the launch of the 3DS (GamePro Staff 2011), as, perhaps admitting some degree of facetiousness, there is not much more we can do.

We need only consider the markedly different ways in which the word 'legacy' is used. In everyday parlance, as in the terminology of the culture and heritage sectors, 'legacy' conjures images of bequests, inheritance and the continuity of generations. For the technology industries, however, 'legacy systems' are a liability, 'obsoleted' hardware and software that, despite the best efforts of supersessionary discourse, is still in use and must be supported and catered for. We will return to the way games alter over time and probe deeper some of the ways in which backwards compatibility actually worsens for some titles with successive firmware revisions. For now, it will suffice to note that backwards compatibility, even when offered, does not unproblematically recapture the experience of the original gameplay.

Whether we can go as far as to suggest that this approach to backwards compatibility betrays a begrudging interest is perhaps a matter for debate. However, we can certainly see that, whether wittingly or otherwise, the gradual diminution of backwards compatibility and the progressive forgetting of previous generations of gameplay signals a clear message to those who are part of or observing the games marketplace. Old games will eventually, inevitably, become obsolete and, by virtue of the material lack of suitable hardware, will become impossible to (re)play. I want to suggest that the handling of backwards compatibility represents one powerful and effective way that the videogames industry closes down access to its old titles. While its intentions may be to fix attention on the next generation, or even the next raft, of games for understandable commercial benefit, one consequence is the systematic devaluing of the old games that are subsequently displaced in the marketplace. The logic of progression and obsolescence, of renewal and replacement, and the discursive construction of the console as technology progressing and developing towards a mythical upgraded perfection, serve to relegate previous hardware and, by virtue of the intimately close ties with the delivery platform, serve to code previous games as inferior and unworthy.

The best game is the next game

> Of course, what's really exciting about Microsoft Kinect is what it promises for games … I can't wait for Kinect 2.
>
> *(Johnson 2010, reporting from the pre-launch demonstration of Microsoft's Kinect motion controller peripheral for Xbox 360)*

Of course, while the existence of platforms and backwards (in)compatibilities facilitates the management of access to old games in quite literal ways by allowing and disallowing the use of old software on current and future generations of readily available and supported hardware, these are by no means the only mechanisms by which consumers' attentions are fixed on the next generation. Print-based and online magazines perform an important role in shaping attitudes towards old and new, and represent a crucial site in which discourses of obsolescence and technological progress are played out:

> Pokémon Black and White
> Evolution or Revolution?

Although it feels initially inquisitive, the front cover of Future Publishing's *NGamer* Nintendo magazine (issue 59, February 2011) leaves us with little doubt about one thing. Whether *Pokémon*'s latest incarnations represent a quantum leap or merely an incremental improvement to the long-running game series, they are definitely, obviously, inevitably, going to be better than the previous versions. In fact, the four-page review spread concedes that *Pokémon Black/White* is not revolutionary but reminds the reader that,

> Pokémon is not the home of innovation or shocking thrills; it's where familiarity breeds … not contempt, but warm nostalgia. Black/White, for the length of its excellent story mode, simply reminds us what we are nostalgic for: setting out in the wild grass with but one Pokémon to our name and catching 'em all.
>
> (NGamer *Pokémon Review 2011: 59*)

Reminding us of Thompson *et al.*'s (2009) insight into the balancing act between delivering invention and familiarity, *NGamer*'s review deftly invited readers to remember that shocking revolutions in gameplay are not nearly as desirable as the proposition of beginning a new game. Once we have collected 'em all in *Pokémon Diamond* and *Pearl*, *Platinum*, *SoulSilver* and *HeartGold*, *et al.*, what we long for is to start again; to return to the beginning, stripped of all our beastly entourage, and embark on a new adventure. And so, in this case at least, and rather fittingly for *Pokémon*, evolution rather than revolution is just fine. What is important is not that we are confronted with the kind of invention or innovation that might detract from the purity of *Pokémon*'s core gameplay offering, but that we have the opportunity to play a new game.

A few years ago, in *Playing with Videogames* (Newman 2008), I wrote about the operation of magazine culture and the ways in which the various online and offline publications comprising the specialist gaming press not only contributed to the sense in which individual readers/players were able to locate themselves and their ludic practice within a wider community of gamers through letters pages and high-score competitions, but also how the content of these magazines inevitably focuses attentions on the forthcoming. In discussing the 'lure of the imminent', I pointed to the prevalence of previews and features that centred almost exclusively on games or projects that were in development, unavailable and often many months or even years from release. By dedicating so much space to interviews with developers about their upcoming work in which they discuss the enormity of their ambitions for, as well as the technical and creative challenges presented by, their current and future projects, readers are effectively placed at the intersection of the present and next generation. Whether it is through reports on trade shows, Q&A sessions with programming and design teams, or dedicated and frequently lengthy 'previews' sections offering insight into not just which games are being developed but which to be most excited about, the pages of the specialist gaming press brim over with anticipation, communicating palpable longing and desire for the next game. As such, one of the key discursive functions of the specialist gaming press arises out of its virtual contract with game developers and publishers, which sees it managing and shaping desire for forthcoming products. In fact, as we saw in our discussion of Unseen 64, the combination of lengthy lead times of game development and the potential mismatch between generational hardware cycles and publishing schedules means that the future-gazing of magazine features fixes attentions on games and projects that are cancelled and never come to fruition (as with Jeff Minter's *Unity* project, for instance).

We should also understand that it is not simply the presence of previews or features outlining forthcoming games or even the proportion of a given publication's page count that these materials occupy that is of interest. The previews and in-development features are themselves typically framed within the magazine by titles that proclaim 'The Next Best Game In The World Ever Is … ' (*Nintendo Official Magazine*) or 'audience excitement' ratings tools that graphically quantify the degree of anticipation that the news of the forthcoming game should elicit in the reader. Xbox World 360's Anticip-O-Meter is one such device and sits somewhere between the health bar in a videogame, a TV talent show's clapometer, and a blood pressure monitor. To be clear, although the Anticip-O-Meter is perhaps the most audaciously named, it is far from the only example of a future desire measurement indicator that we see in the contemporary gaming press. *NGamer*'s are footnoted by a suitably Nintendo-themed 'Fireball-o-Meter', while *GamesMaster*, the UK's highest-circulation multi-format magazine, records and codifies excitement levels in its 'Anticipation Rating'. This five-star rating system suffixes every previewed game, based on an assessment of the title's likely impact and potential for innovation and, accordingly, communicates the degree to which its eventual (though not inevitable, as we note with *Unity*) release should be anticipated. One consequence of each of these sliding scales of expectation is an overall levelling of desire as swathes of games are coded as highly anticipated or 'one of our most wanted games' (the GamesMaster 5-Star rating). As such, in the face of certain major, high-profile releases such as *Bioshock*, for instance, the Anticip-O-Meter is barely able to contain or communicate the hysteria.

> And that's why we're so excited about BioShock that if our Anticip-O-Meter TM wasn't capped at Five, it would be rated so high that the meter would burst off the page and finish somewhere in the middle of the Crackdown review.
>
> *(Dale 2007)*

We would do well to remember here that, as *NGamer*'s review of *Pokémon Black/White* ably demonstrates, the kinds of innovation and promissory notes that often impress and which are typically foregrounded in pre-release stages are not always indicators of a game's eventual quality which might benefit from being a continuation of the familiar. Nonetheless, what we see painted in the pages of the specialist gaming press is a picture of a medium and a marketplace in a constant state of flux where the best game is the next game. The notion of progression and inevitable improvement, whether through the more common trope of revolution or the promotion of a more evolutionary strategy that equally prizes new versions of old gameplay designs and structures is keenly felt. Examining the coverage immediately prior to the launch of Nintendo's 3DS handheld console is particularly instructive of the way in which videogames are presented as being in a constant state of flux and illustrates well the negotiations between claims for invention, the security of familiarity, and the ways in which old games systems and software are variously invoked as examples of heritage and lineage, as well as offering yardsticks against which to measure progress.

Given what we have seen of the importance of generations of gaming platforms, we might rightly expect the imminent launch of new games hardware to generate considerable interest. Certainly, hearing that the 'Queues to get just 20 minutes with the shiny new Ninty handheld stretched for hours' reassure us that even games journalists at trade shows with copy deadlines are prepared to wait in line for their few minutes with the new device, and naturally give rise to the question 'Could this be the next-gen handheld we've been waiting for?' (*GamesMaster* 3DS Preview 2010: 43). The implication here is perhaps that the 3DS clarifies that what we believed to be next-gen evidently was not, and this is certainly not undermined by quotes from developers expressing not only their excitement but their relief that the next–next-gen has finally arrived, 'I was waiting for a system with such powerful processing ability' (Keiji Inafune, Capcom cited in Games on Show 2010: 48). Interviews with some of Nintendo's 3D 'wizards' (e.g. Masahuri Sakurai Q&A 2010: 49) only add to the sense of this being a magical technology, reminding us of Arthur C. Clarke's (1973) famous assertion that 'Any sufficiently advanced technology is indistinguishable from magic' and taking a card from Apple and Steve Jobs's book in noting that it is harder still to distinguish if you tell people your product is 'magical', as with the iPad. As such, we could hardly expect there not to be interest and excitement centring on how 3DS might add to the lexicon of gaming. What gameplay opportunities does it offer, what interfaces does it present? What games does it ship with? How much will it cost? Even though we might anticipate a good degree of interest in these questions, we might still be somewhat surprised to see just how much of the coverage of the 3DS centres not on what it is but what it will become. In addition to the countless pre-views of in-development games (replete with anticipation ratings), the *GamesMaster* verdict mentions nothing of the launch titles but focuses instead on the potentialities putatively offered by the system:

> Motion control on a handheld is potentially as exciting as the 3D itself, as well. The 3DS' ability to detect not just tilt (ala the iPod, iPhone and iPad) but movement too opens up all kinds of new possibilities for a handheld games console – the likes of which we've not even seen on the Wii … Combine that with the 3D (and a good pair of earphones) and it could be an incredibly immersive experience … But one thing we weren't expecting at all was the augmented reality demo … All that, plus the ability to take 3D pictures, watch 3D movies and whatever else Nintendo is yet to reveal … point to some exciting possibilities for games we haven't even dreamt of yet.
>
> (GamesMaster *3DS Games Preview 2010: 49*)

Even on launch, the foregrounding of the 3DS's potential, which appears to be its most important feature, despite the technological functionality actually on show, is commonplace across the gaming press:

As a tech demo, AR Games is undeniably impressive. However, it's the potential of the technology that's truly exciting – if Nintendo and other developers can push this even further, Augmented Reality gaming on the 3DS could make as big an impact on the gaming landscape as waggle control did with the Wii.

(McFerran 2011)

The editorial positions laid out here map almost perfectly onto that expounded in Sony's PS3 promotional materials that we saw previously, for instance. It is not just that the console is sufficiently technologically advanced as to be future proof, or that it represents a leap from present generations and iterations of hardware (iPhone *et al.*), but also that it promises gameplay and technical capability that are unimaginable – games we haven't even dreamt of. One point in the verdict is especially interesting, and reveals the interrelationship between old and new generations and the sleight of hand that sees the features and functionality of the once-new recede into the background: 'The machine's wireless capabilities are also exciting. The current DS's ability to communicate between systems sounded great but the necessity for a specific game to be running restricted the feature'; however, the 3DS's different implementation ensures that it is 'instantly a more significant feature that will be put into use far more often' (*GamesMaster* 3DS Games Preview 2010: 49). The 3DS occupies a place that is grounded in the DS's existence and success and it is backwards compatible with DS games, though note the variation in 3DS and DS screen resolutions and pixel densities (see Ronaghan 2011; Somers 2011), and see Nintendo's caveat:

> Almost all existing Nintendo DS and Nintendo DSi games can be played on a Nintendo 3DS system in 2D … Select Nintendo DS games that use accessories in the Game Boy™ Advance slot of the Nintendo DS system are not compatible with the Nintendo 3DS system.
>
> *(3DS Backwards Compatibility 2011)*

However, the 3DS is also positioned to address what are now understood as the shortcomings of the original DS features that, while previously exciting, are now recoded as promising but underexploited or inexpertly implemented. The discussion of the April 2011 pre-release announcement of the successor to Nintendo's Wii console, the Wii U, replicates this discourse almost exactly. In the absence of any concrete information prior to the first public airing of the system in June 2011, all is pure speculation. But, where the details are uncertain, the outcome is anything but. Neil Ashurst, head of UK PR for GAME and Gamestation, assures us that

> There is going to be huge interest in what its successor will look like and what new features will be added – especially with the current trend for 3D and high-def gaming. Just like with the Wii before and more recently the 3DS, you know that Nintendo will be challenging the current gaming conventions.
>
> *(Parfitt 2011b)*

A link to the past

The presentation of gaming, games technology, game development and the market-place as being in a constant state of forward moving flux encourages us to conceive of games as what Arnold Pacey (1983) has called 'halfway technologies'. As Sterne (2007: 23) notes,

> When we think of technology, we normally think of it as fully accomplished and reasonably functional – as in the sexy computers we see in magazine ads and on television. But computer technology is more like advanced medical procedures, missile defense, and other not-fully-accomplished technologies. It sort of works, but not in a flawless or entirely predictable fashion.
>
> *(Sterne 2007: 23)*

We can certainly find numerous examples of technologies that 'sort of work' or perform in unpredictable ways, and will return to discussions of the creative uses of glitches later in this book. Similarly, as Pacey (1983) notes, 'halfwayness' derives from the fact that technologies are often developed to solve problems that are only partly appreciated. As an example, we might consider how the Wii remote was initially presented as part of what earned the system its 'Revolution' codename, only to be augmented with the Wii Motion Plus peripheral that realises its 'full' potential and latterly becomes the 'traditional' controller in the context of the new(er) Wii U touchscreen device. What is interesting to note in relation to the magazine discourse under consideration here is how what was once new and full of promise is subsequently coded as 'halfway' as its replacement or successor becomes available. The DS/3DS wireless communications offer us a clear example, just as the Wii Motion Plus reveals limitations of the Wii that might not have been evident until the peripheral's release. However, although hardware revisions are perhaps the most obvious examples of 'halfwayness', we might also consider how games themselves, and in particular sequels and remakes, contribute to this discourse.

Videogame sequels have come to be something of a contentious topic within developer and player communities. The apparent reliance of publishers on sequels and licensed games is a consequence of the rising costs of development and publishers' subsequent aversion to risk taking (see Newman 2004). In fact, there may even be a commercial imperative to produce sequels, as Rouse (1999) notes that 'computer game sequels tend to make more money than the original work upon which they're based', while developers often argue that because of technological refinements and streamlining of code, videogame sequels are often superior to their predecessors (e.g. Kronschnabl and Rawlings 2010). Regardless of the reason, the argument typically plays out along the lines that this situation stifles innovation and creativity, giving rise to bland conformity in the marketplace. Interviewed in *The Economist* (2004), Scott Orr, a former executive at Electronic Arts, notes that 'We are seeing less and less innovation, because the stakes are so high', while analyst Michael Patcher claims that 'All licensed and all sequel game titles all the time will give the consumer the impression that the market will never get interesting' (cited in Taub 2004). However, we might ask whether a closer inspection of the discursive framework within which sequels are encountered by potential players reveals an altogether more complex set of processes at work. While Jess-Cooke (2009) observes that film sequels are invariably unsatisfactory to audiences, Atkins (2006: 138) notes that videogame sequels always promise, and in many cases deliver, more than their predecessors. We should certainly not forget that even if it does not present revolutions in gameplay or structure, *Pokémon Black/White*, like each iteration that preceded it (and we might reasonably assume will succeed them), offers hundreds of new Pokémon to catch and new adventures to embark on. The sequel, then, is not merely a rehash of a successful formula, but is coded as an opportunity for new gameplay and performance. Perhaps we might suggest that the relationship and continuity between original and sequel and between subsequent sequels represents an extension of the operation of the familiar structure of games that typically sequences, orders and portions out gameplay into levels within a given title.

If we return to the Nintendo 3DS, we see that the principle that Atkins identifies actually operates not only in relation to sequels but may also be seen at work in the practice of remaking and reinventing games. *The Legend of Zelda: Ocarina of Time* (*OoT*) is frequently lauded as one of the high-water marks of achievement in game design and implementation. Since its release in 1998 on the Nintendo 64 platform, the game has won countless accolades, receiving 'perfect' review scores from specialist magazines including *Weekly Famitsu, Edge, Electronic Gaming Monthly, GameSpot* and *IGN*. As of 2011, review aggregators such as *Gamerankings* note that it remains the highest-rated game on any platform (Gamerankings OoT 2011) and it routinely tops the 'best game' charts of journalists (see Edge Staff 2009, for instance) and players (see joossa *et al.*'s 2009 *GameFAQs* poll). As Curran notes, 'The result was phenomenal exceeding the expectations of the most slavish Nintendo fans' (Curran 2004: 60), while for *Edge* 'the game singlehandedly restores the faith in both the creative might of Nintendo and in the power of the videogame as an entertainment media. A work of pure genius' (Edge LoZ Review 1998: 87).

OoT is one of a small number of games that continues to be valorised while other titles fade into obscurity or are replaced by superior successors. However, actually playing *OoT* presents something of a challenge, as it was originally released in 1998 for the Nintendo 64 console, whose cartridges are not directly compatible with any currently supported Nintendo system. However, the game has been re-released and remade for more recent systems. In 2003, it was bundled as part of the *Legend of Zelda: Collector's Edition* promotional disc that accompanied, for instance, pre-orders of the Game-Cube-native *The Legend of Zelda: The Wind Waker*. In 2007, *OoT* was released on the Wii Virtual Console, while most recently the game has been remade in 3D for the Nintendo 3DS handheld, making it available in some form on Nintendo's current console and handheld platforms. It is worth noting, however, that these re-releases are not exactly what they seem and there are some significant variations between versions. The GameCube and Virtual Console versions offer what are, to all intents and purposes, the original game, with some variation in the case of the *Master Quest* additions, along with changes in display resolution and not to mention different controllers and interfaces that affect the feel and even the operation of some elements of gameplay. (We will return to some of the changes that arise from controller differences and the presence and absence of vibration features, for instance, in the final chapter of this book.) However, the most recent release of *OoT, The Legend of Zelda Ocarina of Time 3D*, is a rather different proposition and presents an opportunity to revisit and re-evaluate this most cherished videogame in light of the capabilities of current technology.

Such is the significance of the title (particularly coming on the 25th anniversary of the launch of the original *Legend of Zelda* title on the Nintendo Entertainment System) that *NGamer* dedicates a full page to its preview. Its coverage raises some interesting points in relation to the discourse of progression and does a highly effective job of recasting even this apparently perfect game as, in fact, a 'halfway' title. In fact, the opening of the preview powerfully asserts the 'halfwayness' of the Nintendo 64, GameCube, DS and Wii in one fell swoop in telling, and adding to, the folklore of Nintendo's ambition for its GameCube console system:

> Nintendo, so the story goes, had 3D in mind for the GameCube, envisioning a special film that, when placed over the television screen, would bring Luigi's Mansion (a prominent GameCube launch title) to 3D life. Looking at Ocarina of Time 3D, we wonder if this wasn't the intention with the N64, too. The game is a miraculous fit for 3D.
>
> *(NGamer LoZ3D Preview 2010: 23)*

Obviously, what we see here is not only the championing of 3D but also the making of a case that asserts the inevitability of 3D. Clearly, with the glasses-free parallax barrier 3D of the 3DS, the allusion to the 'special film' is one that deliberately conjures a clumsy, cludgy fix which harks back to the Odyssey, the first home console which included transparent coloured overlays to effectively 'draw' its play areas on the television screen (see DeMaria and Wilson 2002: 18; Burnham 2003: 78–83). In this opening salvo, N64 *OoT* is cast as a game ahead of its time; waiting for the technology to catch up with its ambition (note Inafune above also). The preview goes on to illustrate (both visually and textually) some of the improvements that the remake presents.

> Spot the difference
>
> How much better does it look?
>
> The World: While geometry is unchanged it is draped in new textures, revealing what were once blurs to be wood, grass and vines. They've also dropped the shabby pre-rendered interiors for 3D spaces.
>
> The Hero: Link is noticeably sharper, boasting greater detail on his face, hair and clothes. And by removing the N64 murk the green on his tunic really pops. This is the best Ocarina has ever looked.
>
> *(NGamer LoZ3D Preview 2010: 23)*

The negotiation of past and present, last and next generation can demonstrably be seen at work here. Of course, it is worth remembering how Nintendo's partnership with high-end graphics workstation manufacturer Silicon Graphics gave rise to the N64 and was, in its day, considered a graphical powerhouse, but is now 'shabby murk'. Launch title *Super Mario 64* was described as managing to 'surpass all expectations, using state-of-the-art 3D technology to amplify the essential charisma of Mario' (*Edge SM64* Prescreen 1996: 30), while the specialist press made copious references to the innovations in texture mapping, z-buffering, alpha blending and tri-linear mip mapping interpolation (see Future Shock! 1997: 15). There is a clear balance between maintaining aspects of the old game – which speaks to reassure the reader that there has in some sense been little tampering with the 'magic formula', and updating and improving it so as to recognise its full potential; a potential that, save for those inside Nintendo who may (or may not) have been envisioning 3D, few if any realised was absent when they encountered the 'perfect' game (though we might recall Unseen 64's analysis of the many changes that accompanied the change in development from *Zelda 64DD* to *OoT* which was a 'mere shadow of his former self'; monokoma 2008). What we see in the analysis of *OoT 3D* is a process that retrospectively exposes the absences and lacks of previous generations of hardware and software and that encourages us to re-evaluate these old systems and games in light of the features, performance and functionality of those which are available – or merely promised as potential – now. What we see writ large in examples such as these is precisely the kind of essentially destructive message that Baudrillard sees at the heart of advertising and marketing discourse, which is dedicated to 'the sole aim not of adding to the use-value of objects, but of subtracting value from them, of detracting from their time-value by subordinating them to their fashion-value and to ever earlier replacement' (Baudrillard 1998: 46).

In its broader sense, as a game that, through the re-release/remake, comes to exist without the specificity of a platform and, simultaneously and categorically, is defined through the platform of its present incarnation, *Ocarina* continues to be lauded. *OoT 3D* creates what is effectively a retrospective or corrective obsolescence that exposes the original N64 version's lack, and encourages desire for what is at once presented as its replacement and what should but could not have always been. Perhaps we should have realised that these features, functions, qualities were absent at the time? Certainly now, the absence is keenly felt. In fact, the new, improved first-person mode of the new *Ocarina* not only calls into question the original, but demands a reconsideration of the newness of other present-generation games.

> We forgot, or perhaps never realised, just how immersive Link's first-person view could be. Unlike modern FPSes, where weapons float too far out in front, Link's items are held tight to his body. Aim the slingshot and the elastic stretches off screen because Link wouldn't be able to see it. In 3D, the sense of peering through the V of a slingshot is wonderfully reinforced. The slingshot is clearly here, the Skulltulas are clearly dead – a kill we've made many times on N64, GameCube and Virtual Console, but never quite like this.
>
> (NGamer *LoZ3D Preview* 2010: 23)

This, then, unlike the conversions for GameCube and Virtual Console, emerges as the (currently) definitive version of *Ocarina*. It reproduces what was apparently 'not broken' and adds what was now apparently missing, thereby positioning the game, and player, at an intriguing intersection between past and present generations. The existence and discussion of *OoT 3D* maintains the life (and continues the potential revenue-earning potential) of an important Nintendo game while simultaneously and decisively obsolescing its original incarnation and ensuring that the loss of the no-longer-available N64 hardware is not felt.

What we see in these journalistic discourses is not just a focus on the next generation that comes through the centrality of previewing and the discussion of in-development titles and the fixing of readers' attentions on what they as yet cannot play, but also a careful positioning of gaming as halfway technology. Although always promising more than that which it replaces and existing in a constant state of progressive flux, the discourse here is more complex than a simple linear model of replacement where the old is obsoleted. What is most interesting about the work of the specialist gaming press is to be found in its invocation of past iterations and generations both as points of reference or benchmarks (better graphics) and also as sites wherein a careful renegotiation of 'the new' that draws on features of the once new, and not only represents, reworks and in some cases repairs them (who realised that the critically lauded best game in the world had 'shabby' graphics?) but, in doing so, encourages us to look back even on originals that are still venerated and see that they now appear to have deficiencies in the light of the new new. Perhaps the *Ocarina of Time* did not seem like a halfway game at the time, but its reworking as a 3DS title demands that we now appreciate it as such as we view it through the lens (or perhaps the parallax barrier) of the current 'next generation'.

Buy now, play later

The fixing of readers' attentions on the imminent horizon of as yet unreleased titles, many of which do not have confirmed release dates (which are, even when confirmed, notoriously slippery, as we shall see in the next chapter), through the widespread practice of previewing and presenting discussion and analysis of in-development projects might initially seem at odds with the interests of retailers and, by extension, publishers and developers. Aside from generating this palpable sense of excitement about what is yet to be released or even developed and committing readers to a continued interest in seeing that which is around the corner, a discourse that proudly proclaims that the best is yet to come seems diametrically opposed to the retailer's imperative of selling games.

In the face of this overwhelming message of inevitable progress it would seem that the most rational consumer response would be to perpetually defer any purchasing decision. At least part of the reason for this apparent mismatch between the discursive practices of journalism and marketing and the mercantile interests of the retail sector comes from the misrepresentation of the specialist gaming press so far presented here. Of course, while previews and futuristic features about new technologies, systems and gameplay are prevalent both online and offline, it is wildly inaccurate to suggest that these are the only materials contained within the electronic or printed pages. Reviews of currently available games (or available at the time of going to press, in the case of print publications with longer lead times) are a staple of all specialist gaming publications, with some offering compendia of previous reviews as buyer's guides that, as in the case of *NGamer*'s regular 'The Best Games Directory' section for instance, are assembled into charts and organised by review score. We might still contrast the balance of reviews to previews in the contemporary gaming press with publications of the 1980s, for instance, where magazines such as Newsfield's *Zzap! 64* and *Crash* routinely boasted of the number of pages of reviews inside (May 1995's first issue of *Zzap! 64* proclaims in excess of 50 pages; see www.zzap.co.uk for more). Nonetheless, contemporary publications still retain their role as arbiters of taste in the present marketplace, offering guidance on today's potential purchases and operating as the ancillary materials to which Barker (2004) refers in framing interest in forthcoming release schedules and scaffolding meaning (see also Caldwell 2008; Gray 2010). Moreover, the availability of cover-mount discs replete with videos of pre-rendered gameplay footage, film-like trailers and even time-limited or level-restricted playable demos of games offers players a first-hand taste of the gameplay waiting for them on – or coming soon to – the retailer's shelf.

However, the apparent mismatch between the discursive practices that produce obsolescence by managing anticipation and desire is not simply a product of the misrepresentation of the content of games journalism. If we probe a little deeper into the practices of videogames retail, we find that some of our assumptions about its focus are somewhat skewed. One of the most striking features of the contemporary videogames retail space is its preoccupation with games that are as yet unavailable to play. In this sense, the videogames store, whether it be online or bricks and mortar, speaks of the same fascination with the future of gaming that we see in the pages of gaming publications. Of course, what is important to note here is that that which is not yet available to play is not the same as that which is not yet available to purchase. As such, contemporary players are presented with copious options and enticements to 'pre-order' games – the forthcoming games about which they read previews, interviews and features in gaming magazines, on gaming news websites and which they have already begun to see or even play at sites such as gamevideos.com and via the demo levels on cover-mounted demo discs. By paying now and playing later, they are literally buying into the future of videogames, both responding to and, through that responsive act, confirming that the best game is the next game. It is worth spending some time exploring the ecology of pre-orders and, in particular, the mechanisms by which consumers/potential players are constructed not only as dedicated and informed fans but also as pioneers and even as parts of the development team assisting in bringing the game to fruition.

Some of the mechanisms will surprise only those who are unfamiliar with contemporary retail. Loyalty cards reward frequent purchasers with points that can be used to fund future purchases and are typically skewed in favour of those pre-ordering games or hardware. As of early 2011, the UK specialist videogame retailer Game offers an illustrative promotion on its existing reward card scheme that further incentivises the pre-order purchase:

> Preorder from GAME and you'll be at the front of the queue for new releases in great games and hot hardware. And for a limited time we're offering TRIPLE REWARD CARD POINTS on selected software Preorders for new releases!
>
> *(Game GoW3 pre-order 2011)*

A hyperlink labelled 'See our hottest Pre-order titles' directs potential players to a list of coming-soon titles, which, by default, is ordered by 'popularity' rather than release date. In this way, the list is effectively cast as a chart that, unlike the Buyer's Guide, which is oriented around review and scrutiny of the completed and played game, maps the anticipation and excitement palpable in the pages of previews into a prioritised purchasing plan. As at April 2011, at the top of game.co.uk's chart (ordered by popularity) sits Epic's *Gears of War 3*:

> Gears of War 3 (Only on Xbox 360!)
>
> Prepare for an action game of EPIC proportions with Gears of War 3, the final chapter in the explosive Gears of War saga!
>
> The final human city of Jacinto may have been sunk by the Locust, but the COG forces, led by Marcus Phoenix and Delta squad, struck a decisive blow in lighting the Locust tunnels aflame. 18 months on and humanity continues the battle in a three way fight against the Locust and new Lambent-possessed foes – and you'll be in the thick of the action in an incendiary duck-and-cover four-player campaign that promises to be one of 2011's Xbox 360 highlights.
>
> *(Game GoW3 pre-order 2011)*

What is so interesting about the *Gears of War 3* pre-order offer is the sheer range of incentives that are offered to entice the potential purchaser:

> Gears of War 3 Epic Edition (With Gears of War 3 BETA Access) (Xbox 360)
> £99.99
> Release Date: 20/09/2011
> Pre-order
> 162 days to go!
>
> *(Game GoW3 pre-order 2011: 11 April)*

At first glance, the urgency to pre-order feels comparatively easy to resist. After all, 162 days is the best part of six months – or thought of another way, six more editions of monthly gaming magazines that we might reasonably assume will introduce us to the potential for new, exciting, 'next-generation' gaming experiences. Certainly, if we can stomach the £100 price tag (perhaps cashing in some of our loyalty points to ease the burden) we may wish to secure the 'Epic Edition' of the game, a lavish package whose contents are the subject of some considerable speculation among fans on the Epic forums prior to release (see swbruni 2011; zGreeNArroWz 2011). However, probing this pre-order package a little deeper, we find some interesting incentives and opportunities that problematise simplistic notions of reserving limited editions or deferred play. The 'Gears of War 3 BETA Access' that is billed as part of the title of the game is particularly telling and presents those who pre-order the final physical disc/package with an opportunity to play the game prior to its retail release:

> Enlist in the most explosive gaming event of the spring: the Gears of War 3 Multiplayer Beta! Get into the Beta by preordering Gears of War 3 through select retailers. The Beta begins April 25 and ends May 15. For those of you who purchased the Bulletstorm Epic Edition (on Xbox 360 only), you get early access to the Beta, beginning April 18. This is your chance to help shape the most anticipated game of 2011.
>
> *(Gears 3 Beta 2011)*

In one sense, particularly in light of the six-month wait until the advertised release date, we might see the opportunity to play the incomplete, still-in-development game as a kind of virtual placation. However, this would be to underestimate the importance of this privileged access. That the beta represents the 'chance to shape the most anticipated game of 2011' casts the player in a role that transcends that of a dedicated fan, eagerly handing over their money in order to assure the delivery of the completed game on the day of its eventual release. While it clearly operates at the level of a 'sneak peek', the access to the still actively developed and changing game casts the player as part of the development team, playtesting and quality assuring the final product that others will play. That the beta version of the game is incomplete and potentially contains bugs and inconsistencies is, accordingly, an important part of the pre-order transaction. As such, *Gears of War 3* is the most anticipated release of 2011 (and certainly this is borne out in the popularity rankings of game.co.uk's chart), which is simultaneously unavailable for six months and available to experience now. The pleasures of engaging with it in its unfinished state derive from being both a player and playtester, fan and de facto developer. In fact, there is more still to the *Gears of War 3* beta access. Playing the beta gives access to exclusive content:

> Not only will you get an early taste of the final chapter in this blockbuster trilogy, but you'll also have access to exclusive content that you can permanently unlock and carry over to your Gears of War 3 gamer profile when the retail game launches on September 20.
> Exclusive Beta Unlockables
>
> − Flaming Hammerburst Complete one match by Sunday, April 24 to permanently unlock.
> − Flaming Lancer Complete one match during the week of April 25 to permanently unlock.

- Flaming Sawed-Off Shotgun Complete one match during the week of May 2 to permanently unlock.
- Flaming Gnasher Shotgun Complete one match during the week of May 9 to permanently unlock.
- Beta Tester Medal – Wear it proudly, Gear. Complete one match in the Beta to permanently unlock.
- Thrashball Cole – Unlock Thrashball Cole to play as Augustus Cole as he was before Emergence Day – a legendary Thrashball athlete known for his ferocious, flamboyant style. Complete 50 matches in any game type to unlock for the Beta period.To permanently unlock, complete 10 matches as Thrashball Cole during the Beta period.
- Gold-Plated Retro Lancer – Before the chainsaw bayonet was deployed at the beginning of the Locust-Human War, the original Lancer assault rifle had a large fixed blade. Complete 90 matches in any game type to unlock for the Beta period. To permanently unlock, score 100 kills with the Gold-Plated Retro Lancer during the Beta period.

Visit one of these participating retailers for your pre-order today!

(Gears 3 Beta 2011)

In this way, the beta version is not simply a test version of the final game. It is not a limited demo but rather has its own unique capacities that may be unlocked through play. Importantly, the beta is not a closed system, and the capacities and capabilities that are unlocked during the beta are carried forward into the final game through the player's profile. What is perhaps most vital to note in Epic's scheme here, however, is not merely that the pre-order is incentivised with access to an in-development version of the game but that pre-ordering this far in advance of the published release date is materially (or perhaps immaterially) rewarded with 'exclusive content' that, in the case of gameplay affecting weaponry and technique, will continue to advantage the player beyond the beta period and that, in the case of the 'Beta Tester Medal', ably distinguishes them as an early-adopter and participant in this beta playing/development phase of the game's genesis. Where we are used to conceiving of reward structures in games being contingent on the capability of players and their ability to master gameplay, we are confronted here with a clear reminder that, in order to even partake in this performative contest, access through purchasing and, in this case, pre-ordering is a pre-requisite. The lure, exclusivity and distinctiveness of these unlockables which are available only through the beta access granted by the pre-order process and which are portioned out (and subsequently revoked) over particular periods, work to create a sense of urgency in the pre-order transaction that belies the *prima facie* fact that there remain 162 days until the game is released.

New lamps for old

Access to exclusive content, limited editions or chances to shape still in-development games are by no means the only mechanisms by which retail practices encourage players to participate in the future of gaming and through which the pleasures and currency of 'old' games are effectively eroded. We should be clear that the drive to accumulate new games does not necessarily culminate in players amassing growing collections of games. The retail transaction underscores the process of obsolescence not merely as the acquisition of the new but also as the replacement of the old in quite concrete ways. Another striking feature of videogames retail is the prevalence of the 'trade-in'. As Henning (2007) reminds us in the title of her chapter on obsolescence and photography, 'new lamps for old' is the de facto catchphrase of the new media and cultural industries. In some senses, we are reminded of Kline *et al.*'s (2003) 'perpetual innovation economy' and McGuigan's position which, drawing on Nicholas Garnham, points to the potential contradiction of the industrially produced cultural commodity:

> it is not typically used up in the act of consumption. The consumer can view a DVD over and over again whereas a loaf of bread cannot be eaten twice. Cultural industries, therefore, adopt strategies of artificial scarcity and perpetual novelty in order to encourage consumers to seek new products.
>
> *(McGuigan 2010: 112)*

However, although we note the continual invocation of novelty, revolution and (re)invention, what we see in the videogames retail space goes further still and involves a rather more literal exchange of new lamps for old. The trade-in is perhaps the most concrete example of the denigration and literal devaluing of old games in the face of their replacements. Again, UK store Game provides the basis for our case study, but its practices are by no means unique and are representative not only of the specialist game retail sector but increasingly of general retailers such as supermarkets. The ability to trade in old games is a sufficiently normalised part of the game retail ecology that bricks and mortar stores frequently and prominently display boards outlining the current exchange value of a range of common titles and systems. According to Game group CEO Ian Shepherd, more than half of the retailer's sales of new are part-funded by consumers trading in old titles. 'Around 50 to 60 per cent of the time, when we were selling a brand new game we were taking in a trade-in against it' (Batchelor 2011).

Game, moreover, employs a technique more familiar to those exchanging their gold for cash – or perhaps to those who have ever been taken ill on a plane. Consumers are invited to fill specially provided 'trade in' paper bags with their old games, return to the store and exchange the old lamps for new. The receptacles bear an uncanny and difficult to ignore resemblance to the sick bags that greet air travellers, and it is extremely hard not to feel that the of old games that soon will fill them should not be treated in the same, slightly unsanitary way – held at arm's length and disposed of in a thoughtful manner. And so, what was in its day highly anticipated and desirable, perhaps even being pre-ordered and played in beta, and whose ludic pleasures were expectantly anticipated up to the final release date, quickly and decisively becomes the games industry's excreta.

The trade-in model, familiar from the motor car industry, is a perhaps unexpectedly normalised part of videogames retail. Indeed, in addition to the accommodation of the kinds of ad hoc trade-ins that fill digital sick bags, we find the trade-in even more embedded into the practices of buying and selling videogame hardware and software. Game's 2011 'Play Now – Trade Later™' scheme is illustrative. The UK launch of the Nintendo 3DS saw a number of pre-release price reductions, with various specialist and non-specialist retailers vying for position and undercutting the system's recommended retail price, by almost 50% in some cases (see Parfitt 2011c on HMV's 3DS UK launch pricing). Additionally, most retailers publicised their trade-in deals and made particular reference to the trade-in value of the most obviously superseded DS Lite, DSi and DS XL consoles (their lack of 3D and the promise of the backwards compatibility of the new system rendering them likely candidates for trading in). HMV's deals were typical:

> pre-order a Nintendo 3DS to get up to £110 off when you trade in a DS console by March 19th 2010
>
> – £110 off by trading in a DSi XL. £5 more than at GAME.
> – £80 off by trading in a DSi. £5 more than at GAME.
> – £50 off by trading in a DS Lite.
>
> *(HMV.co.uk, accessed March 2011)*

Intriguingly, however, Game's offer centred not on the ability to trade in other hardware or software (though this was part of the standard deal) but, rather, drew attention to the facility to 'trade-back' the newly purchased system within the first month for a near full refund.

> Gamers who buy the device for £196.99 from GAME's website will now have the chance to trade the handheld back for £190. They can claim this guaranteed price as long as they do so by April 25th – one month after purchase.
>
> *(Parfitt 2011d)*

Putting aside the retail economics of this situation and accepting that we shall return in the following chapter to a consideration of the afterlife and ecology of games that are exchanged through the trade-in process, here our focus must be on the message communicated in the Play/Trade scheme, which appears less a guarantee of satisfaction and more an odd and potentially conflicting kind of assurance that a month in the company of this revolutionary system might well be sufficient. Detailing the offer, Game's step-by-step explanation plays on both the desirability of the new console and also the potential for its novelty to be exhausted, or perhaps 'used up', within 30 days. The acceleration of the cycle of obsolescence – or at least the periodicity of novelty – reaches a quite astonishing level and we move beyond even the mechanic that removes the old console in favour of the new to one that treats even the new console as something fleeting. Perhaps what we observe in the process of pre-order and trading in, and which operates *in extremis* in the Game 3DS offer, is a shift in the balance between the innovative and familiar that Thompson *et al.* (2009) observe lies at the heart of videogames. The consumer is encouraged to move with great rapidity from a rapturous immersion in the new to a position that simultaneously recognises the tired familiarity of the now old and is desirous of a new new.

While its execution might operate at unexpected extremes, what we see in the combination of pre-orders and the collapsing of newness into ever briefer moments could hardly surprise us in one sense, and there is surely good business sense underpinning this high churn rate. However, for scholars and practitioners of game preservation and history, this backdrop has significant consequences and the practices and models of contemporary videogames retail act in concert with the discursive practices of game journalism to powerfully communicate both the desirability of the next generation and the supersession of that which precedes it. If we consider the effect on the valuing of gaming history and heritage, we might think of these journalistic and retail practices as somewhat self-destructive. Surely we need not look too much further to begin to address Gooding and Terras's (2008) question as to why so little games preservation work has so far been undertaken. This, then, is an industry whose forward movement is almost wholly contingent on the denigration of its own present and past. Even where that past refuses to be silenced, as in the case of Ocarina, it is reinvented and remade with its old, and only now apparent, deficiencies rectified. Although the preoccupation with pre-ordering might be seen as an inevitable consequence of a fascination with a fast-moving future and a desire to fix players' attentions on the forthcoming, it is in reality as much concerned with promoting a 'dissatisfaction with existing product ranges'. At its heart, the contemporary videogames industry is oriented around the production of the 'psychological obsolescence' that Packard (1960) identified as emerging in the business practices of 1950s America. By focusing a large part of their operations on games that exist only as pre-orderable promissory notes, videogames retailers, marketers and journalists are perhaps less Futurist prophets and more 'merchants of discontent' (Packard 1960: 24).

All hidden items revealed!

Of course, videogame retail is not only concerned with selling (and buying back) software and hardware systems, and our assertion thus far expounded in this chapter that videogames are disposed of and replaced with increasing rapidity seemingly fails to account for a range of other materials and texts that appear designed to maximise the longevity of each game. Chief among these ancillary or paratextual materials are 'strategy guides', often colloquially referred to as 'walkthroughs'. These volumes are the products of commercial book publishing, with publishers such as Prima and Brady Games dominating the current marketplace and delivering glossy-covered accompaniments to most major gaming releases. Strategy guide authors often work in close collaboration with the game's coders and artists during the development process to create volumes that not only are released alongside the game but also receive the endorsement of being the 'official' guide. In all their official and unofficial guises, Strategy guides have become a familiar part of gaming culture and a staple of games retail. On one level, we might see the strategy guide as a piece of merchandising, a souvenir or memento in much the same way that we might view the range of high production-value coffee-table books that celebrate the art of games such as *Halo* (Trautman 2004) and *Half-Life 2* (Valve 2004). However, while they are certainly similar in terms of the lavishness of their production and aesthetics, and frequently their offer is embellished with limited-edition reproductions of concept artwork or even collectible posters and postcards (e.g. Hodgson *et al.* 2002), the function of the strategy guide is altogether different and is far more closely tied to gameplay activity.

On the face of it, the strategy guide appears to exist with the sole function of encouraging the deep exploration of games. 'All hidden secrets revealed!' boasts the front cover of Prima's official strategy guide for the *Ocarina of Time* (Hollinger *et al.* 1998). The pages within amply deliver on this promise and offer detailed, full-colour maps and clear, concise instruction on the precise route to be taken through the gameworld, the tactics to employ against each creature encountered, and the location of each and every secret item or weapon. At first glance, then, the glossy pages of these commercially produced volumes, which are often sold in reduced-priced bundles with the game they address, seem to present a powerful counterblast to the arguments we have seen so far which suggest that games are voraciously used up, worn out and replaced. Surely, there can be little in the pages of these extensive volumes that would encourage the kind of ludic grazing that Game's thirty-days-of 3DS-for-£7 offer appears to promote. However, on closer inspection, the strategy guide reveals itself as a rather more complex text that perhaps plays a more pivotal role in the 'using up' of games than its appearance might initially suggest. Moreover, we should be extremely careful not to conflate the content and function of these commercially published strategy guides with those of the player-produced 'walkthroughs' or 'game guides' that have been the subject of most of the, albeit still limited, extant scholarly investigation. It is worth spending a little time disentangling these related texts so as not to confuse the differing ways in which they frame gameplay as either an open and exploratory or closed and finite practice.

In her study of *Legend of Zelda* fans, Consalvo (2003) considers the creation and use of 'walkthrough' texts, which she defines as

> detailed guides to how a player should play a game sequence to find all of the hidden bonuses and surprises, how to avoid certain death, and how to advance past difficult puzzles or trouble spots to best play and win the game.
>
> *(Consalvo 2003: 327–28)*

In fact, while Consalvo's definition is useful in drawing attention to the revelation of hidden items, for instance, its implication that walkthroughs principally focus on aiding the act of completion, or winning, and its construction of the text as one turned to only in moments of desperation, is somewhat incomplete. These player-produced texts are, as I have noted elsewhere (e.g. Newman 2005, 2008), better thought of as amalgams of instructional and exploratory writing. In places, they offer advice and quite literal guidance on strategies and tactics, but this is typically combined with altogether more investigative research into the operation of the game at the most fundamental level. Importantly, the products of the often forensic levels of scrutiny manifest themselves in suggestions for new challenges and frameworks for new ways of engaging with the game. Authors of texts dedicated to Nintendo's *Pikmin* title, for instance, not only concern themselves with documenting the route to solving each of the game's particular challenges and puzzles. Instead, they offer challenges that develop the game beyond the initial goal and that impose additional restrictions (such as limited time). *Metroid*, another of Nintendo's long-running franchises, presents us with similar examples as players devise new challenges that demand the tackling of specific sections of gameplay either with or without particular items of inventory or perhaps by seeking to minimise the amount of damage sustained in virtual combat.

The sharing of newly devised gameplay modes through these player-produced texts encourages us to view these documents as sites that locate gameplay within wider communities and contexts, not to mention the way in which they both codify and regulate notions of expertise and mastery. One thing that becomes abundantly clear after even the slightest scrutiny of these player-produced texts is that 'walkthrough' is something of a misnomer. While major repository sites such as GameFAQs.com which host tens of thousands of these documents retain the historical term 'FAQ' (frequently asked questions), they are perhaps best termed 'game guides'. Certainly, game guides contain walkthroughs, and this is typically presented as a section in the wider game guide/FAQ, but this is only one part of the often lengthy contents. To be clear, then, the walkthrough is the instructional element that guides the reader step by step through the challenges and terrain of the gameworld. It is something akin to a virtual tour and, as Burn (2006) has noted, its mode of address is most usually imperative. Burn draws on Megura's lengthy *Final Fantasy VII* guide to illustrate the voice and mode of address of the walkthrough as virtual tour.

> Once you leave the train, check the body of the closest guard twice to get two Potions. Then head north. You'll be attacked by some guards. Take them out with your sword (you may win a Potion for killing them) and then move left to go outside.
>
> *(Megura cited in Burn 2006: 90)*

In this respect, commercially produced strategy guides and player-produced game guides have much in common. However, while these commercially published volumes and the plaintext documents of gamers might bear some familial resemblance, in some senses they could hardly be more dissimilar. Commercial strategy guides are most often lavish in their production, with glossy covers and full-colour imagery throughout their heavyweight pages. Textual descriptions tour the reader through every point in the game's narrative and structure, outlining each encounter with the enemies that block progress, detailing their weak points and describing the appropriate means via which they may be despatched. At every point, full-colour screenshots, often annotated with graphical overlays that mark the direction of movement of in-game objects or characters, or presented in graphical sequences that illustrate the passage of gameplay time through their multiple, comic-book-like panel layouts, reinforce the textual descriptions, giving the player advance warning and a kind of virtual foresight of what they are about to confront on their own screen. The visual splendour of the commercially produced strategy guide, not to mention its materiality compared with the player-produced text document distributed online, are the most immediately obvious differences, but there is more to the distinction than this alone. The focus of the two documents is subtly but significantly different.

Completing games

As a form of 'reverse engineering', player-produced walkthroughs explore the very extremes and boundaries of gameplay, slavishly documenting each narrative turn, each line of dialogue, every available room, weapon, collectible item and option that is available, regardless of whether they are integral to the ostensible aim of the game or whether they facilitate its 'completion'. Indeed, walkthroughs of this kind problematise the very notion of completion as they signal and map out pleasures unassociated with the apparent objective of gameplay, frequently setting new ludic challenges and establishing supersets and subsets of rules within which to perform. Similarly, we should be mindful of the contexts in which player-produced walkthroughs are encountered and distributed. Alluding to the revisioning of digital files, the plaintext documents collected at sites such as GameFAQs.com are notated by their authors with version numbers that record and communicate the completeness of the text. Importantly, completeness here does not refer to the presentation of a finalised solution to the game which might be taken for granted. Rather, completeness in this context seeks to communicate the degree to which the entire scope or extent of the gameworld's ludic potential is mapped within the text. As we have seen, this very often not only involves documenting what the game appears to offer but also presents newly created game modes or bespoke challenges designed and shared by players. Accordingly, player-produced guides operate at the boundary of creative exploration and careful policing of boundaries as certain styles or conditions of play are revealed, codified and (de)legitimised.

What player-produced guides demonstrate with considerable eloquence is the myriad ways in which games may be played and, most importantly, the ways in which they continue to be played with and by which players continue to 'breathe new life into games long after they have slipped off the retail radar' (Newman 2008: viii). Months, years and even decades after the release of the titles which they investigate, we find player-produced game guides updated by their authors as new facets of gameplay come to light or new ways of playing are devised and shared among players (see also Ashton and Newman 2010 on the regulatory function of player-produced guides). Continuing Megura's work on *Final Fantasy VII*, Baxter's (2010) guide, a veritable codex that explores the 'Lucky 7s' feature of the game, was released and updated four times in 2010. A full thirteen years after *FFVII*'s release, we find a new 'Possible challenge idea':

> play a game to level 99, and carefully calibrate every character's final Nominal HP to be one of those listed in the Bonus Table at the end. This way, every character could be fixed at 7777 Max HP always. Though that would be insanely powerful, it would certainly be a challenge to attempt it.
>
> *(Baxter 2010)*

The community exploring Nintendo's *The Legend of Zelda: Ocarina of Time* reveals a similar ongoing interest. Devin Morgan's *The Legend of Zelda: Ocarina of Time FAQ/Walkthrough* (Morgan 2011), also available at GameFAQs.com, is a case in point. Initially published in 1998 when the game was launched, it was still being updated in June 2011, with previous 2009 and 2010 updates adding detail on tackling the specific challenges of some of the denizens. As is commonplace, much of Morgan's material is derived from (and scrupulously credited to) other Zelda players.

Even in this brief examination of their contours, we clearly see that at least part of the objective of the player-produced text is to eke out every last gameplay opportunity. This documentation of the gameworld and its operation extends to, and sometimes beyond, its expected extremes and veers into unanticipated, although sometimes repeatable and often exploitable, coding bugs and glitches (see Newman 2008 on the myriad *Pokémon* glitches, for instance, and the recuperative work of gamers who incorporate these anomalies into the canon of fan discourse). By contrast, the commercially produced strategy guide contains few if any of these encouragements to explore the spaces of the gameworld or to conceive of the game as malleable material to play with and remake.

Being centred on the didactic instruction and virtual tour of the walkthrough, the strategy guide is far more obviously concerned with encouraging players to progress onward through the game rather than to explore its outer limits. It is notable, for instance, that the discussion of bugs and glitches, documented either for completeness or because they might be exploited for gameplay advantage, and the setting of new challenges, for instance, that we find in player-produced texts, do not feature in commercial strategy guides. That publisher- or developer-endorsed texts do not foreground the inadequacies or malfunctioning of their products does not come as much of a surprise and, on a practical level, many of these inconsistencies and their potential for ludic exploitation, arise only through the intense, deductive play which necessarily comes post-release/publication. However, the presence and absence of materials beyond the virtual tour or 'solution' offered by the walkthrough speak of different uses and different relationships with the game. It is for these reasons that we will argue here that, while the player-produced guide opens up the game by encouraging replay and an ongoing ludic (re)exploration, the commercially published strategy guide, despite its appearance and apparent similarity, is better understood as taking part in the closing down or 'using up', in McGuigan's terms, of the game that is its subject.

If we return to the official *Ocarina of Time* strategy guide (Hollinger *et al.* 1998), we begin to detect the difference in objective. The Prima guide boldly asserts that its coverage includes:

> Detailed maps of every city and dungeon
> Strategies for defeating all the enemies
> Locations of all Heart Containers and Gold Skulltulas
> Solutions to all puzzles
> Bonus items revealed
>
> *(Hollinger* et al. *1998: OBC)*

The word 'solution' is absolutely key here and speaks of a kind of completion that we do not so readily detect in the player-produced guide. As I have noted in *Playing with Videogames*, the degree to which they open up or close down the ludic potential of a given game is a key distinguishing feature of commercially published and player-produced guides:

> while a range of materials encourage players to explore and replay the game many times over, the inclusion of a checklist that details all of the available 'Shine Sprites' in Super Mario Sunshine, Prima's Official Guide encourages the gamer to consider their ultimate acquisition as the conclusion of the game. The final tick brings closure, completion and thereby may be seen to speak the language of supersession by moving the focus from the present and onto the (purchase of the) next game. As we shall see, Game Guides frequently serve to lengthen the engagement with a given videogame far beyond the exhaustion of the 'official' modes of play and challenge the notion of 'completion'.
>
> *(Newman 2008: 97)*

On the face of it, then, while the commercial strategy guide might appear to encourage the mining of the game's extent, it in fact serves to communicate the finite nature of the gameplay whose challenge may be completed and whose puzzles can be 'solved'. In the case of Prima's *Super Mario Sunshine* guide, it is possible to read the Shine Sprite checklist, like the lists that locate every Gold Skulltula or Heart Container in the *Ocarina of Time*, not simply as devices against which to measure gaming prowess or expertise, but as mechanisms that quite literally set out the extent of what the game offers. In this way, attainment of each Sprite moves the game closer to exhaustion. In fact, as so much of the strategy guide is dedicated to the delivery of the didacticism of the walkthrough, the linearity and materiality of the book both communicates progress through the game and, conversely, speaks of the impending exhaustion of its potential to deliver gameplay. In this way, we are perhaps better advised to see the strategy guide not as the invitation to replay and revisit the game so as to reveal its continually changing and malleable contours. Rather, the comprehensiveness of its revelation of secrets and the definitiveness of its solutions suggest that the strategy guide performs an important strategic function in communicating how the game is 'used up'. In this way, by promoting the movement along the singular pathway mapped out by the, often 'officially' sanctioned, walkthrough rather than laying out the potential for the exploration of malfunction or suggesting the immersion in new modes of gameplay codified by players and often deploying new or restricted subsets of existing rules, the strategy guide reminds us of McGuigan's insight into the industrially produced cultural commodity which is not typically used up in the act of consumption. Even if the *Ocarina of Time* does not physically wear out as it is played in the way that McGuigan's loaf of bread disappears in the act of consumption (though we should be mindful of bit rot and material deterioration as well as the inevitable supersession as sequels and remakes refocus attentions and improve on the original), the strategy guide eloquently communicates an altogether more immediate exhaustion of the game: its capacity to offer new play. In this way, *Ocarina* quite literally becomes used up by the act of play, just as the inevitable *Ocarina 3D* strategy guide will signal the exhaustion of the technologically advanced remake.

Whether we wish to suggest that strategy guide authors and publishers are complicit in any scheme to wear out the videogames to which they turn their attentions, the fact remains that these volumes contribute to the creation of the context of forward movement, in which videogames are worn out and used up, within which game preservation work operates and potentially struggles. There can be little doubt that the commercial strategy guide performs a markedly different function to the player-produced game guide. In closing down rather than opening up gameplay, in exhausting rather than enlivening gameplay opportunity, it does not render obsolete the game at play, per se. Rather, in defining and demarcating the extent of available gameplay by declaring the revelation of 'all' hidden items, in mapping out and confirming a singular gameplay objective or goal and codifying its attainment or completion as a moment of closure, the strategy guide brings to an end the game as a playable object. We do not see enticements to replay with new challenges, as we do in the case of player-produced guides. Instead, in the strategy guide walkthrough, we are more likely to encounter guidance on how to minimise distraction and diversion so as to maintain progress towards the goal.

> For 10 Rupees, Talon gives you 30 seconds in which to pick out his money-making chickens. If you win, you get a Bottle full of Lon Lon Milk. You need a Bottle in which to keep things such as potions, Fairies, and even fish, so play this game until you win.
>
> *(Hollinger* et al. *1998: 19)*

The reassurance that this is not a sideshow distraction is helpful for the player keen to progress to the next sequence of the adventure (or perhaps to the next page of the strategy guide), but Talon's mini-game appears disconcertingly random and pro-mises to gobble up valuable time. Fortunately, the guide offers some advice on how to complete the section and get back on track with the quest to rescue Princess Zelda:

> There's no easy way to distinguish between the regular and Super Cuccos, so you must rely on luck – or a little trickery. You can pen up the regular Cuccos in the niche between the stairs and the table Talon is resting against, where they'll stay out of the way during the game. When Talon tosses his three Super Cuccos into the room, he'll be surprised that you could find them so fast but he won't realize why.
>
> *(Hollinger et al. 1998: 19)*

The level of detail of the instruction is clear in this example and the player is given few opportunities to get lost as a consequence of any tactical inability. What is par-ticularly interesting is that the relentless slicing of the game into bite-sized chunks of action, linearly arranged and progressing towards the end of the game/book, serves to restrict the possibility of any wilful divergence from the pathway or any detour that is its own reward. Where finishing, revealing and solving are the watchwords, any diversion from these goals is effectively presented as a waste of time, and certainly the idea of dealing with something as unpredictable as 'luck' must be routed around. The strategy guide, therefore, is not an invitation to explore the gameworld but is perhaps, rather, more akin to a tourist trip itinerary; it is a document that both leads one through the territory and simultaneously encourages the (in some cases literal) ticking off of the sites seen before moving onward to the next destination. Importantly, once all of the destinations on the list have been successfully acquired within the game, the strategy guide makes it clear that the final destination for the game is either the back of the cupboard or the trade-in, as its potential for play is comprehensively exhausted.

In this chapter, we have seen the ways in which a variety of journalistic, retail and marketing practices contribute to the production of obsolescence in relation to videogames by drawing on notions of halfwayness and hardware and software that is always in forward motion, progressing towards inevitable improvement either through sequel, remake or upgrade. Similarly, we have begun to see the ways in which games are framed as being 'used up' and 'worn out' through the very act of play and the mechanisms by which they may be literally disposed of in exchange for new challenges. Of course, what we have overlooked here is that these old 'used up' games do not inevitably end up on Sterne's (2007) trash piles. As the discussion of player-produced game guides begins to suggest, old games do not simply disappear, and many are kept alive through creative and inventive acts of play – the very same play that is codified as destructive in the strategy guide. Moreover, while we have presented the trade-in in terms of finality and expiration, in reality, this is potentially the beginning of a new chapter in the game's life as it moves into the hinterland of the pre-owned space. As such, for all the focus on the new and as-yet-unreleased that we see in marketing and journalistic discourse, what we find in the lived experience of gameplay is an altogether more mixed economy of old and new. In the following chapter, we will begin to explore the ongoing 'afterlife' and residuality of games as they move beyond novelty and negotiate a position between benchmarks of technological progress, affordable access points, stylistically recovered fashion items and valued parts of a shared cultural heritage.

3

OLD GAMES

Residual media

Of course, old games do not simply vanish. Even in the light of their apparently self-evident obsolescence and replacement in the marketplace by technologically superior successors, sequels or updated, improved remakes, old games and old systems linger on. As Moore (2009) notes, 'many users will persist for years, gradually upgrading and delaying obsolescence and even perpetuate the circulation of older cultural commodities'. Some continue to be used, perhaps alongside or perhaps instead of the new. We should be clear that these are not necessarily acts of overt resistance but a result of practicality and household provisioning. New hardware, new software, new peripherals, whether desirable or desired, remain costly items and the investment of both time and money in old systems may make them hard to simply discard.

As we have seen, differing but typically patchy approaches to backwards compatibility mean that libraries of games, as well as additional hardware such as controllers and memory cards, make the decision to shift from one platform to another, even an updated iteration of the same platform, an extensive and expensive proposition. As such, while we should recall Sterne's comments on the way that the 'halfwayness' of technology makes it potentially easy to reject, as it either does not work or has deteriorated over time, becoming troublesome and unreliable, we should be mindful also of his assertion that it is the cost of computing that frequently drives its longevity: 'the memory of dropping well over $1,000 (and probably considerably more) still lingers' (Sterne 2007: 25). Considered in this light, it is understandable that the initial launch price of the PS3 console, clocking in at in excess of £400 (*sans* game and with a single joypad), as well as the ongoing investment in software and peripherals, should continue to prove significant and persuasive even in the face of subsequent technologically advanced console releases. However, Sterne also interestingly points to the way in which the memory of expenditure may potentially create a strong desire to retain costly technological devices even after they cease to be useful, or at least after they remain in constant use. Moving them into marginal spaces such as garages, basements and lofts, where they are stored in the belief that they must still retain some value, they exist in a kind of hinterland, neither exactly wanted nor unwanted. For archivists, the importance of this simple fact is difficult to overstate:

> when a newer system (e.g., PlayStation 3) supersedes an older one (e.g., Atari 2600), the older one will often sit like a fact in benighted spaces such as attics, thrift stores, garages, and closets − all prime hunting grounds for computer game collectors. The ephemera that for most people drift toward oblivion get picked up by archivists and cleaned off, catalogued, stored, studied, used, and reused. Trash becomes treasure, obsolescence newness and utility.
>
> (Thompson et al. 2009)

While specifically describing the position of the archivist or collector, positions to which our discussion will return later in this volume, Thompson *et al*'s statement reminds us that games have rather more complicated lives than the new/obsolete binarism we have seen created in the narratives of games retail and journalism. What is important to appreciate here is not merely that 'trash' (that is, games seemingly at the end of their lives) might be recontextualised and recuperated as 'treasure' by those with particular interests, preoccupations or specific cultural knowledges, but that, despite the best efforts of marketers and retailers to code these games as used up, worn out and superseded, they take part in complex symbolic journeys as they move through different categories from 'unreleased' through to 'unused', 'unwanted' and beyond.

It may well be, as Sterne (2007) encourages us to consider, that games hardware and software, like all new media technology which is defined by the inevitability of its own future decomposition, are a trash pile waiting to happen, but we should be clear that, despite the best efforts of marketers, these devices, systems, media do not unproblematically or automatically flip between new and old, desirable and trash (see also Straw 2000 on 'scavenger-like record collecting tendencies' and 'marginal reissue labels' for parallels with the music marketplace). The immediacy of Bart's fiery disposal of the Gamestation 252 that we saw at the beginning of the previous chapter plays on the rapidity of the discursive construction of obsolescence that we see in the contemporary videogames marketplace, and we certainly recognise the ways in which players are implored to upgrade and replace, if not actually destroy, the old. We recognise also the often rather opaque and imprecise claims that are made for the innovation that is offered by the new. However, we should take care not to simply assume that all players slavishly obey these narratives of upgrade and dispose of their existing hardware and software as soon as they are instructed.

As Sterne notes, obsolescence is a complicated condition that is not only a product of marketing discourses, and the journey towards 'trash' is one that is rather more circuitous and involves various categories. Considering the personal computer, Sterne observes 'a series of symbolic transformations: it travels through categories from new, to useful, to obsolete, to unused, to trash' (Sterne 2007: 23), drawing on Thompson's analysis of the ways building stock becomes 'rubbish' according to decisions about the degree of maintenance that will be lavished upon it. As such, buildings fall into disrepair when decisions are made to no longer maintain them. Conversely, we might also observe decisions to impose durability upon more materially fragile buildings – wattle and daub versus concrete, for instance. Sterne's allusion to building upkeep demonstrates not only that some of the processes of obsolescence and supersession that create trash, often for commercial ends, are not unique to the computing industries, but also that obsolescence is frequently a socially imposed condition. Groups determine which items are protected from deterioration and which are ignored, forgotten and left to decay. The key point here is the decoupling of the physical or material deterioration and decay of the object from the social relations that surround it and govern its status as durable or obsolete. If old and new coexist, we might understand this coexistence as a potential contrivance rather than just a product of the differential resilience of items. If old games exist alongside new games it is not necessarily because they are not yet worn out or irretrievably decayed, but might be because they have been chosen to have durability 'imposed'.

In order to better understand these processes, the persistence of old media technologies, the coexistence of old and new, and to explore the myriad meanings that are bestowed on 'obsolete' technologies, we might profitably turn to studies of 'residual media'. Writing in the introduction to what is perhaps the definitive collection on residual media, in which Sterne's chapter appears, Acland (2007b) forcefully identifies what he sees as an unhealthy and unhelpful fetishisation of the new and the rehearsal of precisely the kinds of marketing discourses that we have seen in the previous chapters blighting much contemporary media scholarship. In proposing the study of residual media as a corrective to contemporary scholarship's fetishization of the 'new', he notes that

> a paucity of research has concentrated on the tenacity of existing technologies or on their related materials and practices that do not magically vanish with the appearance of each successive technology … An inappropriate amount of energy has gone into the study of new media, new genres, new communities, and new bodies, that is, into the contemporary forms. Often, the methods of doing this have been at the expense of taking account of continuity, fixity, and dialectical relationships with existing practices, systems, and artifacts.
>
> *(Acland 2007b: xxiii, xix–xx)*

To some extent, such an approach recalls Carolyn Marvin's desire for a consideration of new media in the particular historical moments of their birth or production, or in other words 'when old technologies were new', as she has it in the title of her book (Marvin 1988). Focusing on attempts to recover the specificity of points at which technologies were introduced and during which their meanings were still not fixed and were being formed through patterns of adoption, adaptation and use, such studies challenge the simplistic coupling of 'new' with 'today'. In a similar vein,

Gitelman and Pingree's (2003) knowing and wittily titled *New Media, 1740–1915* presents a genealogy of new media based around a series of case studies that seek to recover the forgotten or ignored histories from the 'causal plots of technological innovation offered by some historians' (Gitelman and Pingree 2003: xv). This volume, as well as Gitelman's later *Always Already New* (2008), which examines the ways in which specific media such as recorded sound and digitally networked text emerged and are subsequently encountered and studied as historical subjects, invite us to consider the 'new' of previous eras. We might also want to draw parallels with science fiction author Bruce Sterling's call for a 'Dead Media Handbook' (Sterling 1995; see also Bak 1999). In his 'Dead Media Manifesto', Sterling notes the almost obsessive interest in, and claims made for, the technologies of the present moment and opines the lack of consideration, or perhaps even the memory, of those media that have not merely become obsolete or vanished from view but have perished altogether:

> Plenty of wild wired promises are already being made for all the infant media. What we need is a somber, thoughtful, thorough, hype-free, even lugubrious book that honors the dead and resuscitates the spiritual ancestors of today's mediated frenzy … We need a book about the failures of media, the collapses of media, the supercessions of media, the strangulations of media, a book detailing all the freakish and hideous media mistakes that we should know enough now not to repeat, a book about media that have died on the barbed wire of technological advance, media that didn't make it, martyred media, dead media.
>
> *(Sterling 1995)*

However, while Sterling's work is without doubt as provocative as it is entertaining, and the contributions of Gitelman and Pingree, Marvin and others share many of the same interests as those writing in Acland's (2007a) collection, there is a key difference. Where Marvin proposes a form of media history that calls for the consideration of new media *when they were new*, residual media studies invites us to encounter and contemplate new media *now they are old*. This is a subtle but essential temporal and conceptual difference that encourages us to break from the rupturing narratives of technological 'progress' and revolution (which the study of new media when they were new does not necessarily presuppose) and instead demands the recognition and exploration of the resilience of old media, the complexity of obsolescence as a lived experience, and the ecology of contemporary media as one in which old and new rub along together, each informing one another and bestowing meanings upon one another. If we twist Sterling's manifesto, in recognising that old media do not 'magically vanish', we see that the study of residual media is perhaps less concerned with an exhumation of the deceased but rather with a study of what we might term the 'living dead'.

In this chapter, we will turn our attentions to two distinct ways in which the games are reanimated or perhaps resuscitated. First, we will (re)consider the practices of contemporary videogames retail. In particular, our lens will fall on the fate of the games that were traded in to purchase the newer, better replacements – daring to look inside the trade-in 'sick bag' of old games. The pre-owned marketplace might seem like a site of abundance and easy access where old games are widely, and often remarkably cheaply, available. However, our analysis will problematise this reading and, by probing some of the detail of the practices and principles, will suggest that the pre-owned market serves the supersessionary discourse as strongly as the futurism of pre-ordering. Second, we will explore the responses of videogame publishers to the pre-owned market as well as the ways in which their 'back catalogues' are exploited through 'retro' collections. In particular, we will investigate the impact and consequences of the coding of old games as 'retro' and the particularities of their collection and packaging. Finally, we move our attentions to some of the ways in which players breathe continued life into games and systems through cataloguing, documentation and archival work as well as through exploratory play. In contrasting player-produced walkthroughs with the strategy guides we saw in the previous chapter, for instance, we will consider how different motivations relating to durability and obsolescence are revealed.

The living dead

Thus far, our discussion of contemporary videogame retail has focused on new, or even unreleased, games. As we have seen, the availability and foregrounding of pre-orders helps to focus attentions on the future of gaming and contributes to the sense of continual change and progress. Working in concert with other advertising and marketing practices and the forward-looking focus of much specialist games journalism, we see obsolescence and supersession invoked and produced through the construction of an economy of perpetual innovation and upgrade. We have noted, too, that the games retail marketplace is distinctive not only in the veracity of its advertising and promotion of the new and forthcoming but also in the way that it encourages replacement of the old. Old games may be traded in against these new purchases, thereby recouping some of the residual monetary value of the previous purchase and offsetting it against the literal 'buying in' to the vision of newness and the processes of technological update. Up until now, we have conceived of these processes, wittingly or otherwise, as serving to demote old games, which become bargaining chips or technological benchmarks by which the superiority of the successor may be measured. Leaving aside for now the brute fact that, as studies of residual media suggest, there is considerable potential for lag in this system, as some players either do not want to or cannot afford to take part in the culture of continual upgrade, it remains the case that the normalisation of this 'new lamps for old' value model persuasively communicates the privileging of the new at the expense of the old. However, we must take care not to simply cast the old, replaced game as junk. The traded-in title does not simply disappear but rather, begins a new chapter in its symbolic journey as it is transformed into a 'pre-owned' title.

The pre-owned marketplace for videogames has become a hugely important part of the retail ecology and is a key site for encountering old games. Specialist videogame retailers such as chains like Game and Gamestation, as well as numerous independent stores, have long resold the pre-owned titles traded in by purchasers of new games. Even in 2009, Game's CEO Lisa Morgan claimed that 'It represents nearly 18 per cent of our total sales and this is growing as more and more customers see what great value it is' (Elliot 2009). We have noted also that the extent of the pre-owned marketplace has grown significantly, with Game claiming in 2011 that 50 to 60 per cent of its new sales are driven by trade-ins (Batchelor 2011) and GameStop reporting that 'pre-owned game products accounted for 47.4 per cent of the company's profit for the three months ending October 2010' (Parfitt 2010). However, we should not think that it is only specialist videogame retailers who engage in the resale of second-hand games. Supermarkets such as Tesco and Asda have similarly added pre-owned sales to their retail offer. Asda's 2010 announcement of its 'Buy-Play-Trade' scheme is illustrative:

> Customers can bring in their unwanted games and trade them in against other titles or exchange them for money on a 'Buy, Play, Trade' card which can be redeemed against future game purchases. It used to be restricted to games specialists but the market is now said to be worth £500 million ... we're delighted to be able to offer the service to the majority of our customers.
>
> *(Trina 2010)*

While we have previously centred on the coding of old games as 'unwanted' and the discursive production of supersession through the sequentiality of retail schemes entitled 'Buy-Play-Trade', it is clear that pre-owned schemes do not simply wear out these old games but rather transform and recirculate them, making them available again for new players. On the face of it, then, we might see the existence of the pre-owned market as a powerful counterargument to the position we have taken so far in relation to the privileging of new games and the silencing of the old. The apparent abundance of old games to choose from surely puts the lie to any assertion that new games dominate, and demands that we rethink our position on the eradication or silencing of old games. We are perhaps reminded of Straw's analysis of the video rental store as a site for accessing old movies, as well as an environment in which old and new were in dialogue. Drawing on the work of Janelle Watson (1999), whose consideration of 'modes of accumulation' foregrounds the way cultural artefacts are 'stored, displayed and disposed of', Straw sees the video retail environment as performing a complex and dualistic function:

> In the age of the videocassette, new films in theatrical release displaced those that had come before them, as they always had, but older films piled up behind new releases to an extent unknown in the days before home video. In this accumulation, older films served as perpetually available tools of instruction for anyone wishing to renew a contact with contemporary cinema.
>
> *(Straw 2007: 6)*

For Straw, then, the video store exists as a kind of archive of movies which, by virtue of its accumulation of older films, provides access points for viewers. Moreover, as in the case of *The Shawshank Redemption*, for instance, the video market might even offer a lifeline to movies that made little impact in their first-run theatrical release. By intervening in the process that would previously have seen the disappearance from the silver screen equate with their disappearance from view altogether, the accessibility and accumulation of the video store ensures that these movies remain, or in some cases become, available as cultural resources. For Straw, in disrupting the cycle of novelty the video store is responsible for an effective slowing of the process of obsolescence and the 'reshaping of cultural time':

> Expanding the availability of films from the past, it has acted as a drag of sorts on the forward movement of cinematic culture, slowing the disappearance and commercial obsolescence of films as they pass out of their theatrical runs. In this, the video store is an inertial force.
>
> *(Straw 2007: 5)*

There are some interesting parallels here between Straw's 'inertial' video store and the pre-owned marketplace of contemporary videogames retail. Certainly, there is an apparently similar accumulation of old titles that arises as a consequence of the widespread practice of trading in old games for new. In this way, we might well argue that the effectiveness of the discursive production of obsolescence is significantly undermined by the very existence and availability of these catalogues of old titles. While we have seen that the release of *FIFA 11* might be conceived as an implicit or sometimes explicit criticism of *FIFA 10*, which is rendered undesirable and may be traded in by some as part of the new transaction, it nonetheless remains the fact that *FIFA 10* exists, as it becomes part of the pre-owned catalogue. And so, despite having the date of its own apparent expiry written into its name, *FIFA 10*, just like *09* before it, remains available to buy and is saved from the trash pile. In fact, we might argue that it is the very existence of the pre-owned market that ensures that *FIFA 10* continues to exist, precisely because it is traded in in part-exchange for its replacement, thereby assuring its transformation into a second-hand market item.

Clearly, a number of important questions arise. Chief among them is why anybody would buy *FIFA 09* or *10* when *FIFA 11* is available. For Straw, in the case of videos, the answers are clear. The video store offers points of access, ways of reconnecting with contemporary movies, ways of uncovering movies that one missed in their first run theatrical release. While it would be unfair to claim that these motivations were not at play in relation to pre-owned videogames, it is worth revisiting some of the claims of pre-owned retail operators that we have seen above for an alternative answer. In discussing Game's pre-owned successes, Morgan's position is telling: 'this is growing as more and more customers see what great value it is'. Asda's announcement of the launch of its pre-owned scheme is similarly elucidated in terms of pricing and value for money:

> There are some amazing games coming out but parents can't afford to keep up. For example, you can pick up a pre-owned copy of Gears of War for just

£8 that was £50 when it first came out two years ago. 'We're making it even easier for customers to save money every day,' says Andrew [Thompson, head of games at Asda]. Pre-owned games manager Greg Walton sets and reviews the prices each week to keep them competitive, based on the price of the new game, how well it's selling and how much stock we have.

(Trina 2010)

It is not merely a case of supermarkets and specialist retailers 'making it even easier for customers to save money every day', as Asda's head of games has it above, and the 'setting and reviewing' of prices warrants some investigation, as it is here that we see a surprising rate of depreciation that opens up an often sizeable gap between new and pre-owned and that forces us to reconsider the inertial effect of pre-owned games retail. In 2010, *Which?*, the independent European consumer rights organisation, conducted a survey of the second-hand game marketplace. The study focused on the trade-in transaction through which retailers acquire and accumulate pre-owned titles. Under an article with the banner headline 'Video games lose value faster than used cars', *Which?* reports that,

During our research we discovered that gaming blockbuster Call of Duty: Black Ops, released just three days prior to our research and originally bought brand new, lost as much as 70% of its original value when presented to stores that buy pre-owned games.

(Which? 2010)

While there was some variation in the price offered by different retailers to players wishing to trade in the Xbox 360 version of *Black Ops*; with HMV offering £25 and Gamestation £18.80, Blockbuster and Game offering £16.80 and £16.70 respectively, the depreciation is considerable. Although those unfamiliar with the operation and economics of the pre-owned market might find the scale of the price drop difficult to comprehend, what might be even more surprising is the rate at which the price plummets. For a game purchased on the day of its release for £44.99, this depreciation occurs after just three days. As the *Which?* survey details, *Call of Duty: Black Ops* is not a special case, and the rapid, and inevitable, depreciation of new videogames as they undergo the symbolic transformation into pre-owned titles through the act of trading in is a material fact of the contemporary marketplace.

This is not to say, of course, that the traded-in game is sold for such a lowly price when it (re)appears on the retailer's shelf. Indeed, part of the reason for the emergence and promotion of pre-owned markets may be found in the economics of first-/second-hand margins. Speaking at Develop, the UK-based videogame trade conference, in 2010, Niall Lawlor, managing director of retailer GameStop Nordic expounded, 'We discovered the used business was a way of preserving our margins ... If we hadn't got the used business we wouldn't be here' (Martin 2010; see also Brown 2011). We will return to the issues of the higher margins offered to retailers on the first sale of pre-owned games and their economic motivation for developing the second-hand videogames market. For now, however, we should consider the longer lifespan of the pre-owned game.

The dramatic devaluation noted by *Which?* is just the first in a potentially lengthy, ongoing series of depreciations. Over time, most games continue inexorably to lose exchange value. To be clear, some games do retain, or even regain, value over time. This is most typically a function of their scarcity, which often arises from initially limited releases or short production runs, or by virtue of their continued valorisation in 'best game' lists published in specialist magazines and websites. For some titles, their age also acts to help their transformation into vintage rather than second-hand as they become distant from contemporary play and players in much the same way as Gregson *et al.* (2000) note in relation to items of clothing that acquire value as they become removed from the viscerality of recent wear. As such, the Dreamcast game *Shenmue* continues to command a premium, but, even in the context of Dreamcast games, it is part of an overwhelming minority. For those other titles, it is a journey, if not quite a race, to the bottom, whereupon they languish on shelves, becoming the ruins of videogames.

The hastily handwritten, easily updatable A-frame whiteboards that stand outside numerous games retailers detailing today's trade-in prices speak of the continuing decline in value and successfully communicate a sense of urgency about the impending transaction. Similarly, purchasers of older pre-owned titles will no doubt have encountered the multiple layers of price stickers affixed to the game box. Peeling off each label to reveal one below bearing a higher price is an informative, if some-what depressing, form of gaming archaeology that speaks eloquently of the inevitable decline of old games and their journey towards obsolescence and trash. The predict-ability of the availability of games in the pre-owned market, a predictability that speaks of the wearing out of games and is accompanied by the equally inevitable decline in face value, is made clear in Game's early 2011 introduction of a system of pre-ordering for pre-owned games (see Brown 2011).

As such, what we see invoked in the pre-owned marketplace is a different kind of comparison between old and new where the new remains desirable but is positioned as potentially out of reach because of the high price it commands. The continued depreciation of pre-owned games ensures that these gaming experiences are, even-tually, or perhaps in some cases quite rapidly, available to less affluent players unable to access them at the time of their first release. Before we probe further, it is worth briefly reminding ourselves of Watkins's (1993) insightful analysis of obsolescence presented in *Throwaways*. For Watkins, our attentions should be centred as much on the ways in which particular people or groups are rendered obsolete as a result of their inability to access the most up-to-date of technology as they are on the repla-cement and supersession of the technologies themselves. The social consequences of access to technologies are significant and Watkins notes the ways in which this is used to code the obsolescence of different categories of users, who are variously granted and denied opportunity for engagement.

What we see in the pricing differential between new and pre-owned games is perhaps a powerful reminder of the way in which certain groups are disallowed access to new games and what are apparently the most technologically advanced media and experiences. As such, although the pre-owned market might on one level be seen to offer access to games to those who initially cannot afford them, giving access where none was previously afforded, we should not overlook the fact that this ability to access is granted only once these games and systems have been used, once they are second-hand. Accordingly, they are, in Watkins's terms, somebody else's 'throw-aways'. It follows that, in something of a reversal of our *prima facie* assessment of the pre-owned marketplace as an abundant, accessible, contextualising archive of old games that exists in the manner of Straw's video store, we might argue that the new game is rendered yet more desirable as a consequence of the pre-owned marketplace and the operation of its pricing structure. At the very least, even if we stop short of considering it to be complicit in manufacturing the commercial and desirability gap between new and old, it is certainly worth noting that the pre-owned market does little if anything to challenge the 'naturalness' of the differential.

Skin and bones

It should be clear already that while it bears some similarities, in other regards the nature of the pre-owned videogames market is significantly different from the video store situation that Straw describes. Game, Asda and GameStop *et al.*'s shelves are not filled with old games because of any recognition on the part of publishers that the titles are of commercial, let alone cultural value and the games are neither re-releases nor back catalogue inventory. Rather, the pre-owned market is a product of retail margins and, most importantly, trades exclusively in second-hand games. In this regard, it perhaps has more in common with the charity, retro and thrift shops that are the subject of research by Gregson *et al.* (2000), Clarke (2000) and Gregson and Crewe (1997), among others. Clarke (2000: 88) usefully reminds us of the impor-tance of second-hand purchasing as part of the everyday household provisioning, and certainly the narratives we have seen presented above by retailers play on the afford-ability of the pre-owned offerings. Moving further into a consideration of the con-texts of these purchases and extending what they perceive as an often-rehearsed argument about chains of production and consumption that are linked to first-cycle consumption, Gregson *et al.* (2000: 101) draw attention to the importance of con-sidering the spaces of exchange as well as the processes of encountering items in dif-fering states of repair that must be dealt with, and in some cases quite literally cleansed of their previous associations. In the thick description of strategies for dealing with the preparation of items of clothing for sale and the negotiations of purchasers with the resulting garments, Gregson *et al.* foreground the desire to remove all traces of the previous owner. Scrubbing, cleaning, steaming and ironing to remove all trace of the previous body of the unknown Other and its problematic stains, leakages and odours become the preoccupation of the charity-store worker and customer operat-ing in different back and front zones of the store (after Goffman 1959). In fact, as Miller (2000: 80) humorously notes, what we see here is an inversion of the more usual idea of people removing their clothes, to reveal one in which the clothes remove their people (though note the contrast with some eBay purchasers of used underwear, who seek the intimacy of an unknown but still putatively present previous owner; see Petit 2006). The negotiation of olfactory and visual boundaries mediates much of the charity- and retro-store shopping encountered by Gregson *et al.* and is illustrated in their fieldnotes.

> We cross the road and the first thing we both say is 'car boot sale', and yes it is, because stuff in this shop spills out onto the street in front of the shop … The clothes look as though they're covered in layers of grime and even flicking through things is more than an effort.
>
> *(Gregson* et al. *2000: 109–10)*

While a survey of the cleanliness of individual videogame stores is beyond the scope of this project, and discretely avoiding any allusions to the Game group's trade-in 'sick bags', there are useful parallels to be made here. The whiteboards detailing the latest trade-in prices spilling into the street might be considered enticements to enter the store, but what is often the handwritten, dry-wipe amateurism of their production often jars with the backlit store logo, and is just as likely to connect the retail experience with that of the boot sale. Equally, the occasionally troubling garments might remind us of some of the tattier, well-handled boxes with their multiple layers of price stickers, or the glass cabinets of MegaDrive and GameBoy cartridges, each individually priced at just a few pounds or even pennies, as they have torn labels and are missing their boxes and instruction manuals, or even the copy of *FIFA 09* which, as of mid-2011, was widely available in the UK on PS3 for just 99p. Coated in greasy fingerprints and with elements damaged or even missing, these are the grubby realities of technologies of which Sterne (2007) reminds us. Although we do not find quite the same desire to cleanse the game as we do the second-hand garment (though perhaps, in light of stories of ecstasy tablets being found inside pre-owned copies of *Grand Theft Auto IV*, some more purification might be beneficial; see Chalk 2009) nor quite the same desire to restore newness to the second-hand game, we should note the availability of disc-cleaning services:

> If your game is slightly scratched we might still be able to help. We have 'disrepair' machines in store that can remove superficial scratches and restore the game to its original condition.
>
> *(Trina 2010)*

The comparison with charity shops, however, is perhaps most keenly felt in the act of exploration, in the search for the desirable game. This, as Pitts notes, frequently involves just the same kinds of negotiations and encounters with unwanted detritus as one rummages through the layers of 'throwaways'. Most importantly, the impact of the activity is an unsatisfactory one that possibly even tarnishes the games themselves.

There's something distasteful about sifting through this sort of cruft – especially when you really get in there, elbow deep, rooting through unknown titles smeared with fingerprints and sticker glue. It makes me feel like a vulture hunched over some bit of carrion. This is not prime cut. This is skin and bones.

(Main 2011)

Though it may not be the case for everybody, as we will see later in this chapter, for Pitts, the act of searching through these obviously discarded materials that not only bear the signs of wear but also demonstrate their own history as potentially long-term retail objects, being covered in the residue of the glue from sale and pricing stickers, as well as the evidence of being previously sifted through and discarded again, is far from pleasurable. We would do well not to overlook the actual conditions and contexts within which players and consumers come into contact with games, and this impacts greatly on how they are understood and valued. There has been a tendency in academic game studies to focus on textual formations and audience responses to games and gameplay at the expense of a consideration of the means and mechanisms by which these games come into the hands of players in the first place. If we consider Pine and Gilmore's (1999) *The Experience Economy* and its assertions about business and retail as staged performances that simultaneously precede and constitute the sale, we begin to get a sense of how significant the manifest devaluation and depreciation of old games might be. While the acquisition and ownership of the object remains an important outcome of the transaction, Pine and Gilmore's conceptualisation of the experience economy suggests that consumers seek and derive pleasure from closer associations with, and performance within, the channels of desire that encourage and frame consumption. In the case of the pre-owned market, its presentation of 'distasteful skin and bones' constructs an ambiguous narrative at best, and a context and consequence that, for some at least, has to be carefully negotiated.

Of course, it is not only the perceived value of second-hand games that is affected by these experiences, and we should follow Gregson *et al*'s (2000) call to consider the concurrence of second-hand and the first-cycle retail spaces that have tended to be characterised as dominant. Drawing on the earlier work of Gregson and Crewe (1997), we might profitably consider the 'relationality and simultaneity of second-hand and first-cycle spaces of exchange' (Gregson *et al.* 2000: 101–2). Indeed, we might argue that this is particularly essential to a study of games retail, given the closeness of the pre-owned and first-cycle games spaces of exchange. It is essential to remember how normalised the trading in of pre-owned videogames has become. One does not have to travel to a specific second-hand videogame retail space and, as we have seen, the pre-owned is no longer the preserve of specialist game retailers and is commonplace in general entertainment retailers, and even supermarkets. A key characteristic of contemporary videogames retail is the intimacy of the relationship between new and old. In fact, we find pre-orders and pre-owned physically proximate and rubbing against each other, altering each other's meanings. Set against this context, it is instructive to re-evaluate the consequence of the deep depreciation and, in particular, the rapidity of these price reductions on videogames. We see the creation of a situation similar to one that Straw notes in relation to the video store, but accelerated to an almost blistering rate. While the accumulation of videos creates context and multiple points of access, Straw observes complexity in the relationship between old and new movies where the existence and operation of the store 'contributes to the acceleration of first-run film culture. It does so, in part, through the ways in which it has helped reduce the typical run of a film's theatrical release, and so increase the rate of turnover in commercial cinemas' (Straw 2007: 5).

The speed of the depreciation of *Black Ops* that we noted above speaks of the dramatic reduction in the first-cycle lifespan of the new game. Somewhat conversely, then, it is the existence and demands of the pre-owned marketplace and the desire of retailers to generate pre-owned inventory for resale that undermines the longevity of the new, first-cycle release. However, rather than de-privileging the new, the continued depreciation of games to the point of 'skin and bones' and the incentivisation of replacement through trade-in continues to discursively position and normalise the new and the pre-orderable as the fetishised objects of ultimate desire. In this way, while the pre-owned market may initially appear to counterpose the narratives that produce obsolescence by making available old games and transforming them into newly consumable objects, it is possible to argue that it in fact contributes to the validation and even to the acceleration of the process of wearing out and replacing in exchange. The position outlined here bears some of the characteristics of the charity shops described by Gregson *et al.* (2000), as, while it may well be possible to see some of the provision of context, points of access and the skewering together of old and new as outlined by Straw (2007), the rate of increase of commercial turnover is a clear and important consequence. It is essential that we understand the complexity of the contribution of the pre-owned to the valuing, in commercial and cultural terms, of old games and the normalisation of processes of renewal, replacement and iteration.

'Parasitic, abusive thievery'

Of course, we should take care not to present the pre-owned market as the product of the videogame 'industry' per se. Instead, we should appreciate that it is, as we shall see, very much the creation of the retail sector and runs contrary to the wishes of many involved in the creation and publishing of games. Indeed, in recent years, videogame publishers and developers alike have taken an extremely critical view of the practice of reselling old games. The motivations and interests of developers and publishers might be somewhat different from those of others interested in game history or matters of long-term preservation, but their response and, in particular, the strategies and actions that have been, and continue to be, put in place have far-reaching consequences and impacts.

Understandably, and perhaps predictably, the contentiousness of the pre-owned marketplace centres on the revenue model it establishes. More specifically, it centres on the fact that, as developers and publishers see it, the pre-owned revenue model effectively cuts them out and exists as a transaction between the consumer and retailer. While publishers earn their share from the game's original, first-cycle sale, it's subsequent journey through trade-in and resale as a pre-owned object is one that does not directly benefit the publisher financially. 'Directly' is an important qualification here, as it is possible to argue, as some retailers do, that even though the transaction does not contribute funds to the publisher, it may be responsible for driving further sales and enlivening the marketplace more broadly. We shall return to this argument later, but for now, let us consider the ways in which the objections are articulated. There is (perhaps reluctant) recognition and acceptance of the attractiveness of lower-cost games to consumers, but these are typically combined with a palpable sense of frustration regarding the negative impact on profitability. As Andrew Eades of Relentless notes:

> From the gamers' point of view it's really good because you can effectively pay a tenner buying a game, which is great, which is maybe where the price point for games should be … But of course we can't really reduce the price point of games if the only profit we're getting is off of that first sale. That's why retailers aren't the most popular people with game developers right now.
>
> *(Eades in Lee 2008a)*

However, there is also some recognition of the complexity of the situation as being one that does not simply trade in offering consumers cheap games, but rather one that proffers multiple possibilities and in which consumers develop their own retail strategies. Eades recognizes that the pre-owned marketplace may be encountered by consumers as a way of managing the risk. Not only does it potentially present games at a lower initial price (if the pre-owned game is purchased) but, perhaps as interestingly, it exists as a means of regaining some residual exchange value by trading in unwanted or disappointing purchases.

> People feel that they've got a safety net because if it is a game that they don't like or is full of bugs then they can take it back and trade it – that safety net is appreciated by the gamer and that's partly the reason it exists. If we weren't guilty of selling rubbish then we wouldn't have such a big problem.
>
> *(Eades in Lee 2008a)*

While Eades might attempt to shoulder some of the blame, or at least tacitly lay the blame at the door of developers and publishers 'guilty of selling rubbish', it is surprising to note the position of some other development luminaries. David Braben, for instance, co-developer of *Elite*, the seminal 1980s 'space opera' for the BBC B micro and now chairman of Frontier Developments, paints a position that initially seems familiar, yet on closer inspection reveals a lack of confidence in the longevity of games.

> Games like BioShock and Assassin's Creed, where they're perfectly valid games, but once you've played them they go into the pre-owned section.
>
> *(Braben in Lee 2008b)*

Ultimately, Braben's position is a rather curious one in being less critical of the existence of the pre-owned marketplace as part of a system that actively encourages the
'wearing out' of games through trade-in and resale but rather, being one that profits
from the inevitability of games being used up. Braben's point here is that single-
player games such as *BioShock* and *Assassin's Creed*, being based around a strong narrative core that apparently reaches its ultimate conclusion or resolution in much the
same way as a film or novel might, necessarily lack longevity, as they present players
with no reason to replay. This position might seem curious and it is not abundantly
clear why videogames would not be capable of rewarding repeated engagement in
the way that we know that movies, novels and music are, yet Braben is not alone in
positioning videogames as essentially fleeting experiences. Andrew Oliver, co-founder
of Blitz Games Studios, voices a somewhat similar sentiment that speaks of the
inevitability of a rapid 'using up' of games through play:

> Arguably the bigger problem on consoles now is the trading in of games ... I
> understand why players do this, games are expensive and after a few weeks of
> playing you've either beaten it, or got bored of it so trading it back in to help
> pay for the next seems sensible when people are short of cash.
>
> *(Oliver in Crossley 2010)*

Later in this chapter, we will reconsider this position in light of those players and
practices that are precisely dedicated to eking out every last drop of available gameplay from their games. Here, it is sufficient to note that there remains some confusion
and difference of opinion as to precisely why the pre-owned market exists. What is
absolutely unequivocal, though, is the characterisation of contemporary retail's
second-hand sales, whether it is THQ CEO Brian Farrell's (Ingham 2010)
announcement of attempts to 'reduce the impact of used games' or Andrew Eades
noting that 'platform holders, developers, and publishers are saying "we're not really
happy with the way you are treating our games in the pre-owned market"' (Lee
2008a). Oliver's assertion is illustrative: 'So while retail may be announcing a reasonable season, the money going back up the chain is a fraction of what it was only a
few years ago. This is a much bigger problem than piracy on the main consoles'
(Oliver in Crossley 2010).

The comparison of pre-owned sales with the issue of piracy begins to deliver a
clear sense of the manner in which the business is seen by many videogame publishers. Let us not forget that piracy remains one of the global videogames industry's
bêtes noires. Trade organisations like the US-focused ESA note that 'Global piracy is
estimated to have cost the U.S. entertainment software industry over $3.0 billion in
2007, not including losses attributable to Internet piracy' (ESA 2011b), while the
United Kingdom Interactive Entertainment Association operates an IP Crime Unit
with a 24-hour telephone hotline dedicated to reporting incidences of software
piracy. That videogame publishers might wish to speak of the threat of pre-owned
retail markets as being of greater impact than intellectual property infringement
and software piracy; indeed, the fact that they are presented as 'threats' at all

is enlightening. An appreciation of the way in which these retail practices are considered might also help us to make sense of the depth of feeling that is often exhibited. As Fahey (2010) notes,

> 'Parasitic.' 'Abusive.' 'A huge issue.' 'A critical situation.' 'Extremely painful.' 'Thievery.'
>
> Strong words. You might expect those kind of comments about piracy, drug dealers or baby-snatchers. Or drug-dealing baby-snatchers. But those are direct quotes from senior publishing executives about the second-hand games market. And that's just a small sample – the well of discontent over pre-owned sales goes much deeper.
>
> *(Fahey 2010)*

The language of videogame publishers' response to the impact of pre-owned retail is an unambiguously confrontational one. Whether it is calls to 'take action against pre-owned sales' or assertions that the sale of pre-owned games 'cheats developers' (Pakinkis 2010), even the most cursory survey of the games-trade press leaves one in no doubt that swords are drawn. Delving deeper, we find evidence that this is not simply posturing. As a direct response to the perceived threat of pre-owned sales, a number of publishers have adopted schemes whereby first-cycle purchasers are rewarded with an authentication code that may be redeemed online in exchange for additional downloadable content (DLC). Importantly, these codes are single-use, meaning that once they have been used they cannot be reactivated. Coupled with the fact that the content is linked either to a specific individual's online account or even to the machine onto which it was originally downloaded, this makes a simple transfer impossible. As such, the pre-owned game is materially, or perhaps virtually, deficient. By design, it is manifestly inferior and in a most literal way has been, at least partly, 'used up'. THQ's *Smackdown vs. Raw 2011* was among the first games to deploy such a single-use DLC code. While reinforcing the case that the revenue flow back into publishing is essential if new development is to be funded, thereby con- tinuing the economy of perpetual innovation, the position set out by Cory Ledesma, creative director for THQ's wrestling game series, is one that trades on notions of player loyalty and betrayal:

> I don't think we really care whether used game buyers are upset because new game buyers get everything. So if used game buyers are upset they don't get the online feature set I don't really have much sympathy for them. That's a little blunt but we hope it doesn't disappoint people. We hope people under- stand that when the game's bought used we get cheated … I don't think anyone wants that so in order for us to make strong, high-quality WWE games we need loyal fans that are interested in purchasing the game. We want to award those fans with additional content.
>
> *(Ledesma interviewed in Pakinkis 2010)*

In view of the extremity of this position, and following considerable consternation in the gaming press and among fans (see Watts 2010 and the discussion in the comments threads, for instance), Danny Bilson, executive vice president of core games at THQ, attempted to clarify the situation:

> What I care about the most is building great games people are excited to buy. If all of that revenue is going outside of the people who are making the games, it's really tough for us to fund them. It's that simple. But we also don't want to punish the used gamer. So one of the things you're going to see us do, in addition to what is called the online lockout, which sounds a little punishing, is we're also going to be giving some downloadable content with that card. For instance, on our next WWE title, if you buy it used and there's a $10 fee to unlock all the online. It also unlocks the first DLC pack. So the used consumer feels they're getting something for their money, not just a getting out of jail card. We're trying to make it positive. But really what we have to be concerned with is new is premium, used is used. We've got to build our software to demonstrate that.
>
> *(Yin-Poole 2010)*

The situation that is created here is an intriguing one. Because publishers are incapable of directly addressing the operation of the pre-owned marketplace and feel the loss of revenue as games are recirculated between players and retailers, their response is to devalue the game itself, making it less desirable, even inoperable, as a second-hand item. By the addition of a single-use code, the game is effectively worn out in its first-cycle incarnation. If we view videogames as units on a balance sheet and titles and franchises as budget headers, we might have a degree of sympathy for this position. However, it is an undeniably self-destructive practice that literally devalues the game, shortens its life and continues to discursively privilege the new at the expense of the old.

Project Ten Dollar

In fact, there is more to the single-use DLC model than simply closing down the possibility of a transformation of the first-cycle game into a pre-owned item. Pre-owned purchasers of 'locked out' games can purchase their own code, thereby (re)activating the features or game modes otherwise absent. In this way, publishers have sought to directly intervene in the pre-owned market and recover apparently lost revenue. However, as we have seen, in order to do this, they must first devalue the game so that it might be 're-enchanted' with the subsequent top-up purchase.

EA has been a particularly enthusiastic adopter of (re)activation codes. Its 'Project Ten Dollar' is a programme similar in operation to that of THQ outlined above and allows/disallows access to downloadable content and upgrades through single-use redemption codes. As Edwards and Satariano (2010) note in their assessment of EA's ongoing business, Project Ten Dollar was greenlit by CEO John Riccitiello with a clear objective: 'One major goal: Grab back some of the revenue EA and others were losing as consumers flocked to used games' (Edwards and Satariano 2010). In the case of EA's *Alice: Madness Returns*, the Online Pass is used to provide console gamers access to the previously PC-only title, American McGee's *Alice*, although the system is slightly complicated, as EA's press release explains:

> EA announced today that Alice: Madness Returns, shipping on June 14, will include a one-time-use Online Pass registration code (for Playstation 3 and Xbox 360) that gives players access to the original cult-classic American McGee's Alice. Players that do not have the code can purchase American McGee's Alice for 800 Microsoft Points on Xbox LIVE® Marketplace and $9.99 on the PlayStation®Network* through the main menu of Alice: Madness Returns. This download for the Xbox 360® videogame and enter-tainment system and PlayStation®3 computer entertainment system marks the console debut for the infamous PC hit. Together, the two games take players through the two dark chapters of American McGee's adaptation of Alice in Wonderland.
>
> * Alice: Madness Returns disc required in console to access American McGee's Alice.
>
> *(Silwinski 2011)*

The asterisk and footnote are vital here and signal that the original game is usable only with the sequel's disc seated in the console's drive. By tying together the two titles and ensuring that the new game becomes the physical gateway, or perhaps a looking-glass, to the original, they appear almost as equally vital parts of the gameplay experience, rather than purchased/bonus content. The scope of the material that is subject to the restrictions of the Online Pass is revealing and EA's corporate website outlines the system in understandably positive terms. We should note the range of features that are allowed/disallowed:

> What exactly is Online Pass and when does it launch?
> Online Pass launches in all EA SPORTS simulation games on the PS3 and Xbox 360 beginning in June with Tiger Woods PGA TOUR 11. It's quite simple – every game will come with a game-specific, one-time use registration code with each unit sold new at retail. With your Online Pass, you'll have access to multiplayer online play, group features like online dynasty and lea-gues, user created content, and bonus downloadable content for your game including, for example, a new driver in Tiger.
>
> *(Wilson 2010)*

In these cases, the Online Pass not only unlocks additional 'bonus' content but potentially stands as a gatekeeper to modes of play and, in particular, either opens up or closes down the possibility of online multiplayer gaming. As such, access does not bestow the qualities of a 'special edition' with desirable 'added extras' or 'exclusive' features so much as it fundamentally reformulates the ludic potential of the game. Interestingly, while its marketing predictably focuses on the apparently self-evident benefits afforded through the scheme, EA's extensive Online Pass FAQ specifically addresses the issue of the scheme's relationship to the pre-owned 'second sale' marketplace. Again, the notion of investment in innovation is foregrounded and the purchase of new games is presented as part of the mechanism by which new new games may be ensured.

> Is this intended to combat second sale?
>
> We actually view the second sale market as an opportunity to develop a direct relationship with our consumers, and with Online Pass everyone has access to the same premium online services and content regardless of how and where you buy the game. In order to continue to enhance the online experiences that are attracting nearly five million connected game sessions a day, again, we think it's fair to get paid for the services we provide and to reserve these online services for people who pay EA to access them. In return, we'll continue to invest in creating great games and offer industry-leading online services to extend the game experience to everyone. I don't think even the harshest cynic can argue with that and instead I think fans will see the value we're committing to deliver when they see all the services, features and bonus content that is extending the life of their products.
>
> *(Wilson 2010)*

The logic of this final sentiment is especially convoluted, as 'extending the life of their products' necessarily involves a functional downgrading of the game's capabilities as it leaves first-cycle and enters the pre-owned marketplace. Capcom's 2011 announcement of the implementation of game-save features in *Resident Evil: The Mercenaries 3D* for the Nintendo 3DS console raises similar questions and creates a situation in which the pre-owned value is significantly diminished. Communicating on the company's blog, Capcom community specialist Shawn 'Snow' Baxter outlines the corporate position:

> In Resident Evil: The Mercenaries 3D, all mission progress is saved directly to the Nintendo 3DS cartridge, where it cannot be reset. The nature of the game invites high levels of replayability, encouraging fans to improve mission scores. The save mechanic ensures that both original and unlocked game content will be available to all users. Second-hand game sales were not a factor in this development decision, and we hope that all our consumers will be able to enjoy the entirety of the survival-action experiences that the game does offer.
>
> *(Baxter 2011)*

Of course, the consequence of this decision is that the pre-owned title cannot be returned to an unplayed state, as the progress of the previous player(s) is impossible to separate from the game code on the cartridge. The situation is unusual, and the game save data that records progress, achievements, unlocked items and areas and so on is typically saved either to the console's memory or to removable memory such as the SD card that the 3DS provides for such purposes. If we recall Gregson *et al*'s (2000) comments on the practices of cleansing second-hand clothing, we note an interesting parallel in that the ability to remove the tangible signs of previous ownership and use is comprehensively closed down here. As Kuchera (2011) notes, this is not a trivial matter:

> Once you've beaten the game, you can't erase your progress and start over. If you want to loan the game to a friend, they won't be able to start their own game from the beginning. You may be able to trade the game into a store or sell it, but I wouldn't suggest buying it from someone used, since you won't be able to start from the beginning and unlock all the content yourself.
>
> *(Kuchera 2011)*

In fact, as Cullen (2011), Dutton (2011a) and others reported, a number of retailers, including HMV in the UK, subsequently declined to take the title for trade-in. For HMV's Gennaro Castaldo, the decision was taken so as to 'avoid any potential customer disappointment for those purchasing a pre-owned version' (cited in Cullen 2011). In response, Capcom's corporate blog was updated to specifically tackle the questions of resale value and the potentially deleterious impact of the decision to disallow erasure of the game-save state on the experience of gameplay for both first-cycle and pre-owned players. Here, then, the specificities of a given player's performance effectively become part of the code of the game. The unravelling structure of the game that gradually reveals options, areas and capabilities is available only once and is decisively written out of the second(hand) playing. Again, we see the game literally used up through the act of play.

> Q. Does the inability to reset the save game data mean that those purchasing a secondhand version of the game will have content missing?
>
> A. Resident Evil: The Mercenaries 3D consists of 30 time-based missions, through which the player unlocks skill upgrades as they progress through the game. Anyone purchasing a copy of the game secondhand would have access to all the missions and skills that the original owner unlocked, in addition to the content that was available to the original user.
>
> *(Baxter 2011)*

At this early point in the operation of EA and Capcom's systems, their impact is difficult to assess. However, it is worth revisiting some of the comments on the relationship between pre-owned and new sales in order to advance our analysis. If, as Batchelor (2011) reports, 50 to 60 per cent of the Game group's sales of new games are part-funded by trade-ins, it is possible that the devaluation of EA titles might negatively impact on new sales. Consequently, as videogames industry analyst Colin Sebastian of Lazard Capital Markets notes, 'It's a double-edged sword for publishers. On one hand, it may discourage some used sales, but on the other hand, it devalues the used games that consumers would otherwise use as currency to buy new games' (interviewed in Brightman 2010).

Switching off: retiring games

While all of this suggests that the potential for re-enabling the features that are locked out through the EA Online Pass and other publishers' single-use redemption coupon systems, there is no guarantee either that players will or, as we shall see, will be able to access them in the future even if they desire. Elsewhere on EA's corporate website, lists of 'legacy' titles no longer supported or playable speak of gameplay that even coupon codes cannot resurrect:

> The decisions to retire older EA games are never easy. The development teams and operational staff pour their hearts into these games almost as much as the customers playing them and it is hard to see one retired. But as games get replaced with newer titles, the number of players still enjoying the older games dwindles below a point – fewer than 1% of all peak online players across all EA titles – where it's feasible to continue the behind-the-scenes work involved with keeping these games up and running. We would rather our hard-working engineering and IT staff focus on keeping a positive experience for the other 99% of customers playing our more popular games. We hope you have gotten many hours of enjoyment out of the games and we appreciate your ongoing patronage.
>
> *(Electronic Arts 2011)*

What is most surprising about the lists of 'games [that] get replaced with newer titles' is just how recent many of these retired games are. As of 2011, the list includes the following '09–10' titles:

> FIFA 09 for PC, PlayStation Portable, PlayStation 3, Xbox 360 and Wii
> FIFA 09 Ultimate Team for PlayStation 3 and Xbox 360
> Madden NFL 09 for PlayStation Portable (all regions), PlayStation 2, PlayStation 3, Xbox 360, Wii and Xbox
> Madden 10 for PlayStation Portable (all regions), PlayStation 2 and Wii
> NASCAR® 09 for PlayStation 2, PlayStation 3 and Xbox 360 (Europe Only)
> NBA LIVE 09 for PlayStation 3, Xbox 360 and Wii
> NCAA® Football 09 for PlayStation 3, Xbox 360 and PlayStation 2
> NCAA® Football 10 for PlayStation 2
>
> *(Electronic Arts 2011)*

We should note that some of the more draconian implementations of DRM through online authentication have met with stern resistance among players. Capcom's announcement of its plans for the PC version of *Super Street Fighter IV* is a case in point. Responding to the piracy that beset the online leaderboards in the game's predecessor, Capcom sought to implement its 'SSA' system, which required that players be logged into a 'Games for Windows Live' or 'Xbox Live' account in order to get full access to the title. Importantly, logins to these services were not simply required to enable online play or access to leaderboards, but would restrict or grant access to large parts of the 'offline' gameplay. Christian Svensson, corporate officer/senior vice-president at Capcom, outlined the situation in a corporate blog post:

> If you aren't signed in to an online GFWL [Games for Windows Live] profile, the offline mode has limited functionality. Obviously there's no online play, access to replay channels or other online-centric features (and this is the part that keeps the online play secure from hackers or pirates). Additionally, you won't be able to save any progress in challenges or settings, won't have access to any DLC you've purchased and all local play will be restricted to 15 of the 39 characters.
>
> *(Svensson 2011a)*

The severity of these restrictions is not inconsiderable. Without an active connection to one of the proprietary Microsoft gaming services, more than half of the character roster is simply unavailable. Quite apart from questions about losing progress as a result of dropped Internet connections even after a successful login (Svensson outlines a process that enables players to save their progress when their connection is restored, presumably having waited with the inoperable game still running on their PCs while their broadband line is fixed), this situation dramatically limits access to significant portions of gameplay. In fact, shortly after this unveiling of this proposed system, Svensson announced its reversal:

> Last week, when I put up a blog about all of the great new features and thoughtful PC-specific design considerations that were added to Super Street Fighter IV: Arcade Edition PC, many folks ignored the goodness therein and zeroed in on the implementation of the offline mode and its limitations. This in turn gave rise to threads on our boards and others, which in turn spawned stories at several web outlets lamenting our approach for protecting the content. To try and make this discussion more constructive, I engaged our fans in the Ask Capcom forum on how best to improve the situation. …
>
> Shortly after launch (it might even be at launch, but we'll see how submission timing and approval goes) we will roll out a small title update that will completely remove the character limitations for offline mode. That is to say, once you've updated, you will be able to use all 39 characters when not connected to the Internet to practice your combo timings, have some fun with a friend on a laptop, or whatever while offline.
>
> *(Svensson 2011b)*

We should take care not to unduly celebrate the removal of this particularly draconian and restrictive system, however. The fact remains that, like many other contemporary games, a large part of the functionality and gameplay in *Super Street Fighter IV* remains reliant on the continued availability of proprietary access and authentication services. On the practical level of long-term access, the contingency of gameplay on these services and networks presents a clear challenge to preservation projects, while, as we see with EA Online Pass, the very existence of the systems is a powerful tool that allows publishers to 'retire' or obsolesce games in favour of their replacements.

Re-animation: re-releases and retro collections

Of course, it is not true to say that videogame publishers are completely uninterested in old titles or that they uncomplicatedly view their back catalogues as threats to their current roster of games. As such, while authentication codes and the withdrawal of online servers may artificially shorten the life of otherwise playable packages or systems, this does not automatically mean that the games disappear. In fact, as we alluded to earlier in our discussion of the pre-release coverage of the Nintendo 3DS version of *Legend of Zelda: Ocarina of Time*, re-releases of old games titles from previous generations have become increasingly commonplace. Online stores such as Microsoft's Xbox-based Xbox Live Arcade (XBLA), the PlayStation Store serving PS3 and PSP, and Nintendo's Virtual Console each give contemporary gamers access to re-released games otherwise unplayable on the new hardware platform. Nintendo's online service, the Virtual Console, directly references this apparent universality and appears, *prima facie*, to signal the eradication of the restrictions and limitations of backwards compatibility and hardware specificity. Accordingly, titles from Nintendo's own catalogue, as well as games originally designed for non-Nintendo hardware platforms such as the SNK Neo-Geo, become available to owners of the Wii.

In Nintendo's case, the nod to its own gaming heritage is seen not only in the availability of the Virtual Console but also in the Wii interface. While we have become well used to hearing about the revolutionary nature of the Wii's 'remotes' (see Jones 2008), turning these controllers through 90 degrees reveals an unmistakable, and not unintended, similarity to Nintendo's very earliest home console controllers (we should note also the continuation of this familiar Nintendo pad design in the Wii U's controller as well as its implicit denigration of the once-revolutionary Wiimote to everyday and mundane, see Boxer 2011 on the Wii U launch at E3 2011, for instance). With a left-handed D-Pad and two momentary switches set to the right, these are essentially NES pads of 1980s vintage. If we needed proof of the halfwayness of even the most putatively innovative technology, it is writ large in the simultaneously forward- and backward-looking Wiimote. That it is supplemented at retail by the Classic Controller, which adds shoulder buttons, a trigger and an analogue stick, all of which are reminiscent of the 1990s-era Nintendo 64 joypad (itself occupying a precarious position between the 2D and 3D gameplay and control), further adds to the idea of the Wii as a viable home to old games (while simultaneously highlighting the difficulty of accessing and interfacing with games designed for different systems with bespoke controllers, an issue to which we will return later in this book). To complement these online points of access, disc-based re-releases exist and frequently present compendia or collections that cover specific game series (e.g. *Sonic the Hedgehog*) or even titles from across a given platform (such as the Sega MegaDrive, for instance). To be clear, then, what we see here is dissimilar to the pre-owned market which trades in objects that pass through cycles and phases of first and second ownership. Rather, these 'retro' game markets, as they are typi-cally known, are oriented around re-releasing new copies of old games. The game within may be old (although this may, as we will learn, be somewhat illusory), but the package, whether physical disc or digital download, is resolutely new.

We will turn our attentions to some of the Sega collections a little later, when we probe deeper into the (re)packaging of, and player responses to, re-releases. First, however, it is worth addressing some general points with regard to the relationship between the commercial re-release of titles and game-preservation activity. As Guttenbrunner *et al.* (2010: 65) note, the availability of services like Nintendo's Virtual Console channel, in concert with publications like *Retro Gamer* and exhibi-tions such as the Classic Gaming Expo in Las Vegas, speak of a public interest in 'retro' games. However, we should be careful to ensure that we do not mistake the interest in games or even the commercial availability of some 'classic' titles for acts of preservation. As a co-founder of the UK's National Videogame Archive (NVA), I have become used to fielding questions, either at public presentations or in press interviews, that interrogate the need for formal game preservation in the light of each of the three current home console systems having stores and channels that give access to re-releases of old games.

There are a number of ways to answer these questions, some of which we shall leave aside for further discussion later: namely the 'authenticity' of the reissued/ replayed game in relation to the original, both from a technical and contextual per-spective. However, equally important and more pertinent to our discussion here is the issue of selection. Cultural heritage projects such as the NVA, like any operating within contemporary institutions of memory, cannot seek to be completist in their collecting and are necessarily governed by policies and guidelines that set out para-meters, boundaries and interests. Clearly, the Virtual Console is also a curated col-lection of retro titles and does not present the entirety of a back catalogue but, rather, selected titles from a range of different platforms and systems. Practically, it is difficult to imagine any other viable system, yet what remains important here is that the selection process remains utterly inscrutable and rests in the hands of publishers and platform holders with their own particular motivations and interests, which need not be consistent with long-term preservation goals. As commentators like Kohler (2006) have noted, there is also considerable disparity between the libraries in different territories:

The list of titles that Japanese Wii buyers will be able to download from Virtual Console in 2006 is up now, and it's safe to say that it's significantly better than the US list. I mean, way, way better: they're getting Street Fighter II, Donkey Kong Country, Super Mario World, Super Castlevania, Contra III, Link to the Past, and New Adventure Island while we get the shaft, according to the list NOA [Nintendo of America] sent out this evening. If this list is right, we're not even getting Super Mario Bros. at launch.

(Kohler 2006)

Leaving aside any qualitative discussions about which roster is the better, that the lists are different is suggestive of a predictable influence of regional marketing and potential sales decisions on the selections. We should not be surprised by this (see Serrels 2011 on the economics, legality and experience of locking hardware and software to specific geographical regions). Nor is it a criticism as it is nowhere stated that the intention of the Virtual Console or any other retro-release service is to preserve games. However, while they may not be concerned with providing long-term security, and while they are doubtless important in raising the awareness of retro games and either generating or reflecting public interest in games beyond their first release, as Guttenbrunner *et al.* (2010) note, we might argue that systems like the Virtual Console are not only no more likely to deliver long-term preservation solutions than any other platform-dependent gaming service but may even work against preservation by galvanising attitudes and discourses of old versus new media. We should recall the fact that Virtual Console purchases are locked to the specific Wii console onto which they were originally downloaded, with no end-user opportunity to transfer the games to a new system. Accordingly, the re-released game has the same longevity as the Wii platform (or, in fact, the life of that particular console). As such, and as with the case of the pre-owned videogame market, it is possible to argue that some of the decisions and business models that operate in relation to re-releases and the retro-games marketplace are actually injurious to preservation activity and play a contributory role in the devaluing of the old with regard to the new. Here, we will focus on a number of factors. First, we will consider the pricing of retro games and the ways in which games and collections are packaged and presented. We will then move on to considerations of some of the ways in which old games are not just re-released but reinvented for the retro market, as well as explore the ways old games are referenced in the design of new titles. In this way, our discussion will focus on retro re-releases from both a publishing and a development perspective.

Just as with the pre-owned market, the pricing of re-released games acts as a powerful indicator of their apparent value in relation to new titles. Where second-cycle ownership brought inevitable depreciation, in the retro marketplace of XBLA, PlayStation Store and Virtual Console, we see initially low price points for re-released games. At a time when new console releases for each of the major consoles typically command prices of £40+, with handheld releases retailing at £30+, we find re-releases offered for just a few pounds. Thus it is that the new *Super Mario Galaxy* title for the Wii launched with a retail price of £40 while the re-release of 1985's NES *Super Mario Bros.* was the equivalent of £5 (in fact, 500 points, as Virtual Console purchases are made through proxy 'points cards'). In fact, in the case of the Virtual Console, we see a tiered pricing structure that effortlessly communicates, in monetary terms at least, the value placed on various platforms within the closed ecology of Nintendo's store. Importantly, while there is staggered pricing, variations are not between individual titles per se, but rather between the original platforms. As such, *Super Mario Bros.* retails at 500 points because all NES titles retail at 500 points. The absence of granularity in pricing might match that which we see in the first-cycle market and, consequently, is perhaps not too surprising. What is somewhat more problematic, however, is that the variation between platforms appears broadly to be oriented around the unstated but self-evident principle that games originally released on more recent platforms command higher prices. As of early 2011, the Virtual Console pricing structure is as follows:

Commodore 64	500
NES/Famicom	500
Sega Master System	500
TurboGrafx-16/PC-Engine	600
TurboGrafx-CD/PC-Engine CD-ROM	800
MSX	700
Mega Drive/Genesis	800
SNES/Super Famicom	800
Neo Geo	900
Nintendo 64	1000

WTF, only 40 games?

As we noted above, online stores and channels such as the Virtual Console are not the only distribution routes for re-released games, and while the first *Sonic the Hedgehog* game is available for download for 800 points (more costly than *Super Mario Bros.*, being an NES game that was originally released seven years later), it has also been available on DVD/Blu-ray disc as part of series of re-releases specifically revisiting the *Sonic the Hedgehog* oeuvre as well as the output of the MegaDrive platform, for instance. Let us briefly consider the Ultimate MegaDrive Collection (known as Sonic's Ultimate Genesis Collection in the US) released for Xbox 360 and PS3 in 2009. Collecting 40 titles from across the MegaDrive/Genesis back catalogue (in fact, ultimately offering 48/49 games, as some additional titles are unlockable through play), most of the *Sonic the Hedgehog* titles and their spinoffs (e.g. *Sonic & Knuckles*, *Sonic 3D Blast*, *Sonic Spinball*) are included, along with *Altered Beast* and titles in the *Phantasy Star* and *Golden Axe* series. At the time of their original release in the UK, MegaDrive cartridges retailed for approximately £40 (with some titles such as *Sonic 3* weighing in at significantly more).

In keeping with what we have seen in the Virtual Console, the compilation of almost 50 of these MegaDrive titles in a single collection immediately speaks of the way in which the perceived market value of these games has fallen over time. If we couple this with the fact that the Ultimate MegaDrive Collection was first released as a 'low cost' title costing £24.99, we note that the average value of a MegaDrive game has fallen from £40 to just a few tens of pennies. Of course, the disc is also subject to the same processes of depreciation as any other new release and exists now as part of the pre-owned game market, further diminishing the monetary value of each of the titles in the collection.

What is most surprising, however, is the critical response of players to the collection. While by no means universally negative, there is considerable consternation expressed in the reviews regarding the value of the collection. The following comments are drawn from Amazon.co.uk's customer reviews.

> 'Ultimate' Collection? 32Mb of games on a Blu-ray disc?
> I am a massive fan of the Sega Megadrive and have been looking forward to this release since it was first announced. Seeing the list of games was an abrupt smack in the face. Let's do the maths, shall we? (as I can, ahem, vouch for the size of every ROM) ...
> There are 40 Megadrive games at a total of 31 Megabytes of data. This was taking the Michael on a DVD release for the PS2 (or even on a UMD for the PSP), but for a format that can store 50 Gigabytes of data, it's an insult. Sega's entire back catalogue of Megadrive games only comes to around 800 Megabytes – they could fit that several times over on a DVD ... This is extremely cynical of Sega.
>
> *(Happy Space Invader 2009)*

> Wtf, only 40 games?
> Ehm, why would they only put 40 games on a blu-ray disc ... its like taking a pinch of an apple, and just let the rest of it rotten. and besides that ... where are all the good games i used to play? i cant remember all the names becouse i was probably 5 years old, but that ninja game i used to spend hours and hours to complete ... oh yeah they remembered the sonic and golden axe games ... but if you look at the fact that one game rarely fill more then one MB its an insult to release it on the PS3, a PS1 would run this piece of fail
>
> *(Mogensen 2009)*

What is most revealing about this criticism is not so much that it looks back unfavourably at the games in terms of the way they play or even the way they look or sound, compared with high definition, surround-sound titles like *Call of Duty* or *Metal Gear Solid 4*, though some reviewers do make such comparisons. Rather, the criticism in these two reviews centres on technology and the apparent mismatch between the capability of the modern host system and the demands of the re-released game. The selection of titles is conceived as problematic ('only 40 games?') in terms not of the variety of gameplay or any notably missing titles, series or genres. Nor is the criticism levelled at the implementation of the games or the use of different joypads. Rather, the limited selection is a matter of storage space. In these critical reviews, we see the games reduced to bits and bytes. They are data to be stored and delivered on increasingly generous discs. With each game evidently occupying just a few megabytes, it is, in the opinion of both reviewers, an 'insult' to collect together so few of them. What is so curious about this position is that the objection seems to centre as much on the gigabytes of unused storage space on the DVD/Blu-ray disc as it does on the actual games that are encoded on the disc. This reduction of games to data and the levels of awareness of storage capacities of different platforms' disc formats is, we might argue, a clear consequence of the discursive production of videogaming as a technical realm that we saw at the very outset of this book. In fact, some of the awareness of the file sizes of individual games originally delivered on cartridges in the 1990s that are alluded to in these reviews is, without doubt, connected to the availability of these games as downloadable (often illegally downloadable) ROMs ('I can, ahem, vouch for the size of every ROM').

It is worth pausing for a moment to consider the parallel shadow economy of ROM downloading. Quite apart from the (il)legality of emulation and videogame ripping and sharing (see Conley *et al.* 2004), the existence of 'ROMs' and the technicalities of their distribution reveal much about the peculiar tension between the interest in old games and their putative cultural and economic value. (St)ripped down to the barest of code, ROMs deny the downloader the paratextuality of the instruction manual or box art. In fact, ROMs perhaps serve to make the original game, divorced from its context and robbed of its materiality, even more distant. More tellingly, ROMs are typically distributed by the thousand in zipped files. And so, in just a few minutes, entire console back catalogues – every game released in every territory – are available for browsing and playing on a PC, Mac, mobile device or modified console. The completism of the collections allows detailed scrutiny of differences in Japanese versus European releases, for instance, and can be seen as a vital investigative resource. That these ROMs are packaged into collections of many thousands speaks implicitly of these games' perceived value. However, the availability of ROMs is surely not the only factor in play here. If we recall Sony's marketing messages that frame the PS3 as a supercomputer of almost unimaginable power and boasting the most capacious storage facilities ('one of the most advanced technologies you'll ever place in your living room'; Sony Computer Entertainment Europe 2007), we can hardly be surprised to see players so *au fait* with these details and so willing to use these criteria to judge what they are being expected to play and pay for.

Now in HD – remastering videogames

In fact, the notion of unused capacity is not only fuelled by these marketing discourses, and we should take some time to explore the nature and composition of the re-release packages themselves. As we have seen on a number of occasions throughout this book already, what appears on first reading to provide evidence of disruption to the cycle of obsolescence and the promotion of the new and forthcoming might, on closer inspection, be seen to operate firmly within this dominant discursive position. Many of the packages that contribute to the market for newly packaged 'retro' games are not simple re-releases. To be clear, by 'simple' I do not mean here to draw attention to the complexities of emulation that inevitably arise in the translation from game code designed to run on one system to another, typically more contemporary platform with different processing capabilities and available interfaces. Certainly, as we will see in the final part of this book, the issues surrounding 'simple' acts of emulation and the recreation of audiovisual representation and gameplay experience present considerable challenges to players and preservationists alike. Here, however, it is useful to focus on exactly what is being re-released in these retro collections.

The Sega MegaDrive Ultimate Collection is a case in point. Among the collage of images made up from the original box art of the 40 included games which speak of the generosity of the collection, the following text is emblazoned in neon blue: 'Play the originals that started it all ... Now in HD!' (Sega Ultimate Collection 2009). Importantly, then, these are not intended to be seen as recreations of the original 1990s MegaDrive titles, but rather, are to be encountered as updated, enhanced versions. Sega's European marketing and support website for the collection is similarly emphatic in declaring this a 'Hi-definition Upgrade: All titles included in the collection have been converted to vivid hi-def (720p) visuals to truly enhance that classic 2D experience!' (MegaDrive Collection n.d.). As such, the collection reveals an interesting tension that positions the back catalogue as a rich seam of gaming potential and of history and heritage while simultaneously upgrading, updating and enhancing. By bringing these games up-to-date, their original incarnations are effectively demoted and comprehensively designated as belonging to a different era – or generation. Sega's High Definition updates are by no means unique. Sony's release of the God of War Collection speaks of a similar desire to revisit the past in order to update it and demonstrate the potency of the present. Announcing the release, Anthony Caiazzo, product marketing manager at Sony Computer Entertainment America, noted that,

> Now fans and newcomers to the series can experience the epic journey of God of War and God of War II in 720p HD form. Both titles have been remastered with anti-aliased graphics, running at 60 frames per second for a smooth gameplay experience, only on the PS3 system.
> This is your chance to experience God of War in its true form.
>
> *(Caiazzo 2009)*

Throughout 2011, Sony has consolidated these remakes and reissues into a 'Classics HD' range that revisits PS2 titles, updating their graphics, music and effects to bring them into HD and surround sound. Among the high-profile re-releases is a double-pack of Fumito Ueda's *Ico* and its half-sequel *Shadow of the Colossus*. While recognising the durability of the aesthetic of the games, 'Their hazy, bleached visuals, sorrowful air and vague stories make them seem like half-remembered children's books' (Welsh 2011), there is a clear sense that these two games now presented in surround sound, HD and 3D, are ripe for 'updating'.

> Ico's aesthetic may have held up over the years, but if you return to the original PS2 game now, it's surprisingly blurry in all its prettiness. With the PS3

version, everything's still bloomy and mysterious, but the detailing has come to life. Suddenly, you can see individual shafts of light streaming through windows, you can get more of a sense of performance from the characters, you can even make out rough patches on the brickwork and leaves on the trees. The art may be unchanged, but the sharper presentation has brought this world of grass and stone and cloudy sky into focus. It's understated, but it's beautiful.

You know, a bit like Ico.

(Donlan 2011)

In his discussion of the award of *Eurogamer*'s 'game of the week' accolade to the HD reissues, Welsh (2011) poses an intriguingly reflective question. 'Are HD remakes erasing the past even as they restore it?' The question intimates that it is the very act of revisiting, remaking and re-releasing that might give rise to such erasure. However, more than this, we might reasonably examine the ways in which the new 'enhanced' version is situated within a discursive construct that recasts the original as an always inferior expression. The reviews of the games situate them in a complex relationship with their historical reference points. As he continues, Welsh foregrounds the technical and creative trade-offs that it is now evident had blighted *Shadow of the Colossus* from its outset. 'Shadow of the Colossus, severely compromised on PS2, can now run as its makers intended' (Welsh 2011). Indeed, *Digital Foundry*'s in-depth technical analysis of the reissues goes into yet further detail and comprehensively positions the original titles as lacking and technically constrained:

The low resolution of the original release means that an HD remaster presents both challenges and opportunities. In scaling up to either 720p or 1080p, the chance to 'unlock' the full detail of the original artwork is mouth-watering … The immediate impression you get from the HD version of Ico is that Bluepoint has done a good job in making the visuals shine in high definition. The low-resolution 'fog' has lifted, allowing the full detail of Team Ico's original art to be PROPERLY appreciated. There's also a 'full pixel' mode that liberates the PS3 version from the borders of the original game, giving the game much more real estate on-screen – boosted all the more by the move from the original's 4:3 aspect ratio to the full 16:9 widescreen experience.

(Ico Tech Analysis 2011, original emphasis)

Cast in this light, the new versions appear less as enhanced or definitive statements. Rather, they represent the current best attempt to realise the vision. In doing so, they become enmeshed within and serve to normalise the process by which all games stand simply as the current state of the art, as iterative updates. The 'game' is at once fluid and elusive, with only specific implementations or attempts to realise and capture it being fixed. And that fixity solidly grounds them in a moment that will inevitably pass and inevitably be superseded. Indeed, even in these reviews, the limitations of these new versions come under intense critical scrutiny, paving the way for future iterations:

Juxtaposed with that is the dreamy emptiness of the setting itself, and it's here that the HD reworking really does its stuff. It's a shame that the frame rate's capped at 30 frames per second rather than 60, perhaps, but seeing the game's assets in 1080p resolution is a bit of a revelation.

(Donlan 2011)

Moving on to Shadow of the Colossus and it's safe to say that the game is something of a disappointment for those with 3DTVs. The actual gameplay benefits of the 3D mode are difficult to quantify, and the sheer scale of the game world doesn't feel adequately represented … Performance is the real issue here, though. In many respects, running Shadow of the Colossus in 3D is highly reminiscent of playing the PS2 game. We see the same problems with frames rendered over-budget causing sustained frame-rate drops: the smooth 30FPS of the 720p version regularly drops down to the 20 and 15FPS we experienced with the game's original release. In really stressful scenes, we've actually witnessed it go lower than that.

(Ico Tech Analysis 2011)

Games reviewer Ben Croshaw reveals a related anxiety over these remakes that is born not only of an uneasiness with an erasure of the past but also with the way in which putative problems are addressed and 'corrected'.

You may remember me getting quite excited about the planned HD re-release of Silent Hill 2, to my mind the pinnacle of the survival horror genre, and of most game storytelling in general. But I have grown concerned at reports that the developers intend to re-do the voice acting. Yes, Silent Hill 2's voice acting is less than stellar. Guy Cihi, the voice of protagonist James Sunderland, was an American businessman living in Japan who was only at the auditions to escort his daughter. He'd never voice acted before and never would again. But you know what, that's a much more interesting story than some jobbing voice actor coming in, doing the lines and pestering the producer for cab fare home. That gives Cihi's role in the game's production an almost legendary quality. Besides, the stilted awkwardness of Silent Hill 2's dialogue gives the game an even more off-kilter feel that adds a lot to the intended atmosphere.

(Croshaw 2011)

Lest we consider this to be a recent phenomenon linked with the current 'high definition' era of PS3 and Xbox 360 gaming technology, we should note that this updated/remastered re-release strategy has been in operation for a number of years. Nintendo's *Game & Watch Gallery* collections (released 1994–2002), for instance, brought *Game & Watch* titles to the GameBoy and, latterly. GameBoy Advance handhelds (with *Game & Watch* collections released for Nintendo DS in 2006 and 2008). However, they did so in contrasting ways. Each *Gallery* release offered an 'original' and 'enhanced' version of the game. Notwithstanding the difficulties of reproducing the *Game & Watch* series' LCD images and their dual/wide screens on single-screen GameBoys with different aspect ratios, the 'original' modes sought to emulate, or perhaps simulate, the audiovisual presentation of the 1980s title. The 'enhanced' versions, on the other hand, left the gameplay mechanics largely unchanged but re-dressed the games in the manner of contemporary titles, adding full colour graphics, rich animation and music and sound effects. Whether or not they enhanced the experience for players is, for our purposes here, beside the point. What is important is that in a single package we see evidence of the simultaneity of the selective erasure and recovery of gaming's past. The original game is at once inspiration and benchmark by which to measure the subsequent improvement and technological development. This perhaps puts us in mind of Namco's *Ridge Racer* series, which, since its appearance in the home originally on the PlayStation one, has been preceded by fully playable versions of 1980s Namco Coin-Op games during disc loading. As such, what was once the state of the art in interactive entertainment and technological performance is, in a stroke, recast as a diversion that quite literally can be run on the new system while it is doing something else. Such is the multitasking potency of the PS2 that old games can run as a background process, while the aesthetic contrast between, for instance, *Xevious* and *Ridge Racer* clearly offers an invitation to comparatively assess the technical superiority of the new platform. Once racing commences, we note that the in-game, on-car advertising uses names and phrases recovered from Namco's gaming catalogue, which are literally propelled around the newly created world of the PlayStation console.

We notice a similar process at work in a number of games, with some recent examples explicitly making reference not only to titles in the developer or publisher's back catalogue but to former instances and incarnations of themselves. To take but two examples, both *Super Mario Galaxy 2* and *Metal Gear Solid 4* invoke their own heritage in particular ways, but perhaps with similar effects. In the case of *MGS4*, protagonist Solid Snake's flashbacks to earlier episodes in the complex narrative of the multipart *MGS* serial are presented in the audiovisual style of the earlier game in which they originally featured. Thus, the high-definition, surround sound is occasionally punctuated by virtual recreations of PS one-era graphics and sound. Indeed, an entire level of the original *MGS* game is played out as a flashback, replete with what now appear as low-resolution textures and polygon shearing. This flashback to a previous moment is both continued evidence of creator Hideo Kojima's playful command of game design and representation (see Newman 2002 on *MGS1*'s playful breaking of the 'fourth wall', for instance), but serves also to powerfully underscore the potency of *MGS4*'s graphics and audio engine by drawing explicit attention to the distance travelled between first and final instalments.

In *Super Mario Galaxy 2*, we find numerous references to the *Mario* universe, with recurrent characters, themes and generic locations even though the various titles are narratively unconnected. However, one particular back reference is notable. Buried within *Galaxy 2*'s myriad levels is a recreation of the first level from *Super Mario 64* painstakingly recreated, though delivered in the new graphics engine and apparently self-evidently benefitting from 14 years of technical progress. What is most striking about this level, though, is that, despite being a remodelled version of the space within which *Mario* leapt from 2D to 3D, it is somewhat pejoratively titled the 'Throwback Galaxy'. The contrasts and comparisons around which these flashbacks and throwbacks are overtly oriented might encourage us to consider whether their function is to enhance continuity or to interrupt the sense of flow by drawing attention to the state of progress. Or perhaps they perform some of the same function as *The Simpsons*' Itchy and Scratchy cartoon interludes, whose exaggerated, stylised 'cartooniness' serves to enhance the verisimilitude of *The Simpsons* itself by drawing attention away from it as a piece of animation. What is interesting to note in the videogame case, however, is that it is the history of the form, indeed the history of the specific game series, that is deployed as a means of demonstrating the superiority of present over past.

What we begin to glimpse in the commercially released retro packages, the flashbacks and throwbacks, and the discourses constructed around them, is a subtle but significant shift in the relationship between videogames and technology. The ability to experience *God of War* 'in its true form' works to decouple 'the game' from the specific technologies of any given historical implementation. As such, *God of War* is rendered as gameplay potential that is both realised and restricted by the technologies of any particular console or computing generation. The seemingly endless re-releasing of the *Sonic* and *Mario* series similarly positions these as games that are at once associated with particular consoles, perhaps trading in the nostalgia of the MegaDrive or NES, but which are not restricted by their limitations which become apparent as upgrades and enhancements are made available. For Croshaw (2011), the situation not only raises questions regarding the integrity of the gaming experience, but also highlights the vagaries of access provided through re-releases:

> The PS2 had perhaps the best library of games in the entire history of the medium, but now their availability is subject to the whims of publishers and their flighty HDifying ways.
>
> *(Croshaw 2011)*

Now in 3D – perfecting the perfect game

The re-release of *Legend of Zelda: Ocarina of Time* for the Nintendo 3DS console provides us with a useful case study that richly exemplifies these points. Recognising that 'It's considered by many to be the best game of all time', Hinkle notes that

> Developer Grezzo (Line Attack Heroes) has implemented a noticeable overhaul of the graphics. Updated character models, anti-aliasing, higher-resolution textures and a smooth, consistent framerate (whether 3D is turned on and off) all represent major improvements over earlier versions of the game.
>
> Seeing it side-by-side with the GameCube port made some changes seem even more dramatic. The 3DS version of Hyrule looked more vibrant and alive, with more complex building models and livelier townsfolk giving the

impression of an actual castle town, as opposed to the barren, lifeless square encountered before.

(Hinkle 2011)

As we saw in our earlier discussion of magazine previews of the 3DS release, this encouragement to recall the game as a high-water mark of gaming achievement, yet one which is now self-evidently, and inevitably, flawed in its implementation as a result of the passing of time and unstoppable march of gaming technology, is a key feature of Nintendo's own presentation of the re-release. Speaking at a trade show roundtable discussion, designer Eiji Aonuma presented the re-release as an opportunity to redress the deleterious effects of the N64 interface:

> You know the Water Temple? Who thought it was tough or even horrible? I've lived with that for the last ten odd years. But with the 3DS we have a touch screen. You had to take off and on the iron boots constantly, right? So I'd like to lay the evil shame to rest, and add a feature to make the iron boots control much easier.
>
> *(Transcribed in Harris 2010)*

In a particularly revealing interview published by Nintendo as part of the 'Iwata Asks … ' series, Shigeru Miyamoto speaks of the motivations for recreating this most feted of games. As Iwata notes, 'you began this remake because you wanted to see Hyrule in 3D, and because you wanted to improve the quality of The Legend of Zelda: Ocarina of Time'. In discussing the development, Miyamoto not only draws on ideas of update and upgrade, thereby inviting direct comparison between the new and original versions, but also seeds the notion of the game as a creative vision always and already limited rather than enabled by the technological capabilities of console iterations. As such, just as the development of console technology is constructed as non-negotiable and forward moving, so too is the game implicitly reconstructed as poised to take advantage of new capacities and capabilities as they arise:

> MIYAMOTO: Well, there were several reasons. One major reason was that, at the time, we'd barely gotten the games to move in terms of the polygon counts or wire frame processing.
> IWATA: Yes, you couldn't do more than that back then.
> MIYAMOTO: I felt that I wanted to aim higher.
> IWATA: You mean you'd always wanted to remake them some day?
> MIYAMOTO: I had, yes.
>
> *(Iwata Asks 2011)*

It is worth noting here that the operation of this process of replacing videogames through update bears some important differences from the operation of product-cycle obsolescence in other new media industries. *OoT 3D* is not merely 'tweaked' or 'freshened' in the way Smart (2010: 87) notes of US and UK mobile phones that enjoy life cycles of just a few months. Importantly, while frame rates and polygon counts are, indeed, part of the focus of the updating and enhancement work, *Ocarina* also gains new gameplay functionality. This is not, then, a respray, though we should not underestimate how significant changes in visual or auditory representation can be in relation to media encountered in the deep experiential manner that videogame play demands. As with the *Sonic* collection, which adds multiplayer options to some of the titles, *Ocarina* gains new gameplay modes or has interfaces and methods of engagement and interaction significantly modified in its updated form. By using the gyroscopes built into the 3DS, aiming Link's bow and arrow is an altogether more visceral undertaking than in the N64 incarnation, which used the joypad's analogue stick, while interfaces become differently tactile by virtue of the intimacy of the 3DS stylus, which sees the player touching, grabbing and moving objects in a putatively more direct and certainly markedly different manner.

At all levels, then, *Ocarina* is rendered as revisitable, updatable and subject to enhancement and modification. Importantly, *Ocarina* is not rendered obsolete or outdated per se, just in its now painfully and obviously limited N64 imagining. As Miyamoto continues, 'The biggest reason for me personally was that I myself wanted to see the majestic scenery of Hyrule in stereoscopic 3D.' What we observe here is not merely a breathless overturning of the old as it is replaced by the new – this is still *Ocarina*, not a new adventure set in Hyrule – but rather an emerging sense of historical process that constructs *Ocarina* as a game as the veritable epitome of half-wayness. It is only ever capable of being delivered within the current technological envelope. It follows that Iwata may be right in noting that 'To me, it feels as though there's a healthy, active respect for the masterpieces of the Nintendo 64 era'. There is also a palpable sense in which the N64 as a technological and gaming platform is comprehensively designated as obsolete. Its limitations and restrictions become manifestly apparent in the light of the improved capabilities of the current 3DS platform, which, accordingly, allows game design 'masterpieces' such as *Ocarina* to be revisited, enhanced and brought up-to-date. The trick here is to present *Ocarina* as both timeless and of its time. In being re-released, updated and enhanced to take advantage of the technological developments that have occurred in the 13 years since its first release, *Ocarina* becomes both superseded, outdated N64 cartridge and cutting edge, next-generation title. Moreover, in being re-released to exploit the current state of the art in technology, interface and audiovisual representation, *Ocarina* ceases to possess a definitive form. Joining *Sonic the Hedgehog*, *Super Mario Bros.*, *God of War*, *Parachute et al.*, *Ocarina* is positioned as a potentially endlessly re-expressible 'master-piece'. In years to come, there is little to suggest that 3DS will be not be resigned to obsolescence, as was the N64 platform before, and *OoT 3D* will transform again into a new, temporarily definitive instance.

Clearly, the videogames industry is not unique in revisiting its past and it is interesting to consider other places and ways in which old media and technology are invoked in contemporary design and positioned in the marketplace. The electronic music scene, for instance, has cultivated a very particular relationship with the technologies and aesthetics of its history and heritage. Revered and recuperated not only for their authenticity and history but also for their sonic qualities and flexibility, analogue synthesizers such as the Minimoog, Jupiter 8, Prophet 5, Korg MS-20 and ARP2600 enjoy a cult status among aficionados. Moreover, a considerable literature has amassed, documenting these technologies, their creators and the artists that used them and breathed life into them through performance (e.g. Jenkins 2007; Pinch and Trocco 2002; Vail 2000). One notable difference, however, is the continued commercial viability, creative value and mass-market acceptance of these 'vintage' 1970s and 1980s synthesizers long after the hardware has gone out of production. Recreations of each of the synthesizers above, and many more besides, are readily available as software plugins and stand-alone applications that run within the otherwise pristine 24-bit 96KHz world of Digital Audio Workstations like Pro Tools HD *et al.* Indeed, a version of the Korg MS-10 is available for the Nintendo DS as a 'full price' title. As such, while vintage games might not be able to command a premium price, a vintage synthesizer evidently can.

What is particularly interesting about these recreations of analogue synthesizers, though, is the attention to detail even where those details could be considered quirks, weaknesses or even flaws of the original systems. The replication of analogue oscillator drift, for instance, might initially seem curious, as digital control sought to rid the audio world of such imperfection; yet this quest for 'authenticity' makes sense when seen and heard alongside plugins and effects units whose sole purpose is to reduce bit-depth (simulating 8-bit sampling, for example) or to introduce the wow, flutter and saturation of analogue tape, or the crackle and pops of vinyl recordings. In software, of course, the imperfection is not only predictable but controllable and, above all, perfectible. It should be noted, also, that this is not simply an issue of the desirability or 'authenticity' of analogue, as a range of digital instruments, including the Roland D-50 and Korg Wavestation and M1, are recreated with similar attention to detail. The Fairlight iPad app that simulates the 1980s CMI sampling workstation retains its slavish level of detail, down to the audible key clunks that accompany the otherwise silent touchscreen operation, the seemingly interminable load times of floppy disks and even an option to incorrectly set the power supply, thereby blowing up the app and sending clouds of thick smoke up the screen.

The embracing of the vagaries and imperfections that are stylistically and aesthetically recovered and reproduced in the music technology marketplace are rarely seen in relation to games, but there are some examples to be found. Perhaps echoing the emulation of analogue synthesizer recreation, Capcom's *MegaMan 9* is an interesting, if comparatively rare, proposition. Although created to run on PlayStation, Xbox and Wii hardware, it is designed within the technological limits of Nintendo's 1980s NES console and exists as a virtual continuation of the popular series. Here, the word 'limitations' is particularly apposite, as Capcom's development team has artificially recreated the effects of overloading the 'original' hardware. This, then, is not an emulation of old hardware, but rather, a new game designed to exhibit the imperfections of a 20-year-old system for aesthetic effect. Speaking about the decision, producer Hironobu Takeshita, explains,

> there were some things, like you couldn't have more than three enemies on
> the screen at once, so we had to make sure that that's how it stayed in our

game. In the part with the dragon with the flame, [there should be] flickering, and whatnot. In the options of this game, you can adjust that, unlike the old games. We purposely put some of those old-school bugs into this game, so it does recreate that feel.

(Takeshita interviewed online in Nutt 2008)

Much like the bitcrusher, tape saturator and simulated voltage-controlled oscillator drift, these are the qualities of vintage, 'obsolesced' systems recreated for the experiential and aesthetic pleasure of the player, yet now placed wholly under their control. Not only is the game mastered through play and performance, but the limitations of its technological implementation are conquered through the march of platform progress and development.

The re-released videogame as an act of enhancement through re-engineering, rather than simply as a matter of reissuing, should remind us of Ashton's analysis of tension in the videogames industry's relationship with its past as a marker of historical viability, source of inspiration and benchmark for assessment of progress, 'eras[ing] the past whilst simultaneously seeking to recover it as part of an evidence-base for future development' (Ashton 2008).

In some senses, then, the enhanced, updated re-release performs some of the same discursive work as the illegally downloadable ROM. This might initially seem somewhat perverse, yet what both practices engage in is a process of liberating the game from its context or the specificity of any given instance of its implementation. The ROM, of course, does not in itself change the game, though the vagaries of its execution under emulation might, either by virtue of its imperfect reproduction or as a product of deliberate efforts to modify its appearance or intervene in its operation by applying graphical or audio filters, adjusting input devices and mappings, or altering the speed at which the game plays out.

Ultimately, while Guttenbrunner *et al.* (2010) are right to note that the retro market speaks of an interest in old games, the processes and practices of re-releases and, in particular, the upgrading and enhancing of old games to bring them up to date serve also to highlight the clear tension, on the part of publishers and perhaps developers, between the old and new, and the possibilities of the then and now of technological generations. From a preservation perspective, the subtle decoupling of the game from its specific delivery platform has particularly far-reaching consequences, not least because it problematises the very idea of definitiveness, as we shall see in the following chapter. However, more than this, the updating and upgrading of new games that are brought into HD and finally delivered as they were intended, at least within the confines of current restrictions which will inevitably lift in the future, confirms the obsolescence of the original incarnation and expression. It does this because it essentially confirms the eventual obsolescence of every expression – even the current one. In doing so, videogames confirm themselves as archetypally 'new' media defined, as Sterne (2007) notes, by their own eventual and inevitable replacement.

4

GAME(PLAY) PRESERVATION

Now what?

Of the two key questions that this book set out to tackle, thus far we have primarily centred our attentions on the first, in seeking to account for the reasons for the comparative lack of concerted game preservation activity noted by critics such as Gooding and Terras (2008) and others. Throughout Chapters 2 and 3 we have encountered a series of publishing, retail, advertising, marketing and journalistic practices that seek to discursively cultivate specific attitudes towards both old and new games. The resulting situation is one in which the new is decisively privileged and promoted and the old is constructed either as a benchmark by which to measure the progress of the current and forthcoming 'generation' or as a comprehensively worn out, obsolete anachronism to be supplanted by its update, superior remake or replacement. The criticality of this situation should not be underestimated. While material and digital deterioration remain significant and comparatively well-documented (if not well-understood or wholly predictable) impediments to the longevity of games, they are far from the only ones. As Donahue (2009) notes, the games industry's lack of interest is a key factor. Given the kinds of practices we have seen throughout this book so far, we might not be greatly surprised to find that an industry characterised by Kline *et al.* (2003) as one that self-consciously styles itself as a 'perpetual innovation economy' has not led attempts to focus attention on, or to resurrect, its past. These prevailing conditions of apparently irresistible forward motion and continual, self-consuming flux are the context for game preservation activity and go some way to explaining the lack of extant preservation activity, and not only the absence of industry collaboration but also what Donahue identified as the absence of interest in the project.

As such, and almost without exception, scholarly investigations of game preservation such as the PVW project and the IGDA's White Paper recognise the importance of industry collaboration and partnership, whether for the reasons we have identified above or so as to gain access to materials that are otherwise impossible to source, or to potentially work towards circumventions of technical or legal impediments to preservation (whether these be issues of intellectual property or digital rights management, see Anderson 2011). For Gooding and Terras (2008: 1), the position is clear: 'We must understand the reasons for the current lack of computer game preservation in order to devise strategies for the future.' However, while we might wholeheartedly concur with this sentiment, devising these strategies is a far from simple task and it is to this question that we shall turn our attentions in this final chapter of this book.

One thing is clear: the need to act swiftly is keenly felt throughout the current commentary on games preservation. We need to act 'before it's too late', implores the IGDA's White Paper. But what can we do? Perhaps more importantly, what *should* we do? Or, more prosaically, and in the parlance of digital preservation,

> what are the significant properties of digital games which we should seek to maintain and what are their relative degrees of importance? Without this knowledge, we are poorly positioned to select an appropriate preservation strategy from the options available.
>
> *(McDonough* et al. *2010 123–24)*

Ascertaining the 'significant properties' of games is absolutely key, and much of what follows here is an attempt to establish some principles and, most importantly, tackle some of the presuppositions about what game preservations can and should be that have begun to circulate even in the project's nascence. As McDonough *et al.* (2010: 14) have it, we need to be able to answer difficult, seemingly simple, even simplistic, questions such as 'What makes Mario Mario?'. Which aspects, qualities, properties of games have to be preserved and, for that matter, which can and cannot be preserved? Much of this discussion will centre on issues of play and how, and whether, play fits into the preservation process. We should take great care to remember that videogames are playable, and whether we wish to term it their 'interactivity' or 'ergodicity', it is this participative, performative dimension that moves games from the textual or technological to the experiential and creates significant challenges to preservation in terms of look and feel. That games can be played is one thing, and identifying how they might be played in the future by researchers or patrons of museums and collections raises questions in relation to preservation and exhibition. However, beyond a recognition that games might be best considered as always in or at play, we should probe deeper still and think about the potential for wide differences in playings based around gameplay choices and player knowledge and competencies. Given the variety of possible playings, we might question any attempt to define a singular set of 'specific properties' for a game. Specific for whom?

It is essential, then, that we interrogate the extent to which these various playings or performances are constitutive of 'the game' or, to put it in the language of a ludic approach to game studies, the extent to which play is 'configurative' (after Moulthrop 2004). The conceptualisation of the relationship between 'play' and 'game' impacts greatly on the contours and scope of the preservation project and it is worth spending some time unpacking some of the presuppositions about play and playability that underpin both academic game studies and extant game preservation scholarship and practice. In particular, attending to these foundational questions should force us to consider the location of play and whether it should be treated as an outcome or object of preservation activity. Though it is informed by a broadly ludic approach to game studies and an acute sensitivity to the centrality of players' configurative performances, the position espoused in the final analysis of this book might come as something of a surprise to both preservation and game studies acolytes alike.

In the remaining pages of this book, I hope to show that the extraordinary 'instability' of games that we might note, for instance, in their existence less as fully formed objects for play and more as suites of resources to be played with (see Newman 2005, 2008 for a fuller discussion of playing versus playing *with*) significantly calls into question the efficacy of some of the currently dominant strategies of digital preservation. While we might want to stop short of reading this as a statement asserting the impossibility of doing game preservation, as Giordano (see Sterling 2011) begins to suggest, I want to propose that a recognition of the videogame as an unstable, moving target invites us to rethink as to what can and should be preserved. Moreover, and perhaps most initially controversial if not downright perverse, I wish to suggest that playable games might have a limited lifespan. This is not to say that there remains no long-term record, but that the long-term ability to play might not, cannot and perhaps even should not be the objective of the game preservation project.

Before we turn our attentions to issues of play, playability and the (im)possibility of providing meaningful long-term experiences of videogames, it is important to interrogate more deeply the question of their 'instability'. Thus far, we have equated instability with the the mutability of games at play and we shall return to questions of configuration and performance later in the chapter. It is worth tackling the question from an altogether more practical level also. The simple fact of the matter is that there is no such thing as a videogame. Even if we temporarily set aside questions of whether and how it might be played and what the impact of these playings might be, locating the 'object' of preservation presents itself as an unexpected challenge, as 'a game' is rarely static over time.

Instability: ports, patches and conversions

Prior to issues of performance and the changing nature of the game in and at play, here our focus zooms in on what may be an even more fundamental instability in the fabric of the game to-be-played-with. As media that are routinely ported (transferred and translated) to different operating systems and platforms with differing hardware and software capabilities; patched (updated to fix bugs or modify gameplay mechanics); or translated and modified for release in different territories, digital games simply cannot be conceived of as static objects or texts. For Giordano (see Sterling 2011), this 'extreme fragmentation' presents a key challenge for archivists, and even avid fans, as keeping track of the minutiae of variation is a far from trivial task. As we shall see below, as a game is ported from one system to another it gains or loses features or may have modifications made to its operation. Sometimes these missing, added or modified features may be obviously significant, sometimes they are imperceptible to all but the cognoscenti of gamers; but missing, added or modified they remain, nonetheless. Similarly, as the game is modified or 'patched' over time, its contours necessarily change, perhaps leaving successful playing techniques impossible to execute and necessitating the development of new strategies and tactics. My point here is that, before we get to considerations of the ways in which it is (re)configured through the performance of play, in fact regardless of whether it is ever played at all, a digital game is a potentially changing, unstable object. What is most important about this instability is that it is frequently formally undocumented. Patches often take place 'silently', with game code being updated online or via automatically installing updates, while different versions of games distributed on disc or cartridge circulate as patches are incorporated into subsequent pressings or manufacture. As Gooding and Terras observe,

> Even when classic games are re-released, they are often updated versions of the original, which raises new questions regarding preservation: does reissue damage archival value? Does reissuing games obstruct possible preservation activities by maintaining commercial value for publishers? Regular enhancements to game code (typically provided by online games) tends to make capture, and future emulation very difficult if not impossible, and the industry shows little interest in making different versions available in the longer term.
>
> *(Gooding and Terras 2008: 23)*

Giordano draws on Capcom's *Bionic Commando* to illustrate the point. Originally released as a Coin-Op game in 1987, it has been subject to a series of conversions and translations as it has made its way to different systems in different countries over the past three decades. Many changes have radically transformed the game and continue to problematise its status as an object of archival or curatorial attention. Listing the wide variety of (con)versions, Giordano notes differences in graphics, backstory and arrangement of objects between the two Commodore 64 iterations destined for European and US markets, as well as the marked differences in musical soundtrack that is rearranged for the home computer/console releases. However, while these issues are significant and affect the audiovisual aesthetics, game design and player experience of the game, these are by no means the only alterations between versions. Capcom's 1988 NES releases differ radically from the arcade original and, indeed, from each other.

> The Japanese version of this reboot, even from the title 'The Resurrection of Hitler: Top Secret', makes clear references to Nazis as the enemy forces and Hitler himself is the final boss, who will be defeated by having his head blown off, in one of the best known scenes in the history of videogames. In America and Europe it was distributed with a different title, a replacement of the Nazi

symbols and the denomination of the antagonists as 'Badds' (yet in the American Instruction manual they are called 'Nazz'). Some kind of free will 'censorship' changed parts of the game rendering (swastika/eagle).

(Giordano translated in Sterling 2011)

In the intervening years, new versions and translations of the game have been released on a variety of console and handheld platforms, with 2008 seeing the launch of *Bionic Commando Rearmed*. This enhanced remake of the 1988 NES title serves as a prequel to the Xbox 360, PS3 and PC game, also entitled *Bionic Commando*, which was released in 2009. To confuse the issue further, *Bionic Commando Rearmed* received its sequel, *Bionic Commando Rearmed 2*, in early 2011. As Giordano notes of *Bionic Commando Rearmed*,

> Every reference to Nazis is cut out. This version, too, will have its own independent sequel. The protagonists in the original Arcade and NES version of Bionic Commando will return in the new version of the brand which will still carry the same name – Bionic Commando. It is a 'sequel,' from the narrative point of view, of the action which takes place in the original games, and yet is a complete revision of the game system, making use of the current state of the art of technology.
>
> *(Giordano translated in Sterling 2011)*

Though it is clearly complex, and continues to unfold with new remakes and (re-)releases that make explicit and oblique references to different titles and (di)versions in the development of the series, the case of *Bionic Commando* is far from unique. What is important to appreciate, however, is not simply that a game might exist in and across a variety of different formats, sometimes changing through time, sometimes existing simultaneously in a marketplace, but that the processes of conversion and translation give rise to both subtly and substantially different iterations of what, on one level, remains the same game. There are a number of related processes at work here and it is useful to distinguish between the 'porting' and 'patching' of games. Sega's *Sonic the Hedgehog* series presents an illustrative case study. Originally released in 1991 for the MegaDrive (aka Genesis) console, *Sonic the Hedgehog* (hereafter *Sonic 1*) has been both ported (converted to run on different hardware platforms) and 'patched' (modified to fix errors or alter gameplay) many times.

Sonic the Hedgehog(s): porting Sonic

Shortly after the 1991 MegaDrive release, Sega released versions of *Sonic 1* for its contemporaneous 8-bit Master System and handheld Game Gear systems. Both of these conversions bear marked similarities to the MegaDrive title and capture much of the essence of the gameplay but, by virtue of the technical differences in the 8-bit target systems, there are many immediately noticeable alterations. Chief among these are the substantial changes to the graphical environment of Sonic's world, with the

Master System and Game Gear versions losing much of the detail present in the MegaDrive title. Indeed, the 8-bit titles differ substantially from one another, with different sprite and background design as well as variations in colour palette. Moreover, level design and structure differ between the three titles, with only three of the original six zones included in the 8-bit versions and the function of the Bonus Levels being altered to become points-scoring opportunities rather than being oriented around the 'sidequest' collection of Chaos Emeralds, as in the 16-bit gameplay. Crucially, while the 8-bit conversions capture the essence of the gameplay and retain Sonic's basic repertoire of capabilities (running, jumping, etc.), the speed of the game is significantly altered. Given that one of the defining features of the *Sonic the Hedgehog* series is seen to be the speed of gameplay, these variations are far from trivial. Indeed, the notion of Sonic's speed (captured most immediately in his name) represented considerably more than a gameplay decision and stood for a definable distinction between Sega and Nintendo in the marketplace. With Sonic becoming a *de facto* corporate mascot for Sega, the speed and intensity of *Sonic the Hedgehog*'s gameplay sat as an explicit critique of chief competitor Nintendo's more ponderous Mario gameplay. And yet, the speed with which *Sonic the Hedgehog* is inexorably associated is not universally presented across Sega's early 1990s *Sonic* games.

While the audiovisual and kinetic shifts are the most self-evident, differences between the 8- and 16-bit conversions are, in fact, legion and comprehensively documented at the many Sonic fansites that continue to operate online, as well as in myriad walkthroughs, game guides and FAQs. It is worth pausing momentarily here to remind ourselves of the importance of the work of videogame fans in the documentation and research of games as historical artefacts and systems. We will return to consider the role of this amateur research and the textual output of fan culture within the formal project of game archiving and preservation at the culmination of this book, but for now we should note that much of the insight into the complexities of *Sonic 1*'s historical journey comes to us though the endeavours of groups of fans coalescing around sites such as Sonic Retro or the Sonic News Network, for instance.

Although, as Giordano notes of *Bionic Commando*, we might be able to identify 'extreme fragmentation' here, with manifestly different titles all sharing the *Sonic the Hedgehog* name, each of these titles is, implicitly at least, a conversion rather than a literal re-presentation of the original title (we might remember our discussion of *Donkey Kong* from the opening of this volume). As such, one might infer that the expectations of players might be managed and that, for the archivist, the 8-bit game might be considered sufficiently different to warrant consideration as a separate, though related, entity. This recalls the discussion of implementing bibliographic frameworks such as the IFLA's Functional Requirements for Bibliographic Records, for instance, KEEP's TOTEM database, and the challenge of defining original works and manifestations (see McDonough *et al.* 2010, esp. pp 24–27).

However, the situation becomes significantly more complex when we begin to consider the almost unending range of platforms to which *Sonic 1* has been converted and ported in the 20 years since its initial 16- (and perhaps 8-) bit launch. *Sonic Retro* lists no fewer than 24 ports of *Sonic 1* and it should be noted that even this number does not include the numerous fangames or the unofficial, pirated or unlicensed versions of the title, such as *Somari*, which ported *Sonic 1* to the Nintendo NES and replaced the Hedgehog with Mario as the protagonist, thereby eroding the platform specificity of Sonic and Mario, blurring the gameplay, design decisions and aesthetic styles of each game/platform/company. One way in which the 24 phone, mobile, console, and embedded TV player ports can be distinguished from Sega's 1991 8-bit console conversions is through their subsequent use of emulation. Each of these newer iterations purports not merely to capture the essence of the experience of *Sonic 1*, as the 8-bit conversions did, but rather to faithfully reproduce the original (which is identified and confirmed through this process as the MegaDrive version) by running the original code.

Even at this stage in our analysis, some clear issues arise when dealing with 'faithful' reproductions and recreations. It will be clear to even the most casual of gamers that many of the console, handheld and mobile platforms and systems on which *Sonic 1* now may be played employ markedly different hardware and software interfaces. Some devices connect to external displays (e.g. television sets), while others, such as mobile phones and handheld consoles, have embedded displays. Each has its own specialities in terms of colour gamut, resolution, refresh rate and so on, some of which are predictable (in the case of embedded displays) and some of which are a function of user preference or of necessity (the family television set) and which might change through time (connecting a MegaDrive to a 1991-era 4:3 aspect ratio CRT television set, versus a 2011 16:9 flat, 1080p upscaling, widescreen LCD or plasma panel). For now, a sense of the potential for variation will suffice, but we will return to a more detailed examination of the impact of different display technologies and systems in our consideration of emulation later in this chapter. Similarly, control systems range from joypads with different configurations of digital/analogue sticks and buttons through to 'classic' iPod clickwheels and iPhone touchscreens wholly bereft of physical buttons, sticks or switches. The enormity of the difference in the experience of controlling and playing *Sonic*, given these variations must immediately call into question the singularity of a *Sonic 1* game. However, if we delve deeper, we find yet more changes.

Let us take the iPod version of *Sonic 1* as a case study. Its use of the clickwheel and comparatively small display might represent the most obvious ways in which the 2007 fifth-generation iPod, iPod classic (2.5 inch, 320 × 240) and third-generation iPod nano (2 inch, 320 × 240) port of *Sonic 1* differs from the MegaDrive version which it purports to recreate. However, there are, in fact, many more changes to gameplay, structure and design. The music, and the operation of the underlying music/audio system, differ from all but the 2010 Nintendo DS version in that it is not emulated but instead streamed. As such, rather than the music dynamically accelerating when Sonic activates a speed boost and decelerating on depletion of the temporary power-up, a new audio track is triggered from the iPod (or DS) memory. This alteration of the timing and synchronisation of the game's audiovisuals is sufficient to disrupt the aesthetic experience of the game as *Sonic 1*. However, of yet more impact than this are the changes to the game's saving system. Where the MegaDrive title included no battery-backed memory to retain players' progress between system power-offs and offered only a minimal number of temporary save points within levels (these allowed players to restart a level from a mid-point rather than save their progress between power-cycles), the iPod version implements an auto-save feature that saves progress at the beginning of any level that is reached. Moreover, where three lives and a sparse availability of extra life-giving '1-Ups' marked the 1991 experience, the iPod player is offered an unlimited number of continues with which to progress though the gameworld. These alterations in the operation and design of the game are not simply noteworthy addenda in the *Sonic* documentation record, as their consequences have a considerable impact on what the game is and how it is played. As Crawford (1984, 1995) has noted, the nature of the save–die–retry mechanism employed in a game goes a long way to contributing to the sense of jeopardy and asks players to manage risk taking and caution. To alter the save-state mechanic in this way might make the game more suitable for the kind of opportunistic gaming that mobile, iPod play engenders, but it fundamentally changes the operation of the game and necessarily affects how a player might approach its play.

What is particularly interesting about the case of iPod *Sonic* is the way in which the specificities of its operation have come to exist as a reference point for subsequent games/players. We need only look at comments on the iTunes App Store to note similar concerns in relation to the more recent iPhone/iPod touch conversions of *Sonic 1*, as well as its sequel. For many players, the first iPod port has become the point of reference and the iPhone version's lack of an extensive save-game function renders this a game in need of update:

> There is no doubt that this is a fantastic game and blah blah blah etc. but it DESPERATELY needs a save option. I know people will say the original didn't so why should this but it really does need it. SORT IT OUT SEGA!!!!
>
> *(therat123 2010)*

> Great game, takes me back to my childhood but it needs a save function. After getting so far it's annoying to have to start from the beginning when it's game over.
>
> *(Bailadon 2011)*

What we see here, then, is that for a constituency of players modifications to the original game mechanic introduced in subsequent ports to different platforms have become the benchmark, and adherence to the original game structure is defined as problematic. This, surely, speaks eloquently of the way in which 'the game' changes over time. In this way, exactly how a player conceives of and plays *Sonic 1* might depend on their point (or perhaps 'port') of entry.

The presence and absence of specific elements in the port is important in defining the scope of what the game may subsequently become through play. Whether or not the level-skip mode is included again hits at the heart of the risk–reward mechanism of the game, and its absence from iPhone versions is a bone of contention among reviewers and players alike. Similarly, the debug or 'Config' mode of the Japanese Genesis version, which, as Surman (2010) has so persuasively noted, reframes the relationship between player and game designer, is not universally available in *Sonic* ports. As such, the ludic possibilities afforded to the player are limited and restricted in different ways in different ports, depending on the specificities of their implementation.

Sonic the Hedgehog(s): patching Sonic

The variation between the myriad versions of *Sonic 1* that each purport to run the original code under emulation is one of the most striking outcomes of even the most cursory investigation of the videogame as an object of potential preservation attention. This is particularly troubling, given the strategic importance of emulation as an archival and exhibition strategy within current game preservation theory and practice. However, the issue that this situation most immediately raises is one relating to the fragmentation of games across platforms and systems and through time. We might argue that this is a documentation issue which, from an archival perspective, might be noteworthy but ultimately not unduly troubling, as the 'original' MegaDrive *Sonic 1* cartridge/code retains its primacy as the reference point for subsequent (con)versions. However, this does not solve the problem entirely. Regardless of whether we consider the 16-bit version to be 'the original' and all other iterations 'derivatives', 'facsimiles' or 'reproductions' that achieve their goal with varying degrees of success (irrespective of the fact that these are presently the only commercially available versions of *Sonic 1* and that no rider to this effect accompanies their official distribution), there remains one further question. Which 'original' do we mean?

It is not merely that *Sonic 1* has been ported, converted and remade through time and for different platforms and systems. Quite simply, there are multiple versions of the MegaDrive version of *Sonic 1*, as the game was patched and updated over time. The extent and parameters of these differences are, again, manifold, but perhaps the most tangible consequence of these modifications to the game's codebase can be observed in the behaviour of the spikes in levels such as the Green Hill Zone, which is the first level encountered in the game. Writing in relation to what is commonly referred to in the Sonic fan parlance as version 1.0 of *Sonic 1*, Walker notes the following:

> In Sonic the Hedgehog 1, there is a bug with the hit system. Usually if you get hit, you flash for a few seconds and are temporarily invincible. But if you get hit and get knocked back, and land on spikes, you get hit again. This usually means you die since you don't have time to recover any rings after the first hit. The first hit may or may not have come from touching spikes – just getting knocked back onto spikes will kill you. This is a very annoying bug and

it is one reason you must take special care to avoid spikes when you see them. Luckily this does not happen with anything else (lava, etc.).

(Walker 2003)

In fact, there is considerable discussion as to whether this initial behaviour was originally intended by the developers and altered later in line with the gameplay of other titles, or whether it constituted an error that was fixed in subsequent releases of the code.

> There is debate as to whether this is indeed a 'bug' or an intended feature, considering that the behavior was changed in Sonic 2 and later. However, many factors (including the actual coding for the spike object) lead to the conclusion that the 'spike bug' is, ultimately, intended behavior that was removed by the Sonic 2 developers ... The 'spike bug' is caused by spikes calling a special routine to hurt Sonic, different from the routine used by every other object in the game that damages him.
>
> *(Sonic Retro 2010)*

While we should again note the rigour of the investigative work of fans who reverse engineer and disassemble the game's code to discern its function, what is most important for our current analysis is that the 'Spike Bug' behaviour was officially changed in some subsequent MegaDrive/Gensis versions of *Sonic 1*. This is not a porting or conversion issue, but rather, an example of a game's code and, consequently, its gameplay being altered throughout its lifecycle on a given platform. Whether or not this is evidence of a bug fix or, as is suggested by some fans, an effective reaction to bring the original *Sonic* in line with the behaviour of *Sonic 2* (a form of 'retconning' or 'retroactive continuity' familiar to comicbook audiences, see Fisher 2007), is immaterial for our present study. What is significant is that multiple versions of *Sonic 1* for the MegaDrive/Genesis can be seen to exist, each of which might lay a reasonable claim to being 'the original', if not by virtue of the time of their release, then as a product of their implementation of the original developers' intent.

To complicate matters still further, where the use of 60Hz NTSC emulators has become commonplace among the many ports of *Sonic 1* that we noted, consistency of emulated ROM is not so standardised. While the iPhone version uses the third (Japanese) ROM, the GameCube compendium Sonic Mega Collection released in 2002 offers three different ROMs from which to choose:

> In Sonic Mega Collection, the version of Sonic 1 you play is the Japanese version.
>
> You can play the US version by pressing, on the info screen for Sonic 1, Up, Z, Down, Z, Left, Z, Right, Z. The American version differs in that the clouds don't move in Green Hill, there's no wavy water in Labyrinth, and the level select is in the wrong order.

To play another Japanese version, which fixes the bug which makes you continue to take hits when you hit spikes even if you're flashing and supposed to be temporarily invincible, hit, on the same screen, Z, Z, Z, Z, Z, Z, Z, Z, Z, Up, Down, Left, Right.

(SonicAD n.d.)

It is important to note that it is not only the MegaDrive game that is patched, but also the various ports that have become the more recent points of access. The iPhone iterations of *Sonic 1* (and *2*) are cases in point and it is only with the latest revisions (as of 2011) that Sega has reinstated the (secretly accessible) level skip functionality that was part of the MegaDrive games. The level skip is by no means a trivial addition to the Sonic gameworld, as it fundamentally alters the player's ability to access levels non-linearly and perhaps even becomes the only means by which some levels are accessed at all. In the absence of the level skip feature, the progression and reward model is recast as wholly contingent on performance and prowess, as Zone 2 becomes available only upon successful completion of Zone 1, and so on.

That the very code of a game might change over time, whether in response to a bug or in order to (re)implement a feature, clearly problematises the location of the object of study/curatorial activity and certainly *Sonic* is by no means unique in this respect. Fans of Nintendo's *Legend of Zelda* series have undertaken similar investigative work, uncovering three different release versions of the *OoT* title. These versions are variously available across different territories and in re-releases and bring some minor changes and bug fixes as well as more major alterations such as increases in the game's video resolution, the (partial) removal of some culturally sensitive iconography and lyrics in the soundtrack, and the change of colour of Ganondorf and Ganon's 'blood' from red to green in battle sequences. Importantly, while some of these changes appear minor, they impact on the techniques available to players, with some strategies only applicable to particular versions of the game (see Aleckermit 2011). In some cases, these changes are quite clearly defined and even foregrounded. Sega's *Virtua Fighter 2* is illustrative. The Saturn console conversion offers two versions of the game that broadly equate with different iterations of the Coin-Op game:

In the Option menu, you can choose between Versions 2.0 and 2.1. Both versions of Virtua Fighter 2 have been released in the arcades and are faithfully reproduced for Sega Saturn. In Version 2.0, new attack levels have been added over the previous Virtua Fighter game. Version 2.1 offers the following changes:

– Expert Mode added
– Jacky's Crescent and Sweep attack levels corrected (for height/blocking)
– Akira's long-range dashing elbow corrected to dashing elbow with foot position change
– Shun's long-range sweep is corrected to sweep without foot position change

- Wolf's punches and elbow attacks added
- Certain moves (such as Akira's Punch/Kick combo) no longer knock an opponent down. It is also more difficult to back away from an opponent (the pause between steps is slightly longer)

(Sega Enterprises 1995: 25)

For those not adept in the nuances of digital martial arts, the meticulousness of the documentation of the changes between *Virtua Fighter 2.0* and *2.1* might come as something of a surprise, yet it is a salient reminder of what we will continue to see as the impact of seemingly minor alterations on the overall experience and performance of gameplay. However, what is perhaps more significant to our present analysis is that the patches that fans have identified in relation to *Sonic 1* occur altogether more 'silently' and often in a wholly undocumented manner. Of course, this process continues today, and in fact potentially grows in prevalence and impact with online distribution networks and Internet-connected consoles, handhelds, mobiles and PCs. Just as the different spike behaviours in *Sonic 1*'s various ROMs were quietly incorporated into new iterations of the MegaDrive cartridge, so online updating and patching brings new aspects of gameplay to contemporary console, PC and mobile games while removing others. In many cases, players might be unaware of the implemented changes. Even where changelogs document the modifications, players may be left with no choice but to update in order to maintain compatibility with changes in the underlying operating system, for instance.

Regardless of the details, the fact that the game changes over time leads to a situation where, depending on the time of purchase, the platform, the number of updates and patches applied, different players playing ostensibly the same game might necessarily enjoy different experiences in markedly, or subtly, different worlds. It might be overly provocative to declare that this fluidity of form, this mutability of code and these variations in implementation mean that there is no such thing as 'a videogame', but we must surely recognise that it is a real challenge to define exactly what we mean when we talk of *Sonic 1*. The problem for curators and archivists of digital games is that, like most other titles, *Sonic 1* is inherently unstable. As Gooding and Terras (2008) and Giordano (see Sterling 2011), among others, note, the videogame is not a clearly definable or easily delineated object, technology or text, but rather, is a growing and mutating collection of many objects. If there is a coherence to it, then, as Gray (2011) notes, the videogame is best understood as an 'entity spanning several platforms, markets and time periods'.

Things and bits

The variations between different versions of what might appear, *prima facie*, to be the same game, as they change over time and across different platforms, hardware and software systems, hint at a number of yet more critical issues that face game preservation practitioners and theorists. While the absence of formal documentation as to *Sonic*'s various alterations, including the Spike 'bug' behaviour, creates one kind of problem, the existence and detail of the *Virtua Fighter 2.0–2.1* changelog gives rise to its own set of challenges. The minutiae of the changes, concerned as they are with characters' foot positioning and the height and reach of sweeping attacks, might seem like a virtual godsend for games history researchers, yet their specificity reminds us of the impact of minor changes on the experience of gameplay. The alterations that mark out *Virtua Fighter 2.1* are principally concerned with the balance of the game and, although they undoubtedly appear almost trivial to the non-adept, perhaps even confirming just the kind of myopically obsessive player stereotypes that game studies scholars have long since railed against, to the *Virtua Fighter* aficionado they are, nonetheless, of vital importance.

Let us be mindful also of the impact that changes in interfaces, hardware and software platforms have on the experience of playing a game. Even the non-adept player will surely be sensitive to the way in which shifting the control of *Sonic* from a directional joypad to a touchscreen does not merely necessitate a change in the approach to gameplay but profoundly affects what *Sonic* is. To some extent, this realisation helps us to answer some of the questions that the routine porting, conversion and mutliplatform release of videogames raises in relation to selection and documentation, and we might reasonably argue that iPhone and MegaDrive versions of *Sonic 1* are more different than they are similar, even though they apparently run the same code. However, just as the recognition of the impact of these alterations might help tackle one type of preservation and cataloguing question, it introduces new problematics which draw into sharp relief the significance and specificity of experientiality, participation, performance and play. What we, perhaps, edge towards is a recognition of the need to better understand that most intangible and elusive of gaming concepts, the feel of the game, or what is often referred to as its 'gameplay'.

Things: videogames as objects

Given the apparent specificity of particular combinations of hardware and software, it is tempting to opt for what Guttenbrunner *et al.* (2010), among others, have termed a 'museum approach' to game preservation. Broadly, and at the risk of over-simplification, we might define a museum approach as being one that is primarily concerned with the collection, care and exhibition of physical objects. That is, games consoles, cartridges, discs, controllers and so on. Common sense might direct us towards such a solution, not least because, if there is something specific about the combination of a MegaDrive joypad, console and the 1991 first release of *Sonic 1*, then acquiring and making available this combination of material objects should be a strategic priority. However, we saw at the very outset of this book that at least part of the reason for the emergence of game preservation as a matter of museum practice and scholarly research interest is the realisation that the material objects, artefacts and products of gaming are disappearing. Material degradation, media decay and bit rot all jeopardise the long-term viability of such collecting regimes, as the objects literally cease to exist (perhaps some time after they ceased to still function). As such, 'While it is necessary to keep original specimens of systems and games for museum purposes, this can only be an approach for the digital preservation of the software for the very near future (short-term)' (Guttenbrunner *et al.* 2010: 76).

On the most practical level, then, an approach based around the continued availability of 'original' objects appears, almost by definition, unviable as a long-term preservation strategy. In plain terms, the fact of material deterioration, as well as the wearing out and rapid replacement of hardware and software through the discursive production of obsolescence that we have documented throughout this book, creates the need for game preservation, rather than presenting viable solutions to it. In fact, the problems are more widespread than this. As Guttenbrunner *et al.* (2010: 76) also note, maintenance is not an inconsequential task, given the proprietary and undocumented nature of much game development and technology:

> Maintaining the original software and hardware to display the data to be preserved may be possible for machines built from standard components, but console video game systems are usually built from custom-manufactured parts. The latter are no longer available once the console system production stops, so they usually cannot be replaced once broken. The same is true for video game software, as most modern systems do only run originally manufactured media as a copy protection mechanism.
>
> *(Guttenbrunner* et al. *2010: 76)*

We might see this as another consequence of the particular business and commercial strategies employed in the contemporary videogames industry, and Kline *et al.* (2003) rightly note that the use of patents and other legal tools to protect development is a crucial component of the engine that drives of the 'perpetual innovation economy'. Certainly, if we consider that access to these systems and gameplay is a key facet of game preservation activity, whether this be to researchers or wider publics, the ongoing robustness of the materials presents real challenges. In the discussion of the hardware preservation practice of the ICHEG, the authors of the PVW final report note that 'In some situations, it is only acceptable for the restoration to occur with original parts (the preferred method). In other situations, original part restoration may be secondary, such as in situations where motherboard components are no longer available' (McDonough *et al.* 2010: 58).

However, the demands of access place particular pressures on hardware that are partly dealt with through duplication, where possible, and partly through restoration and reinforcement practices.

> For components that find their way into Strong's interactive installations, reinforcement or reconditioning may include processes by which the artifact can be made 'bulletproof' for the duration of the exhibit showing. For example, joysticks and other input devices may have to be replaced by versions that can survive the repeated use by patrons of all ages. The museum has used this

technique for the Atari 2600 version of Pac-Man, due to its overwhelming popularity.

(McDonough et al. 2010: 58)

We might also question what we mean by the 'original objects' and how far this insistence on the authenticity of originality should and can extend. Let us consider again the case of *Sonic 1*. Assuming that we are embarking upon a project to preserve and offer for access the game in its MegaDrive incarnation and have laid to rest questions about which of the different 'Spike behaviour' versions of the game we will focus on, we then turn our attentions to questions of display dependencies. As a TV console, and unlike a handheld or mobile device, the MegaDrive has no built-in display and must be connected to an external (audio) video monitor in order for any picture to be seen (or sound to be heard) as audio and video are passed along a single RF (radio frequency) connection. At this point, it is useful to establish which territory's version of *Sonic 1* we will be centring on, as this decision has impacts on the aesthetic and gameplay outcomes as well as posing specific demands on additional hardware requirements. While *Sonic 1* was released for the MegaDrive console (aka Genesis) throughout the world, variations in international television standards, among other things, ensure that different territories received different versions of the game.

One consequence of the various television standards that exist between videogame market territories (notably between Japan, the USA and Europe) is that *Sonic 1* runs at different speeds in different territorial releases. The variation in 50/60Hz TV refresh rates, as well as in resolutions and colour spaces, conspire to mean that *Sonic* is literally faster in Japan, where fewer television scanlines enable the CPU/graphics processor to work more effectively than in Europe. The synchronisation of video and audio also means that *Sonic*'s soundtrack, while identical in terms of arrangement and instrumentation, is pitched down in its European incarnation, where it, in common with the whole game, runs slower than in Japanese or US instances (even the in-game timers that structure play and record achievement run at different speeds with 'seconds' and 'minutes' in Sonic's world lasting longer in Europe than in Japan). As we noted earlier, while a 1991 MegaDrive audience in the UK would probably have known nothing other than the 50Hz version (save for those who imported a US or Japanese console and game), the inconsistency in the release of collections that package the US, European or Japanese ROM running under emulation means that for a contemporary audience, the point of access to Sonic's world is altogether more blurry.

Even once we have alighted on a television standard, the issues do not cease. As J.P. Dyson (director of ICHEG) notes, the scarcity of contemporary displays raises significant issues in terms of collecting, not only because modern televisions and displays exhibit different visual artefacts, but also because they are often incompatible with older console devices. As Guttenbrunner *et al.* (2010) note,

> With analogue cathode ray tube (CRT) displays being replaced by LCD, LED or plasma displays, even the look of original systems changes when they are running on screens using new technologies. When trying to preserve the look

aspect of console video games the original TV artifacts of standard display units that were used when the system was released have to be preserved to recreate the look aspect of these games.

(Guttenbrunner et al. 2010: 75)

In their study of the Atari 2600 game *Star Raiders*, the PVW team encountered at first hand issues of scarcity and compatibility of television sets, with difficulties increasing with progressively newer displays:

[W]ith televisions from the 1980s through 2009, the team experienced problems such as pixelization of image, fluctuation of brightness (photodiode and photoresistor compensation), problems with signal lock (digital tuner problems), problems with sound reproduction (volume, clarity), impedance conversion (conversion from 300 ohm to 75 ohm), and overscan problems (ghosting, artifacts around image edge). The problems are only exacerbated by newer television technologies based upon the conversion to digital TV signals in the United States. The team was already aware of television technologies that have eliminated the possibility of over-the-air input based upon the lack of analog signal as well as the decrease in popularity of VCRs, game consoles, and DVD players that use a direct RF broadcast signal. In such cases, the television is not even capable of receiving the signal, and as such, nothing is displayed.

(McDonough et al. 2010: 60)

In *Racing the Beam*, Montfort and Bogost (2009) stress the strong affinity between the Atari VCS (video computer system) and the CRT (cathode ray tube) television. Elaborating the point, Bogost notes that:

In today's world of huge, sharp LCD monitors, it's hard to remember what a videogame image looked like on an ordinary television of the late 1970s. Emulators like Stella make it possible to play Atari games on modern computers, serving the function of archival tool, development platform, and player for these original games. But unfortunately, they also give an inaccurate impression of what Atari games looked like on a television.

(Bogost n.d.)

As Bogost observes, an essential part of the quality of the Atari VCS gaming experience is actually a consequence of technological imperfection. Afterimages, RF noise, colour bleeding, visible scanlines and the blurring and smearing that are inherent in CRT displays, all combine to become crucial to the creation of the aesthetic of VCS digital play. Nintendo's auteur designer Shigeru Miyamoto notes a similar concern in revisiting his *Super Mario Bros.* title on the occasion of its 25th anniversary re-release. In discussing Mario's 25th anniversary celebrations with Shigesato Itoi, fellow game designer and creator of the *Earthbound* series of Role Playing Games, Miyamoto noted that

> When I see this [Super Mario Bros.] so clearly, it's a little embarrassing. Back then, with tube televisions, it was a little blurrier and the images weren't quite so sharp. The places where we tried to fudge it a bit really stand out!
>
> *(Miyamoto 2010)*

Of course, the specificities and compatibilities of particular display technologies are not the only dependencies of which we should be mindful. Numerous early consoles and games were often supplied with non-digital overlays and additions that enhanced and, in some cases, made possible gameplay. Examples include the Magnavox Odyssey's mylar screen overlays, which effectively drew a large part of the contextualising gameworld and the controller overlays that provided context for the Colecovision controllers, for instance. As Guttenbrunner *et al.* (2010: 74) note,

> This concept was taken one step further by Philips by releasing combinations of traditional board games and video games (the Master Strategy Series) for the Magnavox Odyssey2/Philips Videopac. They were shipped with a game board, playing pieces, an overlay for the keyboard and a cartridge. Playing the game without the added board game was all but impossible.
>
> *(Guttenbrunner* et al. *2010: 74)*

What we see here is at least in part the result of the kinds of business practices that we noted in the first part of this book. The erratic delivery of backwards compatibility and the rapid replacement of hardware systems and software that are no longer manufactured or even supported, in light of their inevitable replacement, contrives to create a situation in which the material objects of gaming disappear quickly from view, even before the ravages of time see the deterioration of their plastics, contacts and circuits. It is because of this catalogue of issues and the fundamental deterioration of the materials, objects and forms that contemporary assessments of game preservation strategy disregard the museum approach as a long-term solution (see, for instance, Guttenbrunner *et al.* 2008, 2010; McDonough *et al.* 2010) and centre their attentions on alternatives that are not reliant on the availability of the physical, material objects of gaming and gameplay.

Bits: videogames as software

Central to software preservation approaches is the capturing of the game's code and, it follows, the decoupling of the means of storage from the means of ultimate access and play. The pressures of bit rot and storage media instability drive the desire to copy the data from the original format to a newer, more stable one. As no current storage medium is known to be free from the effects of data rot or media decay, this process is a necessarily and inevitably iterative one that presently has no end in sight as data are recopied over time as they continually flee the effects of obsolescence and erosion. Data capture is one thing, but of course, it is of little use without a means of accessing it through execution and play. A number of options are presently available. Of the extant software strategies currently promoted within game preservation research and deployed in museums, galleries and archives, emulation (and to a lesser extent virtualisation) is by far the most prevalent and well studied. Alternatives such as code migration and 'source porting', in which code is recompiled to be run on a new, more modern and currently supported platform, are theoretically viable; yet, as Guttenbrunner *et al.* (2008: 3) observe, the proprietary nature of videogame hardware and the typically platform-dependent code that arises in game development where the specificities, capabilities and capacities of particular platforms are harnessed, 'make it next to impossible to migrate a game to a new platform'.

Emulation takes an altogether different approach to software preservation and seeks to maintain the original code while creating what is essentially an interpretative layer that allows one hardware system to mimic – hence emulate – the operation of another. As Monnens (2009: 6) notes, emulation 'involves replicating the exact operation of another hardware and software environment'. Essentially, an emulator is a piece of software that allows one platform (e.g. a PC) to run the program code and potentially deal with inputs and outputs through various peripheral devices (e.g. joysticks and pads) of another platform (e.g. a ColecoVision console). Typically, a modern platform is used to emulate a vulnerable (or vanished) platform. However, while the authorship of emulation software is allowable as an act of investigation and analysis, the acquisition of code to run or system boot ROMs raises a number of legal issues for preservation practitioners (see Conley *et al.* 2004). As McDonough *et al.* (2010) note, 'Emulators are designed to utilize the original executable code from the game. For most emulation systems, this involves extracting and providing a copy of the native cartridge ROM or game CD-ROM.'

From a legal standpoint, this is one area in which industry involvement in preservation projects is urgently needed, and lobbying to redress the often draconian laws that restrict museums and archives in making copies of game code is a key point of priority for many projects. The desire to tackle the legal restrictions on circumventing DRM and gaining access to protecting intellectual properties is at least part of what motivates the calls we have seen to collaborate with the games industry on matters of preservation. Describing the US situation, PVW notes that

> The Digital Millennium Copyright Act's prohibition on defeating technological protection measures makes it impossible for a library to create a preservation copy of games employing DRM and anti-copying measures. While obtaining the permission of the rights owner to make a preservation copy offers a potential path around this obstacle, securing these permissions is complicated by the existence of a large number of 'orphan works' in the field of computer games, and the great difficulties encountered in trying to track intellectual property rights ownership in an industry as volatile as the game software industry. Intellectual property laws also may pose impediments to the development of emulation technology necessary for continuing access to some games.
>
> *(McDonough et al. 2010: 6)*

The state of current legal frameworks and the restrictions on circumventing technical measures of protection such as password-protection or more complex DRM systems (see Anderson 2011: 6–8 on the considerable variations across Europe) are so onerous that even if a developer wished to permit preservation of its intellectual property, the systems, procedures and protocols for doing so do not presently exist in an unambiguous manner, thereby continuing to hamstring practitioners and industry partners alike. As the PVW final report notes, the uncertainty of the exceptions or defences against IP and copyright infringement, as well as the difficulty of tracking down rights holders where games have been (or are suspected to have been) commercially abandoned, 'translates into libraries risking fines of $200–150,000 per game were they to migrate their collection of classic software from 3.5" floppy disks to images stored on hard drives, an act comparable to rebinding a book or creating an access copy of a manuscript' (McDonough *et al.* 2010: 52). What is particularly notable about this situation is thatwhile emulation might seem like the saviour of games in the long term, it is videogames hardware and software manufacturers that have been at the vanguard of those calling for legal measures against emulation and ROM acquisition and distribution; see Sony's action against Connectix (SCE 2000a) and *Bleem!* (SCE 2000b), and Nintendo's corporate position (Nintendo Legal Information 2011), for instance. As Conley *et al.* note, 'Console manufacturers claim that emulation is outright theft, whereas the emulation community considers it a programming feat to be admired. At the center of this controversy is a struggle between fair use and monopoly rights' (Conley *et al.* 2004: 9). However, we should note the success of sites such as world-ofspectrum.org and the UK National Media Museum's 'Games Lounge' initiative in tracking down and securing permissions for distribution and display in specific cases.

Despite the seriousness of these issues, both technically and legally, the advantages that emulation offers appear manifest. Faced with a situation in which we see original hardware and software disappearing at hitherto unimagined rates, the ability to mimic the behaviour of old machines seems almost too good to be true. Consequently, it might not surprise us to hear data migration and emulation portrayed as 'the only viable techniques of long-term preservation' (Monnens 2009: 6). Guttenbrunner *et al*'s (2008: 3) assessment of current console game preservation strategy presents a similar endorsement of the technique, concluding that 'For console games, emulation may be the most promising solution.' However, the situation is not quite so clear cut and the original research presented in PVW casts some serious doubt over the efficacy of these techniques.

> None of these approaches, however, provides a perfect solution to the problem of preservation, and migration, emulation and re-enactment [remaking games rather than emulating them] pose significant risks of altering the appearance and performance of games … Our research on emulation in particular shows that significant visual and aural aspects of the work can be strongly affected by running under emulation. Without a clear understanding of which aspects of a game are likely to be considered significant by scholars in the future, it is extremely difficult to choose an appropriate preservation strategy and preserving games without any change in their appearance and play may simply not be achievable in many instances.
>
> *(McDonough* et al. *2010: 6–7)*

The trouble with emulation 1: vs the original

Both Guttenbrunner *et al.* (2010) and the researchers on the PVW project have conducted extensive studies of videogame emulation, assessing the accuracy of emulation, variations in emulated versions of games and comparing the results with original hardware where that is still possible. Given the positioning of emulation as one of the few viable long-term solutions (Monnens 2009), if not the most promising (Guttenbrunner *et al.* 2008) within extant literature on game preservation, the findings of these case studies are obviously of crucial importance. The brute fact is that current videogame emulation is imperfect. This should not surprise us greatly. If we think about the nature and enormity of the task of running code designed for one system on another with a completely different architecture, the fact that playable videogame emulations exist at all is good evidence of the kind of technological marvel the games industry prides itself upon. Nonetheless, and regardless of how spectacular the achievement might be, emulation is not unproblematic and its use as a game preservation strategy is far from straightforward.

Rather than simply rehearse the detail of each of McDonough *et al.* (2010) and Guttenbrunner *et al.*'s (2010) case studies, here we will concentrate on two key issues that arise: variation between emulation and original hardware and software, and variations between the performance and output of different emulators.

The in-depth case study of Atari 2600 emulation presented in the PVW final report is a function of the project's focus on 1977 title *Star Raiders*. Testing involved scrutinising the output of four different VCS emulators (MESS, z26, PC Emulator and Stella) running on 10 different target PCs with a mix of Windows, Linux and Mac OS operating systems, alongside three original Atari 2600 consoles, multiple copies of the 1970s cartridge and television sets from the 1970s, 1980s and 1990s. Each of the emulators was able to run the extracted *Star Raiders* ROM and present the game in a playable form, though when compared with the original reference hardware, a number of variations were noted:

> there is a perceivable quality difference in the graphical output between the emulator and the original 2600 output for both black and white as well as color televisions (for authenticity, we did some of our testing on 1970s era televisions). The RF/television combination created an experience in which the graphics were not as sharp as the emulated version.
>
> *(McDonough* et al. *2010: 68)*

On the face of it, we might think that the increase in perceived sharpness of image evident in the emulated game displayed on a flat panel should be beneficial. Certainly, the clarity of image reproduction is something of a trope within discourses of 'high-definition' gaming. However, the absence of the blurriness that the CRT television screen imparts actually leads to the presentation of distracting visual artefacts. These anomalies are not the products of poor emulation per se, but rather, arise precisely because the contemporary PC's display technologies do not mask them in the way that the 1970s CRT television screen does. Recalling Montfort and Bogost's (2009) comments on the indivisibility of the Atari VCS/2600 and the CRT television, we begin to appreciate the complexity and extent of the emulation project. Certainly Bogost's (n.d.) call for a 'television simulator' recognises this, and we should note that a number of emulators designed to run on contemporary displays include selectable visual effects that attempt to mimic the effects of raster lines and even the 'fishbowl' effect of CRT televisions. While intriguing, novel and manifestly the product of ingenuity and creativity, these modes typically present little end-user control. More significantly, even though they may simulate some of the visual (in)consistencies of display technologies such as CRT, they do not replicate the extent of their functionality. The light gun is a case in point and is an interface technology whose operation as an input device is intimately tied to the CRT's properties as an output device. While their designation as light 'guns' might lead us to think of them as emitting a beam of light that is registered, they are, in fact, typically receivers. As Baek *et al.* (2005) note,

> They work optically with the screen and do not keep track of location on the screen until the gun is fired. When the gun is fired, the screen blanks for a moment, and the optics in the gun register where on the screen the gun is aimed.
>
> *(Baek* et al. *2005: 688)*

The operation of the light gun is ultimately inseparable from the visual display that it interacts with, and the combination of numbers of scanlines and refresh rates ensures a narrow operating window and a fundamental incompatibility with different types of display. As Baek *et al.* go on to note, 'a light gun designed for a VGA CRT monitor cannot be used with an LCD monitor, and a TV-based light gun cannot be used with a non-TV monitor' (Baek *et al.* 2005: 688).

With consoles of the VCS era and considerably beyond, we should remember also that the television is not simply a visual display, but typically carries audio also and, as such, variations in speaker technology, and even the availability of speakers, impact on the aesthetic qualities of emulation. Accordingly, beyond visual anomalies, differences were also noted in the playback and fidelity of *Star Raiders*' audio:

> the sound quality was also different in the emulated versions. Although the sound approximation of the Television Interface Adapter was acceptable in the emulated version, there were some pitch and timbre variations noted in the audio reproduction when compared to the original experience.
>
> *(McDonough* et al. *2010: 68)*

Clearly, the notion of 'acceptability' in relation to emulation performance is a potentially problematic one and raises a number of questions that relate back to Bogost's (2007) earlier comments on the diversity of audiences for game history and preservation projects. It goes without saying that a general audience wishing to gain a broad sense of 1970s gameplay, design and aesthetics might take a different view and have different, if any, points of reference for comparison from a student of electronic music or digital audio technology, for whom the integrity of playback might be a paramount importance or even the very object of their study. Problems with sound effects and music reproduction (as well as video issues) proved similarly problematic for attempts to emulate (and virtualise) *Doom*, another of the PVW case study games. Some emulators offered no sound support at all, with others offering it intermittently or becoming unstable. However, even the most successful emulation of *Doom* raises a related problem. As a PC-compatible title (subsequently converted and ported to a wide variety of console, handheld and mobile platforms), *Doom* does not have a 'reference' platform in the way that *Star Raiders* does. In common with many PC-compatible titles of today, *Doom* sets out a minimum specification (386 processor, 4MB of RAM, VGA graphics card and a hard disk). However, beyond this basic specification, the game's compatibility with numerous sound and graphics cards, each with different capabilities and specificities, means that now, just as in 1993 when *Doom* was released, its performance, appearance and sound present something of a moving target. In fact, we might argue that the variability in television display type, quality (ranging from black and white with monaural sound through to flat-panel sets connected to AV amplifiers) might problematise the target specification of all but systems with built-in audiovisual displays (mobile phones and handhelds). If we return to Nintendo's *Ocarina of Time* re-release, we note an intriguing caveat in the instruction manual of the GameCube Collector's Edition:

> This NINTENDO GAMECUBE software is a collection of titles originally developed for other Nintendo Systems. Because of the process of transferring software from Game Paks to a Game Disc, you may experience slight sound irregularities or brief pauses during which the system loads data from the Game Disc. Such instances are normal and do not indicate defective software or hardware.
>
> *(Nintendo 2003: 3)*

The trouble with emulation 2: vs other emulators

Moving beyond graphical and sonic (in)consistencies, it is essential that we evaluate the extent and limits of emulation in delivering the experience of play. At the most basic level, this demands a consideration of available interface tools and the nature of interaction. In relation to *Star Raiders*, McDonough *et al.* observe some initial issues that were later overcome with additional peripherals and adapters:

> the mouse and keyboard experience did not properly substitute for the joystick and pad experience of the original. The team later found that an adaptor could be purchased (www.stellaadaptor.com), which would allow the original Atari 2600 joysticks and pads to be interfaced to a modern PC. The adaptor converted the original digital I/O signals from the 9-bin connector to a USB format that could be utilized by z26 and Stella.
>
> *(McDonough* et al. *2010: 69)*

However, in the cases of the games *Mindwheel* (1984) and *Mystery House* (1980), both originally running on the Apple II home computer, the situation was less easily rectified. Here, in addition to wide variations and problems in the rendering of text and graphics (with different fonts used by different emulators), inconsistencies in the operation and mapping of the qwerty keyboard rendered the games unplayable in some instances, and varying markedly from the original Apple II experience.

> By far, the greatest problem the team noted with emulation technology for the Apple II was the inconsistent use of a standard keyboard metaphor when dealing with the Apple II/II+ keyboard. The Apple II/II+ keyboard worked primarily with uppercase encodings, with such machines only allowing key font generation of the uppercase glyphs when typed for certain applications. The inconsistency among emulators leads to inconsistent behavior that is not representative of the original experience.
>
> *(McDonough* et al. *2010: 75)*

The situation presented in the analyses of emulation does not make for particularly reassuring reading if we consider this to be among the only viable long-term preservation strategies for digital games. In each documented case, considerable variation in performance, as compared with original hardware and software combinations, was notable, and in some cases emulators were simply incapable of running the game code under scrutiny. Similarly, the official Nintendo re-releases of *OoT* for Game-Cube and 3DS both receive modifications to compensate for the console's lack of rumble features (as the *Zeldapedia* fansite notes, 'In the 3DS remake, the Stone of Agony is replaced by the new Shard of Agony, which has the same function, but instead of rumbling, produces a sound and on-screen icon, this being due to the Nintendo 3DS's lack of a rumble feature'; Stone of Agony n.d.). Moreover, the cases of *Mindwheel* and *Mystery House* as well as *Doom* and *OoT* make it clear that there is potential for significant variation between the implementations of different emulators. In light of these variations, the optimism of Guttenbrunner *et al*'s (2010: 78) in principle designation of emulation as a viable strategy seems potentially misplaced, or at least underestimates the magnitude of the challenge. '[O]nly one piece of software (the emulator) has to be written to run the library of all games for a console system instead of having to deal with every piece of software for a given system.'

This tendency to overstate the efficacy of videogame emulation is not uncommon, and there is a sense in which emulation is discursively constructed as a virtual black box, in much the same way we saw the videogame console in publishers' marketing materials:

> each time a new console generation is launched, consumers who wish to play the new games must purchase new hardware. Emulation, however, addresses this problem by allowing users to play both new and old games associated with their video game system, as well as those games developed for competing video game systems.
>
> *(Conley* et al. *2004: 10)*

In particular, what is clear from PVW and Guttenbrunner *et al.*'s studies is that, even running on the same target system, different games may require different emulators. The variation between systems and the specific demands placed by each game means that a 'universal' emulator for a given platform, let alone beyond this scope, appears presently unlikely. Certainly, generic or wider scope emulators such as MAME and MESS appear to perform less well than those more dedicated to a particular platform and its nuances (as Guttenbrunner *et al.* 2010 note).

At least part of the problem here is that, at present, videogame emulation is a largely grass-roots, hobbyist arena. As we have seen, projects such as MAME declare themselves, quite proudly, as labours of love. However, while the motivation and dedication should impress us only slightly less than the feats of technical inventiveness that go into the creation of emulation applications, we must surely question whether a reliance on the products of amateur, fan culture is truly viable in the long term.

> Dedicated emulators tend to receive few updates and are frequently discontinued when the authors become distracted from development. Therefore, hardly any emulators exist in a final version that perfectly emulates all games for a system.
>
> *(Guttenbrunner* et al. *2010: 87)*

Indeed, as the PVW team notes, many potential emulation solutions were discarded from their study at an early stage because either they were in development stasis, had been abandoned altogether or their status was uncertain: 'this investigation has also revealed one of the critical weaknesses in the emulator community – as emulators age, they too can fall into neglect and disrepair' (McDonough *et al.* 2010: 69). As such, the emulator is as likely to become an object in need of preservation attention as it is a solution to the problem of preserving the games it initially sets out to make playable. On a related note, we should remember also that emulators are not universally available. According to Conley *et al.*'s (2004) analysis,

> Not all video games and console systems are emulated. The three factors that likely influence whether or not a video game or system is emulated are: console popularity, availability of information regarding system hardware and software, and the technical difficulty of the emulation itself. In general, demand for a suitable emulator for a game system correlates directly with the popularity of a video game console when it was available in the retail marketplace. Consoles possessing a large selection of popular video games are frequently emulated. Thus the emergence of emulators for N64 and Atari 2600 consoles should be no surprise to manufacturers given that historic sales data highlight the popularity of the original systems.
>
> *(Conley* et al. *2004: 5)*

With amateur, hobbyist development focused on those platforms and systems that were most popular or that enjoy the largest library of software, the situation is one in which only the popular and successful survive. And so, just as we might raise concerns about the normativity of a digital game history that fastidiously documented Nintendo, Sega, Atari *et al.* but which made little or no mention of the more 'minor' systems that failed to gain popular or commercial traction, let alone offering any recognition of the legion of pirated and cloned systems circulating in the Far East and Eastern Europe, for instance, so too should we be wary not to assume that fan-derived emulation solutions will present the kind of comprehensive coverage we might seek. Guttenbrunner *et al.*'s (2010) case studies reveal a similar lack of support for comparatively less well-known systems that enjoyed smaller market share, such as the SNK NeoGeo, whose emulations were discarded from the study, due to incompatibilities with the test games. Similarly, the technical demands placed on emulating increasingly complex and powerful systems ensure that there remains a time lag between original platform and emulation, with Guttenbrunner *et al.* (2010) noting a clear correlation:

> Even popular systems of the first four generations are not perfectly emulated today. The more recent the system, the lower the degree of accuracy. Of two tested games on two emulators for the Atari Jaguar only one game was playable. The two games for the Sony PlayStation 2 proved entirely unplayable.
>
> *(Guttenbrunner* et al. *2010: 86)*

As they explain, this lag is amplified yet further where the games under emulation were originally produced later in a platform's lifecycle, thereby typically placing greater demands on target hardware as new middleware, engine development and performance optimisations are exploited. The relentless cycles of renewal and innovation that drive console and PC replacement can be seen to impact greatly on emulation, with a permanent state of technological catch-up (itself reliant on the continuity of developments in PC technology) and the marketplace continuing to guide emulation effort towards the reproduction of popular systems with large libraries of games.

Perhaps, as McDonald (1999), author of *You Will Be Emulated*, states, 'The problem isn't the rise of emulators. It's that there are too few of them.' However, the issue is not simply one of coverage and we must not underestimate the impact of the variations between emulated games and originals, and between different emulations, that are evident in the various case studies we have seen here.

Every (60th of a) second counts

We earlier noted the enormity of the impact of what might at first glance appear to be minor differences and changes. It is essential that the importance of this principle is not underestimated. Nintendo's re-release of its Game & Watch title *Donkey Kong* (DK-52) as part of the Game & Watch Gallery series for the GameBoy handheld console is illustrative.

Seasoned players of Donkey Kong will know the distinctive, Steve Reich-like phasing polyrhythm of the barrels and Mario blipping their collision-course paths across the screen. Indeed, true connoisseurs of the game will soon learn to judge their jumps according to the audio cues of this minimalist composition more than they will rely on reading the visual especially once the pace picks up. In the GameBoy version, the rhythmic beating of Mario against the barrels is not offset in the same way as the original. The result is not only a qualitatively and aesthetically different one, but one that robs the player of part of the fundamental tools of interaction and feedback. The result is a different game. Minutely different. Utterly different.

(Newman 2009)

The precision of technical performance is, as we shall see, absolutely crucial in order to allow the performance of certain styles and proficiencies of gameplay. One-on-one combat games (or 'beat-em-ups') such as Capcom's *Street Fighter* are meticulously scrutinised by their players. Articles such as *Eurogamer*'s 'Face-Off: Street Fighter IV', which compares the Xbox 360 and PS3 versions of the game in the most minute detail, along with websites such as Digital Foundry that provide side-by-side synchronised high-definition video comparisons for frame-by-frame analysis, appear, on the face of it, to do little more than fuel endlessly recursive fan debates about the 'best' platform. Certainly, we know that platform loyalty is one of the bedrocks of videogame fandom and culture (see Newman 2008). However, these analyses are not partisan. What is presented at *Eurogamer* and Digital Foundry is a carefully and skilfully constructed collection of high-resolution images and video showing – in split-screen – identical sequences from the two (con)versions of the game, allowing detailed analysis of the impact of the PS3's lack of full-frame anti-aliasing and its dynamically shifting 720–630p resolution.

The sheer level of commitment and effort that is entailed in producing a video analysis of this kind will be immediately evident, though this alone does not necessarily mark it out as distinctive in the context of fan culture. However, there is more to this than idle curiosity or the self-evident demonstration of playing and media-editing prowess. This hugely compelling and insightful piece of work is invaluable in its own right but, perhaps more importantly for our purposes here, it speaks volumes about the meticulousness, passion, care, affection and knowledge of gamers. Ultimately, what is essential to remember is that analysis such as this is motivated by a desire not only to reveal the technical, but rather to understand and explain the impact of the technical on the experiential. The point of the *Street Fighter IV* video comparison, as I read it, is not simply to reveal the existence of anti-aliasing or graphical artefacts or to ascertain resolution or frame rate for their own sake or to sate the desire for technical knowledge that might be fuelled by marketing discourses such as Sony's 'you don't need to know how powerful the PS3 is'. Rather, the aim of these analyses is to evaluate the consequences of anti-aliasing on gameplay experience. As such, what they reveal is an interest in and understanding of the impact of apparently minute, almost imperceptible changes on the experience of the game – on gameplay.

The investigations go further than the identification of audiovisual distinctions and their impacts, however. The depth of the analyses conducted by *Street Fighter IV* players into the detail of every conceivable attack and defensive manoeuvre reveals the importance of accuracy in the operation and execution of game code. If we look at the discussions and analyses presented in EventHubs.com's (2010) 'How to Read Frame Data: Super Street Fighter IV', for example, we see that the roster of each character's manoeuvres is assessed in relation to the number of frames of animation they take to start up, complete and recover from. It is important to note that these analyses of frame data are not idle or inconsequential investigations, but rather the resultant data contributes to a significant knowledge base for players. Selecting an effective combination of moves for each of the available combatants is facilitated, while truly expert players can read the moves of their attacker from the onscreen appearance of their start–up animations and take evasive action accordingly. These start–up animation routines may last only a fraction of a second (just a few frames of animation running at a 60Hz refresh rate), and the fact that they might be used in this way should give us some idea of how deleterious common emulation performance 'hacks' such as frame skipping might be on the integrity of the digital gamer's experience.

Ultimately, what is foregrounded here is the maximal importance of minute detail in the composition of gameplay experience. The significance of accuracy is not lost on emulator creators, and the differential performance of current videogame emulation applications reflects not only the technical complexity of the task but also, in part at least, the differential motivations of creators and the diminishing returns of improved accuracy in the mass–marketplace. We noted earlier that accuracy was a concern for the curators of the HVSC and, on similar lines, byuu (2011) makes the point particularly forcefully and eloquently in an article detailing his work on *bsnes*, an emulator dedicated to Nintendo's 1990 SNES console. The objective of *bsnes*, unlike other SNES emulators, is accuracy. While noting that 'It is possible for a well-optimized, speed-oriented SNES emulator to run at full speed using only 300MHz of processing power … emulating those old consoles accurately – well, that's another challenge entirely; accurate emulators may need up to 3GHz of power to faithfully recreate aging tech' (byuu 2011). The difference between creating an emulator that is capable of running the majority of games in a generally convincing manner and one that truly, and accurately, recreates the particularities and peculiarities of the target system is the issue with which byuu and *bsnes* are concerned.

With emulators concerned with speed of performance and compatibility with a range of the most popular titles for a given platform, hacks and tweaks to the code are commonplace in order that known problems and inaccuracies can be routed around and compensated for,

> What typically happens is that the problems are specifically hacked around. Both ZSNES and Snes9X contain internal lists of the most popular fifty or so games. When you load those games, the emulators tweak their timing values and patch out certain areas of code to get these games running.
>
> *(byuu 2011)*

For byuu, the issue is finally one of synchronisation and it is this that both makes and breaks the accuracy of the emulator when dealing with those 'edge cases' typically beyond the canonical titles for which tweaks and modifications exist, and puts the lie to any simple assertion that the relative computational power of host and target systems inevitably leads to accuracy in emulation.

> The most common misconception in gauging an emulator's performance is that you can simply look at the clock rate of the primary processor. Unfortunately, this really doesn't tell you anything. The N64's CPU may be clocked at 35x that of the SNES CPU, yet *UltraHLE* requires the same processing power as *ZSNES*.
>
> The primary demands of an emulator are the amount of times per second one processor must synchronize with another. An emulator is an inherently serial process. Attempting to rely on today's multi-core processors leads to all kinds of timing problems. Take the analogy of an assembly line: one person unloads the boxes, another person scans them, another opens them, another starts putting the item together, etc. Synchronization is the equivalent of stalling out and clearing the entire assembly line, then starting over on a new product. It's an incredible hit to throughput. It completely negates the benefits of pipelining and out-of-order execution. The more you have to synchronize, the faster your assembly line has to move to keep up.
>
> *(byuu 2011)*

In some cases, the consequences of speed-over-accuracy emulation might be apparently minor for many players, in that the issues do not unduly compromise or end gameplay and may even be unnoticeable without a reference system for comparison.

> As an example, compare the spinning triforce animation from the opening to Legend of Zelda on the ZSNES and bsnes emulators. On the former, the triforces will complete their rotations far too soon as a result of the CPU running well over 40 percent faster than a real SNES. These are little details, but if you have an eye for accuracy, they can be maddening.
>
> *(byuu 2011)*

However, examples of altogether more serious issues with emulated SNES games abound. Inaccurate audio synchronisation leads to dropouts of music and sound effects in titles like *Earthworm Jim 2*, sub-scanline graphics synchronisation causes video problems with *Air Strike Patrol*, while some games crash altogether, leaving them incapable of being completed and, as a result, unplayable.

> Let's take the case of Speedy Gonzales. This is an SNES platformer with no save functionality, and it's roughly 2–3 hours long. At first glance, it appears to run fine in any emulator. Yet once you reach stage 6–1, you can quickly spot

the difference between an accurate emulator and a fast one: there is a switch, required to complete the level, where the game will deadlock if a rare hardware edge case is not emulated.

(byuu 2011)

As such, if the objective of emulation shifts from speed to accuracy, even a comparatively low-powered console such as the SNES pushes the processing capacity of the current generations of PC hardware. Once the SNES's cartridge-based co-processors such as the SuperFX and DSP-1, which were utilised in games such as *StarFox* (*Starwing*) and *Super Mario Kart*, and which require a laborious and costly reverse engineering process to ascertain their operation, are added into the equation, not only does the task become one involving technical resources, but also a 'level of dedication needed to accurately emulate these games' (byuu 2011). It is worth restating here that consoles such as the PS3, Xbox 360 and Wii are immeasurably more complex than the SNES in terms of their technical architectures, not to mention their often proprietary I/O and online dependencies.

While the conclusions of PVW and other studies evaluating game preservation strategies (such as Guttenbrunner *et al.* 2008, 2010) present a case broadly in support of emulation, it is clear that there are significant limitations and weaknesses that we can identify at technological, experiential and infrastructural levels. Although we might focus on the efficacy of particular audiovisual representations and the strengths and weaknesses of specific emulators or display technologies, in order to identify the best (or at least an acceptable) combination, from the perspective of a game studies researcher interested in game preservation, the question is ultimately concerned with the integrity of the experiences of play. Games are, after all, brought to life in the playing and are, in some senses, always in and at play. Although it is not the intention here to repeat the discussion of configurative play as originally expounded by Moulthrop (2004), it is useful to consider briefly just how central play is, as it is my assertion that, once we recognise, and perhaps reconsider, its place within the game preservation project, we allow ourselves to embark on a markedly different and less technologically focused journey.

The centrality of play

Within academic game studies, it is well documented that digital games are essentially made through the act of play, and while terms like 'interactivity' are rejected by some (e.g. Aarseth 1997) as being ideologically charged, the fact remains that the performance of the player impacts greatly on the structure, form and aesthetic of the game (see Eskelinen 2001; Moulthrop 2004). Most obviously, many digital games make use of branching, non-linear structures or 'narrative trees' that are traversed by players making self-conscious choices (go left; enter the building; etc.). The course of the gameplay experience might be markedly different for players making different choices, with some sections either present or omitted and even wholly new narrative branches or ending states revealed. Moreover, game structure might be contingent on other performance factors. One branch might open up only if a sequence is completed in a particular manner (e.g. within a specific time limit, or having collected a specific number of items) or by demonstrating a particular prowess (e.g. having lost no 'lives').

More than this, videogame play actually describes a variety of related but significantly different practices and performances that are contingent on the differential motivations of players, as well as their skill. Play may be articulated in terms of the 'completion' of games in the fastest possible time, the acquisition of the highest score, or by tackling the challenges in a 'pacifist' mode, dispatching only those enemies that actually bar progress and cannot be avoided. Players may seek to use as few additional capabilities or weapons as possible or may be driven by a desire to acquire every last item of inventory available, even those that are tangential. Play may involve exploring as much or, indeed, as little of the gameworld as possible by engaging in 'complete' or 'low per cent' routes to completion. As such, while some players may never complete a game like *Super Mario Bros.*, others are able to finish the job in just five minutes. For example, see the recordings of superplay at *Speed Demos Archive*, with Andrew Gardikis's 4:59 run the latest to shave seconds off Scott Kessler's 5:11 performance, and one second off his own 5:00 run performed in 2007 (Gardikis 2010). Note also Gardikis's (2008) 19:40 100 per cent time for an all-stages run that does not utilise any of the warp zones.

Additionally, as I have discussed elsewhere (e.g. Newman 2008), the video recording and online sharing of gameplay has become a significant part of the culture of videogames, with players keen to demonstrate their knowledge of the game's potential and their mastery of the system (see also Lowood 2005, 2007 for more on the emergence of 'superplay' and the online collection at the *Speed Demos Archive* for resources). What is notable about these various playings is that they are often characterised by forms of customisation, personalisation and the self-conscious modification of technique and strategy. Players often explore and perform with their games to – and even beyond – destruction, with strategies and tactics exploiting not only the range of moves and capabilities outlined in instructional manuals but also a host of bugs, glitches and other inconsistencies in the operation of the game's code.

We need only look at fan sites such as ZeldaSpeedRuns.com for evidence of the ways in which the exploitation of glitches and bugs in the game have become written into the standard lexicon of gameplay (certain techniques are listed under the 'general knowledge' section, implying their widespread use, while others are coded as being available only to more sophisticated players or to facilitate specific types of play). For some players, even the limits of human ability are insufficient to explore games to their ultimate conclusion. Practices such as tool-assisted speedrunning (TAS) typically involve the use of emulation software and the ability to save the state of gameplay at any point (rather than using the game's own saving regime) so as to perform gameplay as a form of stopframe animation. Built up over many months, these TAS performances are often cast by their creators as artworks whose intention is to push at and beyond the boundaries of what is routinely achievable through play. In addition to the exploitation of the kinds of strategies we have seen deployed by other superplayers and speedrunners, TAS creators make extensive use of further glitches, bugs and other performance and code inconsistencies in games that either would require too great a degree of precision or whose execution is too variable to be used in standard play. *Super Mario Bros.*'s collision detections are a case in point, and recordings of TAS show seemingly impossible jumps through enemies that, in fact, utilise the vagaries of *Mario*'s sprite detection routines and benefit from the ability to 'rewind' and re-record in the event of a failed manoeuvre.

Examples of this creative, exploratory play abound. The canonisation of 'Glitch Pokémon' through in-depth practices of writing, visual art and analytical textual production speak of fans' willingness to explore fully, process and assimilate their findings (see Rita Buuk n.d. and Mandy Nader 2004), while we have seen already the range of walkthroughs for games like *Goldeneye 007*, some of which document in meticulous detail the variety of ways missions can be failed. Discussions of 'cheating' in videogames (e.g. Consalvo 2007) reveal additional layers of complexity in relation to digital gameplay and further highlight the permeability of the game's rulesets and the willingness of players to deliberately play 'against the grain' to maximise their performative reward.

It follows that the ways in which games are played frequently diverge from the ways in which they were intended to be played by their developers and designers, with 'emergent' strategies yielding unanticipated, and impossible to anticipate, results. It will be clear that videogame play need only be obliquely concerned with the ostensible 'aim' of the game as documented in instructional manuals and frequently superimposes additional rulesets that are designed and regulated by communities of players. These might be comparatively straightforward (driving the 'wrong' way around a racing track attempting to avoid oncoming traffic for as long as possible; see Newman 2004 on *Gran Turismo* and *Ridge Racer*, for instance) or more obviously divergent (side-stepping large tracts of the game to access advanced weaponry before the logic of the narrative/structure ordinarily allows, a subversive practice known as 'sequence breaking'; see Newman 2008).

In devising these new strategies and gameplay modes, players sometimes work alone, but very often operate within the context of a community of offline and online players sharing experiences and the results of their investigative playings. As such, gameplay is best understood as a practice that very often takes place within the context of, and is shaped and regulated by, a community of other players, whether this occurs through face-to-face collaborative play, talk and discussion or via the textual products of a fan-culture distribution network such as *GameFAQs* or *YouTube*. Specific tactics, techniques and strategies become available to players as they observe the performances and discussion of others, just as certain techniques are written into or out of the canonical lexicon of available gameplay strategies. Sites such as ZeldaSpeedRuns.com investigate and codify a range of techniques, including, for *OoT*, 'Power Crouch', 'Infinite Sword Glitch', 'Damage Buffering', 'Megajump and Hover Boost', and 'Megaflip', as well as the various 'Sequence Breaks' that allow the subversion of the game's narrative structure by avoiding areas or acquiring objects, techniques and capabilities out of their designated sequence. Conversely, players of first person shooters such as the *Halo, Call of Duty* and *Modern Warfare* series pour scorn on the use of grenade launchers whose accuracy and impact typically leaves them apparently unbalanced and appealing to putatively less skillful players. Their designation as 'noob tubes' reflects the shape of the weapons (typically grenade launchers or bazookas) and pejoratively constructs their use as suitable only for the new, unaccomplished and unskilled gamer (see, for instance, the discussion of 'noob tubes' at *Gamespot UK* (Essian 2011) and the Call of Duty Wiki's (n.d.) outline of the game's various weapons).

Most critically, the gameplay that results from these performances is often unpredictable, emergent and frequently travels in directions unintended and unanticipated even by the designers and developers of the gaming environments within which it is enacted. For these reasons, Sue Morris (2003) terms videogame play a 'co-creative' act in which notions of creator and user, developer and player are effectively blurred (this recalls Surman's 2010 discussion of the 'level creator' facility in *Sonic 2*). Not only do players operate on the system, rules and code to bring 'the game' to life (thereby engaging in play as a 'configurative' practice in Moulthrop's 2004 terms) but also players create their strategies and tactics for play with reference to the advice, guidance and norms of the communities of practice within which they operate. In some instances, this even appears to operate at the expense of the gameplay in its entirety.

Machinima, in which the interactive environments of games are used as the stage for the creation of decidedly non-interactive movies, is perhaps the most extreme and well-known example. Series such as Rooster Teeth's *Halo*-based *Red vs Blue* (see Delaney 2004) and Chris Brandt's (2005) virtuoso *Dance Voldo Dance* routine performed in *Soul Calibur* (see Newman 2008) move beyond the use of real-time game engines as pre-visualisation environments or prototyping tools and present critical spaces in which issues of masculinity and violence, for instance, are interrogated as well as operating as self-consciously reflective examinations of the modalities and conventions of game forms (see Wilonsky 2002; Marino 2004; Lowood 2005, 2007; Cannon 2007). Of course, the production of Machinima is by no means the only way in which gameplay mechanics are subverted and recast, and we might look to the appropriation of motion control systems such as the Wiimote, PlayStation Move and Kinect by experimental musicians and visual artists for further examples. Applications such as *OSCulator*, for instance, facilitate the use of Nintendo Wiimotes as well as accessories such as the WiiFit balance board and nunchuks to create motion-based interfaces for synthesiser plugins and digital audio workstations by converting game control signals to the protocols of audio control, namely OSC (Open Sound Control)/MIDI (Musical Instrument Digital Interface). Like Machinima, these uses do not mark the eradication of gameplay per se. *Prima facie*, *Red vs Blue*'s removal of shooting from the First Person Shooter or *Dance Voldo Dance*'s close choreography that eschews the brutality of combat in favour of erotic, balletic gyrations, might seem to have little to do with 'gameplay' if we define gameplay solely as the actions and performances that the game appears to have been designed to support. However, what these and countless other examples of the creative, investigative, transgressive performances of superplay demonstrate is the videogame's susceptibility not only to be played but to be played *with* (see Newman 2008).

In light of these observations and analyses, it is something of an understatement to suggest that play is important. Certainly, current strategies for game preservation recognise this, and both museum and software-based approaches orient themselves around making games available in playable forms. Whether concerned with the collection of the material objects of gaming or recreating games hardware and software systems through emulation, migration or virtualisation, it is self-evident that being able to play games is the key driver for these projects. And why should it not be? After even the brief discussion of the configurative, exploratory nature of play that we have seen above, with its unexpected, unanticipated contours and its use of emergent strategies and techniques, it is clear that games and 'play' go hand in hand. To paraphrase Kevin Kelly (2010), then, if we pose the question 'what do videogames want?', 'to be played', or at least, 'to be played with', must rank as one of the most convincing answers.

However, there are some important issues raised here. First, as we have seen, neither emulation nor museum strategies are able to unproblematically solve the issues of game preservation. Material objects deteriorate and inevitably disappear, while, as PVW and other projects have demonstrated, emulation presently offers 'acceptable' but significantly lacking recreations to play. Second, as contemporary game studies reminds us, play is more than a process of inputs and outputs into and from a system. It is a socially and culturally situated practice. Sensitivity to the ways games are actually used and what, as a result, are deemed to be the important qualities and characteristics of that game to its players who have learned to use it in specific ways and for specific purposes must then be a key aspect of any preservation activity. Noting these issues, Lowood poses some essential questions:

> There is a difference between preserving game technology and preserving game content, which includes gameplay. Is it necessary to play The Legend of Zelda on the original Nintendo Entertainment System, with the original Nintendo controller and a contemporary television set, in order to gain a historically valid experience of the game? The experience of viewing Birth of a Nation in a palatial theater with live music is different from viewing it on videotape, on our television, at home, and so is reading any rare book in a modern edition or format. Different, yes, but is that difference essential for scholarly research?
>
> *(Lowood 2004: 5)*

In fact, we can develop this point yet further. We might also ask whether attempting to play a game in the absence of the networks and sources of information that originally shaped and informed its playing is similarly problematic. It is certainly possible to argue that encountering a game in a gallery or archival context in the future is not only potentially jarring from a technological or historical perspective, but, in being stripped of the contextualising network of talk, discussion, demonstration and webs of investigation, the game is isolated as a comparatively free-floating text or exhibit rather than part of a suite of complex, interconnected social and cultural practices.

Dead pixels

Ultimately, the study of play reveals a variability, flexibility and malleability in the game that encourages us to view it not as a static object of preservation but as a set of resources to be engaged with and shaped through configurative, creative, exploratory practices. It is small wonder, then, that Guttenbrunner *et al.* (2010: 72) note that their ability to be played means that 'Digitally preserving interactive console video games is very different from digitally preserving static documents'. As we have seen, neither museum- nor emulation-based approaches appear entirely satisfactory or viable as long-term solutions, by virtue either of the inherent shortcomings or the incon- sistencies and differences in the experiences they deliver. Depending on our positions and allegiances, we might consider these shortcomings to be insurmountable pro- blems that cast doubt on the efficacy of the entire project of game preservation or simply as a set of challenges that may be tackled through the deployment of increas- ingly sophisticated technological solutions. Certainly, Giordano's (see Sterling 2011) assessment strongly hints at the fundamental impossibility of game preservation, given the 'extreme fragmentation' we have noted and the intrinsic mutability and instability of games as forms that we see highlighted in examinations of games in and at play. Indeed, at this nascent stage in the development of game preservation strategy, read- ing discussions of the need to define 'good enough' preservation alongside judge- ments of what might constitute the 'acceptable' performance of an emulator in relation to its differential performance compared with original hardware and software might lead us to feel some sympathy for Giordano's position.

However, I wish to suggest that these issues only become problems because of the way we are presently approaching game preservation. The issues surrounding the long-term availability of original hardware and software systems or the variations in audiovisual representations and the interface mappings of particular emulators are problems only because the current objective of game preservation is to retain the playability of videogames in the future. If being able to play games in the future is the aim of game preservation, then the integrity of the experience offered to future players is, it goes without saying, of paramount importance. However, as we have seen, the attainment of this goal of duplicating the experiences of play through cur- rently available means is, if not impossible, then demonstrably unattainable at present. This is not a problem, though, if we reconsider our objectives. Accordingly, I wish to suggest a somewhat radical and apparently counterintuitive alternative.

Let videogames die

By this, I mean to say that games as playable entities may have a limited lifespan and that the objective of game preservation need not be to artificially extend this in per- petuity, but rather, should be to document the period of the game's existence. This is not merely a pragmatic decision taken in the face of the difficulties encountered in deploying a museum or software approach, but rather, a considered position informed by a recognition of the importance of gameplay as a configurative act and as a socially and culturally situated practice. In short, play is not the outcome of game preservation but is its object. The capturing of games in and at play could and, I would contend, *should* be the core objective of game preservation. To be clear, this position is not opposed to emulation or the presentation of original hardware and software, and what is proposed here should not be read as a criticism of either of those approaches or projects. Nor does this position imply that emulation or playability have no place in the wider context of games preservation, interpretation and access. However, it does signal a shift in the focus of game preservation.

Of course, the proposal that game preservation broadens its attentions beyond the playable game is far from a revelation. As Vowell (2009: 12) notes,

> if we place too much emphasis on preserving only published games, we relegate much of the history behind games to the shadows. To challenge this over-emphasis on the game itself, we may consider whether a future historian can learn how a game was made by only playing it, or whether that historian could learn about the history of a development studio and the culture of the development team simply by playing their games.
>
> *(Vowell 2009: 12)*

Vowell goes on to produce a helpfully lengthy list of materials (and types of materials) that might accompany digital game objects and provide contextualisation for future scholars. Among these diverse materials, we find development documentation, budgetary information, PowerPoint pitches, press kits, demos and company newsletters. However, important though these materials are, their designation as context implies a continued centrality of the game as the unit of currency in game preservation. The position I am outlining here represents, in one sense, a reversal of this stance. The game, at least in its playable form, is 'dethroned', and ceases to be the object that is contextualised, interpreted and made sense of by these other materials which, in turn, potentially take on the role of archival documents of games and, most importantly, of gameplay. Among these 'other documents' I include video recordings of gameplay as well as the fan-produced walkthrough texts that we saw earlier in this book, as these represent some of the most comprehensive investigations of game structure, form and ludic opportunity that exist either within or outside game studies. It is worth pausing momentarily to consider the implications of this point. In order to document, record and capture gameplay, that most interactive, configurative and performative of practices, the most appropriate and effective tools reveal themselves to be decidedly non-interactive: static, plain text documents and linear video recordings. In relation to video, we might take a middle ground, as proposed by Guttenbrunner *et al.* (2010: 87), who recognise the benefits of video capture particularly in relation to the absence or failings of other contemporaneous strategies:

The video approach was ruled out in this case study as it lacked interactivity, even though it scored highest in almost all other aspects. In cases where a suitable emulation alternative is not available (e.g., Sony PlayStation 2, Atari Jaguar) it can be the best option until an interactive alternative does become available. It can also be a complementary strategy to emulation for quick access or to verify future emulators' visual and audible compliance. Video recordings of users playing the game can serve as an additional reference for the way games were played with special controllers and even in what context they were played.

(Guttenbrunner et al. 2010: 87)

McDonough and Olendorf's (2011) assessment of the importance of interactivity as well as the dynamic and mutable nature of game structure and resources leads them to a similar conclusion:

Preserving this dynamic component of games and virtual worlds has meant that a purely documentary approach to preservation through the use of screen shots, video capture of game play, textual walk through of game play, etc., was not sufficient. Such documentation might provide a useful supplement to our preservation efforts in many cases, but perhaps the most significant property of virtual environments is their interactivity, and so our efforts have tried to preserve this as much as possible.

(McDonough and Olendorf 2011: 91)

The assumption that an emulation alternative will inevitability be available is, as we have seen, open to question, given the current state of hobbyist development and its tendency to reproduce the patterns of popularity and market share. However, we might question yet further the desirability of a playable solution, even if one were feasible. In its discussion of *Second Life*, the PVW team notes that

The value and meaning of a virtual world is primarily derived from the actions and interactions of its players. Imagine stepping into Second Life, which doesn't even have the benefit of plotlines or non-player characters (NPCs), years after the last user signed off. The world would be empty; interactivity limited to the virtual equivalent of archaeology: examining buildings and prims in an attempt to build a picture of how Second Life was lived.

(McDonough et al. 2010: 29)

Elsewhere in the report, the point is reiterated in relation to *Everquest*, drawing attention not only to the significance of materials external to 'the game' in contextualising gameplay but also to the possibility of their status as the only source of information and documentation of practices and events that are simply impossible to deduce from fresh playing:

Installing Everquest in 2050 will not reveal much about the virtual world
that emerged from the software, how it was built or used, even if future writers
and historians have access to everything needed to run a fully functioning
version of the game. Certainly, there are important reasons for preserving
this software, whether as artistic or cultural content, for technology studies,
or for forms of scholarship that treat digital games and virtual worlds as
authored texts or artistic objects. Still, we also need to think about virtual
world history in terms of events and activities, much as an archivist or historian
would in the real world, and attend more carefully to preservation of forms of
documentation in digital form that are external to virtual worlds as software
environments.

(McDonough et al. *2010: 49)*

Clearly, both *Everquest* and *Second Life* are online role-playing games or software
environments that apparently differ from the comparative containment of console and
PC games like *Sonic the Hedgehog* or *Doom*, and we might be tempted to consider the
issues they raise to be non-transferable. However, as we have seen, gameplay is
invariably socially and culturally situated, informed and shaped by discussions, practices and cumulative knowledges that are at once integral to and external from the
game. While the presentation of contextualising documentary materials may serve to
alleviate some of these issues by breathing some air into the vacuum of the encounter, there can little assurance that the *Street Fighter IV* player in 2050 will benefit from
the a priori knowledge that contemporary players potentially bring, whether this is
gleaned through discussions with friends, read in strategy guides, shared via fansites or
learned through head-to-head competitive play. Let us not forget also that much of
what constitutes *Street Fighter IV* is revealed only through repeated, skilful and self-
consciously directed play. If we factor in multi-player gaming and the availability of
online competitive play, *Street Fighter IV* soon might appear as barren and deserted a
place as *Everquest* or *Second Life*'s environments.

Consider also that games such as the *Final Fantasy*, *Legend of Zelda* and even *Super
Mario* series present not only expansive worlds but worlds whose contours are
revealed only through extensive, iterative play. We might well ask at what point the
playable should be made available in the first place. In common with many games,
Super Mario Galaxy's environments change throughout the game. The act of play is
literally transformative, changing the landscape, opening up some options while
closing down others that have been completed or negated. Gameplay leaves an
identifiable and indelible trace on the world. Indeed, as we saw in the case of Capcom's
Resident Evil: The Mercenaries 3D, this trace is permanent and cannot be erased. Of
course, regardless of whether it becomes hardwired into the code of the game, the
trace of gameplay is both a function of informed choices and contingent on gameplay
performance, prowess, skill and perhaps even luck. One path opens up because a
player decides to fork left rather than right, while another is revealed because, while it
is not declared in the gameplay, a player completed within or outside an unstated
target time.

That so much of what games have to offer is based on contingencies of play must surely lead us to question the primacy of playable games in the game preservation project and encourage us to consider the possibility of a need to a shift the balance from game preservation towards game*play* preservation. In contrast to the position outlined by McDonough and Olendorf (2011) and Guttenbrunner *et al.* (2010), I want to suggest that recognising play as a vital part of what is to be preserved, rather than the outcome of preservation, might lead us to a re-evaluation of the role of the documentary approach. While for many it exists as a valuable supplement to the business of game preservation, I wish to suggest that a documentary approach is well suited to respond to the diversity of play and the susceptibility of games to the con-figurative, transformative acts of play as well as underpinning any project based around the presentation of playability. The centrality of documentary materials, of non–interactive means of gaining access to, and ascertaining the meaning of, a media form that is defined by its interactivity marks an important if somewhat controversial shift of focus.

Videogames are disappearing

To reiterate, this stance is not one that denigrates the idea of playable games, but rather, it is one that questions the extant centrality of playability in game preservation strategy. The continued ability to play remains a valuable and potentially useful means of contextualising and interpreting videogames, in much the same way as handling a replica or original medieval broadsword might give a sense of combat through its heft or the aura of its authenticity. However, just as the sword itself reveals little of the detail of the lived experience of knightly life, neither can the isolated playable game communicate the lived experience of gameplay. Ultimately, a strategy based around the comprehensive documentation of play as it exists now, and in all its diversity, lessens the severity of some of the anomalies we noted in relation to emulated versions of games, as these no longer have to stand as perfect replicas of the originals or, worse still, as a simulacrum that masks the fact that no singular 'ori-ginal' ever truly existed, due to variations in components such as sound and graphics cards, joypads, multibutton mice and audiovisual display technologies. Moreover, the desperation felt in relation to the business practices that use up, wear out and 'retire' games may abate somewhat if we are sufficiently confident to allow games to die in their playable state. The onus therefore shifts to documenting as thoroughly as pos-sible the game while it exists. At the very least, we might argue that the creation of a documentary record of gameplay, audio and visual performance must be a *predicate* for an emulation- or software-based strategy. Without a reliable and trustworthy refer-ence point for comparison, how might we be able to judge the accuracy or efficacy of future attempts to recreate or resurrect? Far from being ancillary materials that flesh out the story of a given game, platform or series, or that help to enrich our appre-ciation or ability to interpret, I would assert that, even if only in terms of their ability to present a referential baseline, gameplay videos, along with walkthrough texts and the other products of fan cultures, are the foundations upon which all preservation effort must be built. As such, the creation and preservation of these comprehensive documentary materials must be a priority.

It is important to remember at this point that game preservation is not simply a project concerned with resuscitating old games. Certainly, the lens of game preservation thus far has tended to focus on 1980s-era titles, and this is at least in part because of the putative threat of their material disappearance, as well as the focus of grass-roots videogame emulation projects on consoles and Coin-Ops from this period (which, as we have seen, is perhaps a function of the technical feasibility of such undertakings). However, a concerted focus on a documentary approach (even, for that matter, if it remains part of a 'contextualisation' or 'reference point' strategy that still retains playability as its long-term objective) reconfigures preservation as a present concern. If we take on board the inevitability of the disappearance of games, which for at least some titles appears unanimously agreed a practical certainty – and we need only look at the documented failings of attempts to preserve *Second Life* in McDonough et al. (2010; see also McDonough and Olendorf 2011) or the business practices of retirement, the subsequent removal of online access to games and the lack of formal support and backwards compatibility for a compelling case – we find that a potentially liberating position unfolds, which encourages a concern for the present and future rather than a wistful sense of a lost past.

But what of the games that have already been lost? Might we be suggesting a 'year zero' approach to preservation? While there is little that documentation can do to capture the stories of play and development that help to explain and make sense of *Jet Set Willy*, *Sonic the Hedgehog* or *Parachute*, these games do continue to exist in some form. That their emulated, re-released selves are not identical to their original releases might present problems where the recreation seeks to stand for the original, but by treating the 2012 emulation as a continuation of the original game rather than its substitute we find the contexts of contemporary play a rich and productive area to document. The cultures and practices of retro gaming, the creation and use of games under emulation are, in and of themselves, vital areas in need of recording and documentation. As such, oral histories, annotated and narrated gameplay videos and walkthroughs as extensive archival documents of gameplay can deal with *Jet Set Willy*, *Sonic*, *Parachute et al.*, as they are now – 'now they are old', as Marvin (1988) might have it. Where the IGDA Game Preservation SIG urges action 'before it's too late', we might shift slightly and recognise that at some point it inevitably will be too late – too late to play these games in their original state, at least.

As we noted at the very beginning of this book, videogames are disappearing, and while it is natural to lament their passing, it does not necessarily follow that the realisation of games' vulnerability to material and digital deterioration, obsolescence and supersession should cast the project of game preservation as one primarily concerned with halting or interrupting these processes. The idea that we might be able to arrest the business and discursive practices that sit at the very foundation of the videogames industry in its broadest sense, and which are, in part, responsible for the disappearance of games and the diminution of their longevity, is ambitious, to say the least. Similarly, the contingency of ongoing access to games on technologies, systems, networks, intellectual properties and rights management systems that are in the control of organisations in whose interest it is to protect their proprietary nature and exclusivity ensures that any attempt to preserve systems and games in playable form beyond their commercially supported lifetimes inevitably operates from a position of disadvantage. Moreover, we have seen that techniques to recreate the conditions of play using different hardware and emulation software, and which attempt to side-step some of the dependencies on proprietary and unsupported technologies and systems that are beyond the control of preservation practitioners, bring with them their own issues in terms of the authenticity of their representations and experiences, as well as requirements for their ongoing support and development.

Ultimately, what is at stake here is the purpose of game preservation as a project. As we have seen, current game preservation work is underpinned by the desire to maintain or recreate games in playable form, which, given the apparent indivisibility of 'game' and the configurative 'play' that enacts it, appears to be a wholly natural position to adopt. However, I want to suggest that the focus on preserving playability is not the logical outcome of recognition of the importance of play. Nor is it the best way to tackle the disappearance of games, which, far from being the problem to tackle, is best conceived as the context in which preservation takes place. Videogames are disappearing and they will continue to disappear, for all the technological and commercial reasons we have seen throughout this book. It might seem an odd, even perverse thing to suggest, but perhaps their disappearance is not a problem per se, or at least might not be the problem best addressed by game preservation. Perhaps recognising that it will not be possible to play today's games in the future is not an admission of failure but a firm foundation upon which to plan.

The decision to embrace the extinction of games in playable forms, and the shift away from conceiving of play as the outcome of preservation to a position that acknowledges play as an indivisible part of the object of preservation, are not merely born of pragmatic frustration with the apparent impossibility of the project or the (im)precision of current strategies to prolong playability. Rather, the decision to focus on the documentation of gameplay as experience and configurative practice, in concert with development documentation and original or emulated playability as part of the wider body of contextualising materials, is born precisely of the recognition that play is not merely important, but that it is too important not to preserve.

Videogames are disappearing and, by default, so too is gameplay. The urgent aim of game(play) preservation must surely be to record as much as we possibly can about games, and the way they are made, played and played with, while they are still with us.

REFERENCES

@molleindustria (2011) 'According to Apple ... ', *Twitter*, 13 September <http://twitter. com/#%21/molleindustria/status/113647144078020609>

3DS Backwards Compatibility (2011) 'Backwards with Nintendo DS Games', Nintendo. com [US] <http://www.nintendo.com/3ds/games/>

Aarseth, E. (1997) *Cybertext: Perspectives on Ergodic Literature*, Baltimore, MD: Johns Hopkins University Press.

About HVSC (n.d.) *High Voltage SID Collection.org* <http://www.hvsc.c64.org/>

About MAME (n.d.) *MAME – The Official Site of the MAME Development Team* <http:// mamedev.org/about.html>

About Unseen 64 (n.d.) *Unseen64.net* <http://www.unseen64.net/about-2/>

Acland, C. (2007a) (ed.) *Residual Media*, Minneapolis, MN: University of Minnesota Press.

——(2007b) 'Introduction: Residual Media', in C. Acland (2007) (ed.) *Residual Media*, Minneapolis, MN: University of Minnesota Press, pp.xiii–xxvii.

Adams, E. (2007) 'Will Computer Games Ever be a Legitimate Art Form?', in A. Clarke and G. Mitchell (eds) *Videogames and Art*, Bristol: Intellect Books, pp. 255–64.

Aleckermit (2011) 'Ocarina of Time: Version Differences', *ZeldaSpeedRuns.com* (posted 2 June 2011) <http://zeldaspeedruns.com/oot/generalknowledge/version-differences>

Alexander, L. (2011) 'Nintendo Addresses 3DS Crash Reports', Gamasutra, 28 March <http://www.gamasutra.com/view/news/33745/Nintendo_Addresses_3DS_Crash_Re-ports.php>

Anderson, D. (2011) 'A layman's guide to the KEEP legal studies', *KEEP (Keeping Emulation Environments Portable) deliverable D2.6* <http://www.keep-project.eu/ezpub2/index.php?/eng/content/download/20703/103715/file/D2.6_laymansguidelegalstudies_final.pdf>

Apple Inc. (2011) App Store Review Guidelines for iOS devices <http://developer.apple. com/appstore/resources/approval/guidelines.html>

Ashton, D. (2008) 'Digital Gaming Upgrade and Recovery: Enrolling Memories and Technologies as a Strategy for the Future', *M/C Journal*, 11(6).

Ashton, D. and Newman, J. (2010) 'Slow Play Strategies: Digital Games Walkthroughs and the Perpetual Upgrade Economy', *Transformations*, 20.

——and——(2011) 'Slow Play Strategies: Digital Games Walkthroughs and the Perpetual Upgrade Economy', *Transformations*, 20 <http://www.transformationsjournal.org/journal/issue_20/article_03.shtml>

Atkins, B. (2006) 'What Are We Really Looking at?: The Future-Orientation of Video Game Play', *Games and Culture*, 1(2) pp. 127–40.

Au, A. (2011) 'Everything Good Old is New Again', *The Escapist*, 7 June <http://www.escapistmagazine.com/articles/view/issues/issue_309/8926-Everything-Good-Old-is-New-Again.3>

Baek, S., Kim, T., Kim, J., Im, C. and Lim, C. (2005) 'IRED Gun: Infrared LED Tracking System for Game Interface', in Y.-S. Ho and H.J. Kim (eds) *Advances in Multimedia Information Processing: PCM 2005*, Proceedings of the 6th Pacific Rim Conference on Multimedia (Part II), Jeju Island, Korea, November 2005, pp. 688–99.

BAFTA (2010) 'Shigeru Miyamoto to receive the Academy Fellowship', BAFTA press release, 24 February <http://static.bafta.org/files/video-games-fellowship-announcement-528.doc>

Bailadon, D. (2011) 'Sonic the Hedgehog iPhone 1.2.6 review', iTunes App Store, 27 June.

Bailey, K. (2011) 'Editorial: Why I'm Still Playing the Game Boy Advance', *GamePro*, 30 March <http://www.gamepro.com/article/features/218682/editorial-why-im-still-playing-the-game-boy-advance/>

Bailey, K. and Kemps, H. (2011) 'A History of Nintendo Handhelds', *GamePro*, 30 March <http://www.gamepro.com/article/features/218671/a-history-of-nintendo-handhelds/>

Bak, A. (1999) 'Dead Media Project: An Interview with Bruce Sterling', *ctheory.net* <http://www.ctheory.net/articles.aspx?id=208>

Barker, M. (2004) 'News, Reviews, Clues, Interviews and Other Ancillary Materials – A Critique and Research Proposal', in J. Burton (ed.) *21st Century Film Studies: A Scope Reader* <http://www.scope.nottingham.ac.uk/reader/chapter.php?id=2>

Barnholt, R. (2011) 'The Good Times and Bad of the GBA', *GamePro*, 30 March <http://www.gamepro.com/article/features/218653/the-good-times-and-bad-of-the-gba/>

Barton, M. (2005) 'Games in Captivity: Liberation, Emulation and Abandonware', *Free Software Magazine*, 8, 10 May <http://www.freesoftwaremagazine.com/articles/liberating_games?page=0%2C0>

Barwick, J., Dearnley, J. and Muir, A. (2010) 'Playing Games With Cultural Heritage: A Comparative Case Study Analysis of the Current Status of Digital Game Preservation', *Games and Culture*, 6(4) pp. 373–90.

Barwick, J., Muir, A. and Dearnley, J. (2009) 'Where Have All the Games Gone? Explorations on the Cultural Significance of Digital Games and Preservation', *Proceedings of DiGRA 2009*, Brunel University, London <http://wiki.igda.org/images/e/e7/State_of_Play_Where_have_all_the_games_gone.pdf>

Batchelor, J. (2011) 'GAME-Trade-in Drives 60% of New Game Sales', *MCV* (online edition), 24 January <http://www.mcvuk.com/news/42669/GAME-Trade-in-drives-60-of-new-game-sales>

Baudrillard, J. (1994) 'The System of Collecting', in J. Elsner and R. Cardinal (eds) *Cultures of Collecting*, London: Reaktion, pp. 7–24.

——(1998) *The Consumer Society: Myths and Structures*, trans. C. Turner, London: Sage.

Baxter, J. (2010) 'The Simple 7777s Guide' (v.1.04), *GameFAQs*, last updated 18 July 2010 <http://db.gamefaqs.com/console/psx/file/final_fantasy_vii_7777.txt>

Baxter, S. (2011) 'About the Save Data', *Capcom-Unity.com*, 29 June <http://www.capcom-unity.com/resident_evil/go/thread/view/7391/27944601/About_the_Save_Data_(Official)>

Bishop, T. (2004) 'Is Music Safe on Compact Disc?', *BBC News* [online], 27 August <http://news.bbc.co.uk/1/hi/entertainment/music/3940669.stm>

BNF (2011) 'Video Games', *Bibliothèque nationale de France* website (posted 31 January 2011) <http://www.bnf.fr/en/collections_and_services/multim_eng/s.video_games.html>

Bogost, Ian (2007) *Persuasive Games: The Expressive Power of Videogames*, Cambridge, MA: MIT Press.

——(n.d.) 'A Television Simulator: CRT Emulation for the Atari VCS', *Bogost.com* <http://www.bogost.com/games/a_television_simulator.shtml>

Boxer, S. (2011) 'Wii U: First Hands-on with Nintendo's New Console', *Guardian.co.uk*, 7 June <http://www.guardian.co.uk/technology/2011/jun/07/wii-u-nintendo-games-console>

Boyd, S. (2005) 'Preservation, Patent Litigation and Prior Art: The Selfish Reasons to Save Our Interactive Entertainment History', *Game Developer Magazine*, May.

Brandt, C. (2005) 'Dance, Voldo, Dance: A Machinima Music Video', Bain Street Productions <http://www.bainst.com/madness/voldo.html>

Brightman, J. (2010) 'EA Sports' Online Pass "Brilliant," EA "Charging Too Little," says Analyst', *Industry Gamers*, 11 May <http://www.industrygamers.com/news/ea-sports-online-pass-brilliant-ea-charging-too-little-says-analyst/>

——(2011) 'Sony's NGP "Dead On Arrival" and 3DS "Gimmicky," says Neil Young', *Industry Gamers*, 1 March <http://www.industrygamers.com/news/sonys-ngp-dead-on-arrival-and-3ds-gimmicky-says-neil-young/>

British Library Board (2008) 'Digitisation Strategy 2008–11', *British Library website*, August <http://www.bl.uk/aboutus/stratpolprog/digi/digitisation/digistrategy/>

Brown, M. (2011) 'Retailer GAME Introduces Pre-orders on Used Games', *Wired.co.uk*, 7 March <http://www.wired.co.uk/news/archive/2011–03/07/game-preowned-preorders>

Buchli, V. and Lucas, G. (2001) (eds) *Archaeologies of the Contemporary Past*, London: Routledge.

Buckingham, D. and Sefton-Green, J. (2003) 'Gotta Catch 'em All: Structure, Agency and Pedagogy in Children's Media Culture', *Media, Culture and Society*, 25, pp. 379–99.

Burn, A. (2006) 'Reworking the Text: Online Fandom', in D. Carr, D. Buckingham, A. Burn and G. Schott (eds) *Computer Games: Text, Narrative and Play*, Cambridge: Polity Press, pp. 82–102.

Burnham, V. (2003) *Supercade: A Visual History of the Videogame Age 1971–1984*, Cambridge, MA: MIT Press.

Buuk, R. (n.d.) 'A Day in the Life of MissingNo.', *Team Rocket's Rockin* <http://www.trsrockin.com/missing.html>

byuu (2011) 'Accuracy Takes Power: One Man's 3GHz Quest to Build a Perfect SNES Emulator', *Ars Technica*, 10 August <http://arstechnica.com/gaming/news/2011/08/accuracy-takes-power-one-mans-3ghz-quest-to-build-a-perfect-snes-emulator.ars?comments=1#comments-bar>

Caiazzo, A. (2009) 'God of War Collection – Blu-ray Disc Compilation Available this Holiday Season!', *PlayStation.Blog*, 31 August <http://blog.us.playstation.com/2009/08/31/god-of-war-collection-blu-ray-disc-compilation-available-this-holiday-season/>

Caldwell, J. (2008) *Production Culture*, London: Duke University Press.

Call of Duty Wiki (n.d.) 'Grenade Launcher', *Call of Duty Wiki* <http://callofduty.wikia.com/wiki/Grenade_Launcher>

Cannon, R. (2007) 'Meltdown', in A. Clarke and G. Mitchell (eds) *Videogames and Art*, Bristol: Intellect Books, pp. 38–53.

Carbone, M. and Giordano, F. (2011) 'Almost the Same Game. Text and Gaming Experience between Continuity of Forms and Changing Context', *Contemporary Audiovisual Geographies*, Udine – Gorizia, 5–14 April 2011 [for English translation, *see* Sterling 2011]

Carless, S. (2006) 'Breaking: Nintendo Announces New Revolution Name – "Wii"', *Gamasutra*, 27 April <http://www.gamasutra.com/php-bin/news_index.php?story=9075>

Chalk, A. (2009) 'Man Finds Ecstasy Tabs in Used GTA Game', *The Escapist*, 8 April <http://www.escapistmagazine.com/news/view/90800-Man-Finds-Ecstasy-Tabs-in-Used-GTA-Game>

Chaplin, H. (2007) 'Is That Just Some Game? No, It's a Cultural Artifact', *New York Times*, 12 March.

Choquet, D. (ed.) (2002) *1000 Game Heroes*, Köln: Taschen.

Chun, W. (2006) 'Did Somebody Say New Media?', in W. Chun and T. Keenan (eds) *New Media Old Media*, New York and London: Routledge, pp. 1–10.

Chun, W. and Keenan, T. (2006) (eds) *New Media Old Media*, New York and London: Routledge.

Clarke, A.C. (1973) *Profiles of the Future*, London: Victor Gollancz.

Clarke, A. (2000) '"Mother Swapping": The Trafficking of Nearly New Children's Wear', in P. Jackson, M. Lowe, D. Miller and F. Mort (eds) *Commercial Cultures: Economies, Practices, Spaces*, Oxford: Berg, pp. 85–100.

Clarke, A. and Mitchell, G. (eds) (2007) *Videogames and Art*, Bristol: Intellect Books.

Cohen, S. (1984) *Zap: The Rise and Fall of Atari*, New York: McGraw-Hill.

ColecoVision Unreleased Games (2011) *ColecoVision.dk*, 8 September <http://www.cole covision.dk/unreleased.htm>

Conley, J., Andros, E., Chinai, P., Lipkowitz, E. and Perez, D. (2004) 'Use of a Game Over: Emulation and the Video Game Industry: A White Paper', *Northwestern Journal of Technology and Intellectual Property*, 2(2) <http://www.law.northwestern.edu/journals/njtip/v2/n2/3/Conley.pdf>

Connal (2010) 'The Museum of Soviet Arcade Games', *A Dangerous Business*, 5 January <http://adangerousbusiness.com/2010/01/05/the-museum-of-soviet-video-games/>

Consalvo, M. (2003) 'Zelda 64 and Video Game Fans', *Television & New Media*, 4(3), pp. 321–34.

——(2006) 'Console Video Games and Global Corporations: Creating a Hybrid Culture', *New Media & Society*, 8(1), pp. 117–37.

——(2007) *Cheating: Gaining Advantage in Videogames*, Cambridge, MA: MIT Press.

Cook, T. (2011) 'Let's Talk iPhone', Apple Press Event, 4 October, Cupertino, CA.

Crawford, C. (1984) *The Art of Computer Game Design*, Kindle ebook <http://www.amazon.com/Art-Computer-Game-Design-ebook/dp/B0052QA5WU>

——(1995) 'Barrels o' Fun', *Interactive Entertainment Design*, 8(3) <http://erasmatazz.com/TheLibrary/JCGD/IEDV8/BarrlesFun/BarrlesFun.html>

Crecente, B. (2011) 'PlayStation Outage Makes Some Capcom Games Unplayable Offline', *Kotaku*, 21 April <http://kotaku.com/#!5794533/playstation-outage-makes-some-capcom-games-unplayable-offline>

Croshaw, B. (2011) 'Extra Punctuation: Keeping Old Games Intact', *The Escapist*, 2 August <http://www.escapistmagazine.com/articles/view/columns/extra-punctuation/9053-Extra-Punctuation-Keeping-Old-Games-Intact>

Crossley, R. (2010) 'Pre-owned a Bigger Problem than Piracy', *Develop* [online], 11 May <http://www.develop-online.net/news/34791/Pre-owned-a-bigger-problem-than-piracy>

——(2011) 'Angry Birds Rio "hits 10m downloads in ten days"', *Develop*, 4 April <http://www.develop-online.net/news/37423/Angry-Birds-Rio-hits-10m-downloads-in-ten-days>

Crytek UK (2011) 'DirectX 11 Ultra Upgrade for Crysis 2', *My Crysis: The Official Crysis Community*, 1 July <http://www.mycrysis.com/dx11>

Cullen, J. (2011) 'HMV to Refuse Resident Evil: Mercenaries Trade-ins in UK', *VG24/7*, 29 June <http://www.vg247.com/2011/06/29/hmv-to-refuse-resident-evil-mercenaries-trade-ins-in-uk/>

Curran, S. (2004) *Game Plan: Great Designs That Changed the Face of Computer Gaming*, Mies, Switzerland: Rotovision.

Dale, A. (2007) 'Bioshock: New Piping Hot Details Leak out of Rapture's Rusting Borders ... ', *Computer and Videogames* [Xbox 360 World] 12 March <http://www.computerandvideogames.com/159824/previews/bioshock/> (also published in *Xbox 360 World* magazine, October 2007, Bath: Future Publishing).

Day, W. (1998) 'Chapter One: The Golden Age of Video Game Arcades', *Twin Galaxies* <http://207.239.218.46/index.aspx?c=17& id = 620>

Def Guide to Zzap! 64 (n.d.) <www.zzap64.co.uk>

Delaney, K.J. (2004) 'When Art Imitates Videogames, You Have "Red vs. Blue": Mr. Burns Makes Little Movies Internet Fans Clamor for; Shades of Samuel Beckett', *Wall Street Journal*, 9 April.

DeMaria, R. and Wilson, J. (2002) *High Score!: The Illustrated History of Electronic Games*, Emeryville, CA: McGraw-Hill/Osborne.

Denerstein, B. (2007) 'What for Art Thou?', *Kotaku*, posted 27 July <http://kotaku.com/gaming/feature/what-for-art-thou-283021.php>

Desjardins, M. (2006) 'Ephemeral Culture/eBay Culture: Film Collectibles and Fan Investments', in K. Hillis, M. Petit and M. Epley (eds) *Everyday eBay: Culture, Collecting and Desire*, New York and London: Routledge, pp. 31–43.

Deuze, M. (2007) *Media Work*, Cambridge: Polity.

DiGA (2004) 'Short Statement Concerning the "Referentenentwurf für ein zweites Gesetz zur Regelung des Urheberrechts in der Informationsgesellschaft" (Consultant's Draft for a Second Law Governing Copyright Law in the Information Society) with Regard to Complex Digital Cultural Artefacts (Computer Games)', *Digital Game Archive*, Berlin, 13 November <http://www.digitalgamearchive.org/works/computerspielebuendnis_ av_eng.rtf>

Donahue, R. (2009) '"Do You Want to Save Your Progress?" Preservation Strategies of the Game Industry, and What Their Users Could Teach Them', *Society of American Archivists Annual Meeting*, Austin, TX, 9–16 August.

Donkey Kong (n.d.) *MobyGames* <http://www.mobygames.com/game/donkey-kong>

Donkey Kong (video game) (n.d.) *Wikipedia* <http://en.wikipedia.org/wiki/Donkey_Kong_(video_game)>

Donlan, C. (2011) 'Ico & Shadow of the Colossus Collection HD – Review', *Eurogamer*, 8 September <http://www.eurogamer.net/articles/2011-09-08-ico-and-shadow-of-the-colossus-collection-hd-review>

Dovey, J. and Kennedy, H.W. (2006) *Game Cultures*, Maidenhead: Open University Press.

Dowdall, T. (2009) 'Guest Op/Ed: Toxics, Electronics and Why Consoles Matter', *Kotaku*, 26 August <http://kotaku.com/#!5345196/guest-oped-toxics-electronics-and-why-consoles-matter>

Dutton, F. (2011a) 'Capcom Defends Resi: Mercs Save System', *Eurogamer.net*, 29 June <http://www.eurogamer.net/articles/2011-06-29-capcom-defends-resi-mercs-save-system>

——(2011b) 'Nintendo Comments on 3DS Error Screen', *Eurogamer*, 28 March <http://www.eurogamer.net/articles/2011-03-28-nintendo-comments-on-3ds-error-screen>

Ebert, R. (2007) 'Games vs. Art: Ebert vs. Barker', *Roger Ebert.com*, 21 July <http://rogerebert.suntimes.com/apps/pbcs.dll/article?AID=/20070721/COMMENTARY/70721001>

Edensor, T. (2005) *Industrial Ruins*, New York: Berg.

Edge LoZ Review (1998) 'Legend of Zelda: Ocarina of Time (N64 review)', *Edge*, 66, pp. 84–87.

Edge SM64 Prescreen (1996) 'Super Mario 64 – Prescreen', *Edge*, 34, pp. 28–30.

Edge Staff (2009) 'The 100 Best Games To Play Today', *Edge* [online], 9 March <http://www.next-gen.biz/features/100-best-games-play-today?page=11>

Edwards, B. (2007) 'Why Super Nintendos Lose Their Color: Plastic Discoloration in Classic Machines', *Vintage Computing and Gaming*, 12 January <http://www.vintage-computing.com/index.php/archives/189>

Edwards, C. and Satariano, A. (2010) 'Electronic Arts: Lost in an Alien Landscape: The leading maker of computer games is struggling as people turn to cheaper, online alternatives', *Bloomsberg Businessweek*, 10 February <http://www.businessweek.com/magazine/content/10_08/b4167064465834.htm>

Egenfeldt-Nielsen, S., Heide Smith, J. and Tosca, S. (2008) *Understanding Video Games: The Essential Introduction*, New York: Routledge.

Electronic Arts (2011) 'Online Service Updates', *EA.com* <http://www.ea.com/1/service-updates>

Elliot, P. (2009) 'GAME: Pre-owned Generates a Fifth of Our Sales', *GamesIndustry.biz*, 22 April <http://www.gamesindustry.biz/articles/game-pre-owned-generates-a-fifth-of-our-sales>

ESA (Entertainment Software Association) (2011a) 'Economic Data', *Entertainment Software Association* <http://www.theesa.com/facts/econdata.asp>

——(2011b) 'Anti-Piracy Frequently Asked Questions', *Entertainment Software Association* <http://www.theesa.com/policy/antipiracy_faq.asp>

Eskelinen, M. (2001) 'The Gaming Situation', *Game Studies*, 1(1) <http://www.gamestudies.org/0101/eskelinen/>

Essian (2011) 'Are Noob Tubes Ruining FPS Games?', *Gamespot UK*, 2 March <http://uk.gamespot.com/forums/topic/27593794/are-noob-tubes-ruining-fps-games&msg_id=328458417>

Eventhubs.com (2010) 'How to Read Frame Data: Super Street Fighter', *Eventhubs.com*, last updated 10 May 2010 <http://www.eventhubs.com/guides/2009/feb/17/how-read-frame-data-street-fighter-4/>

Faber, L. (1998) *Re: Play. Ultimate Games Graphics*, London: Laurence King Publishing.

Fahey, R. (2010) 'Are Pre-owned Sales Killing Gaming?', *Eurogamer.net*, 6 December <http://www.eurogamer.net/articles/2010-12-06-are-pre-owned-sales-killing-gaming-article>

——(2011) 'Going, Going, Gone', *Gamesindustry.biz*, 21 April <http://www.gamesindustry.biz/articles/2011-04-22-going-going-gone-editorial>

Fisher, M. (2007) '"How Very Lacanian": From Fantasy to Hyperreality in Basic Instinct 2', *Film-Philosophy*, 11(3), pp. 74–85 <http://www.film-philosophy.com/2007v11n3/fisher.pdf>

Fleck, J. (2005) 'SNES General Cleaning/Care Guide v1.2', GameFAQs, Version v1.2, last updated 13 December 2005 <http://www.gamefaqs.com/snes/916396-snes/faqs/36361>

Fox, M. (2006) *The Video Games Guide: From Pong to Playstation 3, Over Forty Years of Computer and Video Games*, London: Boxtree.

Franzen, J. (2003) 'Scavenging', in J. Franzen (ed.) *How to be Alone: Essays*, New York: Picador, pp. 195–206.

French, M. (2011) 'NGP-Sony Outlines Handheld Games Vision in Tokyo', *MCV* [online edition], 27 January <http://www.mcvuk.com/news/42729/Sony-outlines-handheld-vision-in-Tokyo>

Fron, J., Fullerton, T., Morie, J.F. and Pearce, C. (2007) 'Playing Dress-Up: Costumes, Roleplay and Imagination', *Women in Games*, 19–21 April, University of Wales, Newport <http://www.ludica.org.uk/LudicaWIG07.pdf>

Future Shock! (1997) 'Future Shock! – N64 is Here!', *Official Nintendo Magazine*, 54, pp. 14–15.

Game GoW3 pre-order (2011) 'Gears of War 3 (only on XBox 360) – Pre-order Information', Game.co.uk <http://www.game.co.uk/lowdown.aspx?lid=15502&cm_sp=gearsofwar-topnav–gearsofwar3>

GameBox64 project homepage (n.d.) <http://www.gamebox64.com/>

gamenthusiast (2004) 'SNES Game Cartridge Save Game Battery Life', *Digital Press: The Video Game Database*, 12–13 December <http://www.digitpress.com/forum/showthread.php?t=47132>

GamePro Staff (2011) 'Remembering the Game Boy Advance', *GamePro*, 30 March <http://www.gamepro.com/article/features/218683/remembering-the-game-boy-advance/>

Gamerankings OoT (2011) 'All Time Best – All Platforms', *Gamerankings.com*, <http://www.gamerankings.com/browse.html>

Games on Show (2010) 'More 3DS Games on Show', *GamesMaster*, September, p. 48.

GamesMaster 3DS Games Preview (2010) 'The Games … ', *GamesMaster*, September, pp. 46–49.

GamesMaster 3DS Preview (2010) '3D Without Four Eyes', *GamesMaster*, September, p. 44.

Gaming goes to Hollywood (2004) *The Economist*, 25 March <http://www.economist.com/node/2541401>

Gardikis, A. (2008) 'Super Mario Bros. Speedrun (nowarps). Best time 0:19:40', (performed 12 March), *Speed Demos Archive* <http://speeddemosarchive.com/Mario1.html#nowarps>

——(2010) 'Super Mario Bros. Speedrun (normal). Best time: 0:04:59', (performed 24 October), *Speed Demos Archive* <http://speeddemosarchive.com/Mario1.html#norm>

Gasking, F. (2010) 'About GTW: how it all began and all that … ', *Games That Weren't 64*, 22 August <http://www.gtw64.co.uk/about.php>

Gaywood, R. (2010) 'The Staggering Size of iOS's Game Collection', *The Unofficial Apple Weblog (TUAW)*, 17 November <http://www.tuaw.com/2010/11/17/the-staggering-size-of-ioss-game-collection/>

Gears 3 Beta (2011) 'Gears 3 Beta Launching on Xbox LIVE in April', *Gears of War/Xbox.com* <http://gearsofwar.xbox.com/Templates/Secondary.aspx?id=2004> [accessed March 2011]

Gibson, W. (2006) 'My Obsession: I Thought I Was Immune to the Net. Then I Got Bitten by eBay', in K. Hillis, M. Petit and Epley, M. (eds) *Everyday eBay: Culture, Collecting and Desire*, New York and London: Routledge, pp. 19–30.

Gilbert, M. (1998/2003) 'Digital Media Life Expectancy and Care', *@OIT*, University of Massachusetts Office of Information Technologies [originally published 1998, updated 2003] archived at <http://www.softpres.org/cache/DigitalMediaLifeExpectancyAndCare.html>

Gilbert, R. (2005) 'Yum ... ', *Grumpy Gamer*, 11 January <http://grumpygamer.com/8911540>

Gitelman, L. (2008) *Always Already New: Media, History and the Data of Culture*, Cambridge, MA: MIT Press.

Gitelman, L. and Pingree, G. (2003) (eds) *New Media, 1740–1915*, Cambridge, MA: MIT Press.

Goffman, E. (1959) *The Presentation of Self in Everyday Life*, New York: Doubleday.

Good, O. (2011) 'Why Would a Game with no Online Play Require an Online Connection?', *Kotaku*, 3 February <http://kotaku.com/#!5751122/why-would-a-game-with-no-online-play-require-an-online-connection>

Gooding, P. and Terras, M. (2008) '"Grand Theft Archive": A Quantitative Analysis of the State of Computer Game Preservation', *International Journal of Digital Curation*, 3(2) <http://www.ijdc.net/index.php/ijdc/article/view/85/56>

Gray, J. (2010) *Show Sold Separately*, New York: New York University Press.

Gray, S. (2011) 'Videogames: The Impossible Archive', *JISC Digital Media blog*, 3 May <http://www.jiscdigitalmedia.ac.uk/blog/entry/videogames-the-impossible-archive>

Greenpeace International (2010) 'Guide to Greener Electronics – Nintendo, January 2010: The 14th (January 2010) Guide to Greener Electronics assessment of Nintendo', *Greenpeace.org* <http://www.greenpeace.org/international/en/publications/reports/nintendo-guide-to-greener-electronics-14/>

Gregson, N. and Crewe, L. (1997) 'The Bargain, the Knowledge and the Spectacle: Making Sense of Consumption in the Space of the Car Boot Sale', *Environment and Planning D: Society and Space*, 15, pp. 87–112.

——and——(2003) *Second-hand Cultures*, Oxford: Berg.

Gregson, N., Brooks, K. and Crewe, L. (2000) 'Narratives of Consumption and the Body in the Space of the Charity/Shop', in P. Jackson, M. Lowe, D. Miller and F. Mort (eds) *Commercial Cultures: Economies, Practices, Spaces*, Oxford: Berg, pp. 101–21.

Grint, K. and Woolgar, S. (1997) *The Machine at Work*, London: Blackwell.

Grossman, E. (2006) *High Tech Trash: Digital Devices, Hidden Toxics, and Human Health*, Washington, DC: Island Press.

Guins, R. (2009) 'Concrete and Clay: The Afterlife and Times of E.T. The Extra-Terrestrial for the Atari Video Computer System', *Design and Culture*, 1(3), pp. 345–64.

Gunter, B. (1998) *The Effects of Video Games on Children: The Myth Unmasked*, Sheffield: Sheffield Academic Press.

Guttenbrunner, M. (2007) 'Digital Preservation of Console Video Games', master's thesis, Vienna University of Technology (completed September 2007) <http://www.ifs.tuwien.ac.at/~becker/pubs/guttenbrunner_games2007.pdf>

Guttenbrunner, M., Becker, C. and Rauber, A. (2010) 'Keeping the Game Alive: Evaluating Strategies for the Preservation of Console Video Games', *The International Journal of Digital Curation*, 5(1).

Guttenbrunner, M., Becker, C., Rauber, A. and Kehrberg, C. (2008) 'Evaluating Strategies for the Preservation of Console Video Games', in *Proceedings of the Fifth International Conference on Preservation of Digital Objects (iPRES 2008)* London, British Library, pp. 115–21 <http://www.bl.uk/ipres2008/presentations_day1/18_Guttenbrunner.pdf>

Ha, A. (2011) 'Angry Birds Maker Predicts the Death of Console Gaming', *GamesBeat*, 13 March <http://venturebeat.com/2011/03/13/angry-birds-console-gaming/>

Hamilton, J. (2011) 'Nintendo 3D "makes gamers dizzy & sick"', *Sun* [online], 1 April <http://www.thesun.co.uk/sol/homepage/news/3499049/Nintendo-3DS-makes-gamers-dizzy-sick.html>

Happy Space Invader (2009) '"Ultimate" Collection? 32Mb of Games on a Blu-ray Disc?', *Amazon.co.uk* (Customer Reviews, SEGA Mega Drive: Ultimate Collection), 8 February <http://www.amazon.co.uk/product-reviews/B001P5HX0Y/ref=dp_top_cm_cr_acr_txt?ie=UTF8& showViewpoints=1>

Harris, C. (2010) 'E3 2010-Nintendo Developer Roundtable Live Blog', *IGN.com* (UK), 15 June <http://uk.wii.ign.com/articles/109/1098500p1.html>

Helft, M. (2001) 'What Makes eBay Unstoppable?', *Industry Standard*, 6–13 August.

Henning, M. (2007) 'New Lamps for Old: Photography, Obsolescence, and Social Change', in C. Acland (2007) (ed.) *Residual Media*, Minneapolis, MN: University of Minnesota Press, pp. 48–65.

Higgins, S. (2011) 'Digital Curation: The Emergence of a New Discipline', *The International Journal of Digital Curation*, 6(2) <http://www.ijdc.net/index.php/ijdc/article/view/184/251>

Hillis, K., Petit, M. and Epley, N. (2006) (eds) *Everyday eBay: Culture, Collecting and Desire*, New York and London: Routledge.

Hinkle, D. (2011) 'The Legend of Zelda: Ocarina of Time 3D preview: Ageless beauty', *Joystiq*, 13 April <http://www.joystiq.com/2011/04/13/the-legend-of-zelda-ocarina-of-time-3d-preview/>

Hodgson, D.S.J., Stratton, B. and Stratton, S. (2002) *Super Mario Sunshine: Prima's Official Strategy Guide*, Roseville, CA: Prima Games.

Hollinger, E., Ratkos, J. and Tica, D. (1998) *The Legend of Zelda: Ocarina of Time. Prima's Official Strategy Guide*, Rocklin, CA: Prima Publishing.

Huang, E.M. and Truong, K.N. (2008) 'Sustainably Ours – Situated Sustainability for Mobile Phones', *Interactions* 15(2), pp. 16–19.

Huh, J. and Ackerman, M. (2009) 'Obsolescence: Uncovering Values in Technology Use', *M/C Journal*, 12(3) <http://journal.media-culture.org.au/index.php/mcjournal/article/viewArticle/157>

Hyman, P. (2004) 'Game Over? Not if Preservationists Have Their Way', *Hollywood Reporter*, 8 October <http://www.hollywoodreporter.com/hr/search/article_display.jsp?vnu_content_id=1000663278>

Hyperion (n.d.) 'Bronzing CD's', *Hyperion*, <http://www.hyperion-records.co.uk/bronzed.asp>

Ico Tech Analysis (2011) 'Tech Analysis: Ico and Shadow of the Colossus Collection HD', *Digital Foundry*, 10 September <http://www.eurogamer.net/articles/digitalfoundry-ico-shadow-of-the-colossus-hd-collection>

Icon (2011) 'Care and Conservation of Plastic Materials', *Conservation Register* <http://www.conservationregister.com/PIcon-careplastics.asp>

IFLA Study Group on the Functional Requirements for Bibliographic Records (1997) *Functional Requirements for Bibliographic Records: Final Report* [updated 2008], The Hague: International Federation of Library Associations and Institutions <http://www.ifla.org/files/cataloguing/frbr/frbr_2008.pdf>

Ingham, T. (2010) 'THQ – We'll Crush Pre-Owned Threat: Publisher to Use "Premium Online" Model to Damage Second-Hand Market', *ComputerAndVideogames.com*, 10 August <http://www.computerandvideogames.com/259308/thq-well-crush-pre-owned-threat/>

Iwata, S. (2009) 'Discovering New Development Opportunities', *Game Developer's Conference*, Moscone Center, San Francisco, CA, 25 March.

Iwata Asks (2011) 'Iwata Asks. Vol. 5 Asking Mr. Miyamoto Right Before Release: 8. I Wanted to Experience Hyrule in 3D', *Iwata Asks*, <http://iwataasks.nintendo.com/interviews/#/3ds/how-nintendo-3ds-made/4/7>

Jenkins, M. (2007) *Analog Synthesizers*, Oxford: Focal Press.

Jess-Cooke, C. (2009) *Film Sequels*, Edinburgh: Edinburgh University Press.

Jobs, S. (2010) 'Keynote speech', *Apple Worldwide Developers Conference 2010*, Moscone Center, San Francisco, CA, 7–11 June.

Johnson, S. (2010) 'E3 Report on Microsoft Kinect', *Tech News Today* (*This Week in Tech* netcast), first broadcast 14 June.

Jones, G. (2002) *Killing Monsters: Why Children Need Fantasy, Super Heroes, and Make-Believe Violence*, New York: Basic Books.

Jones, S. (2008) *The Meaning of Video Games: Gaming and Textual Strategies*, Abingdon: Routledge.

joossa, LagunaticHigh, Yesmar88, ZenOfThunder (2009) 'Contest Bonus: Final Fantasy VII vs. Zelda: Ocarina of Time', GameFAQs poll, 9 June <http://www.gamefaqs.com/poll/index.html?poll=3509>

Kaiser, J. (2010) 'The Dirt on Ocean Garbage Patches', *Science*, 328(5985), p. 1506.

Karppi, T. (2011) 'Digital Suicide and the Biopolitics of Leaving Facebook', *Transformations*, 20.

Kelly, K. (2010) *What Technology Wants*, New York: VikingPenguin.

Kent, S.L. (2001) *The Ultimate History of Video Games*, Roseville, CA: Prima.

King, L. (2002) *Game On: The History and Culture of Videogames*, London: Laurence King.

King of Kong, The (2007) dir: Seth Gordon.

Kline, S., Dyer-Witheford, N. and De Peuter, G. (2003) *Digital Play*, London: McGill-Queen's University Press.

Kohler, C. (2006) 'Japan Gets Way Better Virtual Console Lineup', *Wired (Game|Life)*, 31 October <http://www.wired.com/gamelife/2006/10/japan_gets_way_/>

——(2011) 'Epic Shows Off Its Unreal Vision of Gaming's Future', *Wired (Game|Life)*, 4 March <http://www.wired.com/gamelife/2011/03/epic-unreal-engine-demo-gdc/?pid=965&pageid=33381>

Kokkinidis, G. (2010) 'Remnants of a Disappearing UI', *Design Language News*, 18 November <http://news.designlanguage.com/post/1611663345>

Kronschnabl, A. and Rawlings, T. (2010) 'Why Are Games Sequels so Often Better than Film Sequels and What This Can Teach Us About the Development Cycle', *Develop Conference*, Brighton, UK, 13–15 July.

Kuchera, B. (2011) 'Capcom Crushes Replay Value of New Game by Making Saved Games Permanent', *Ars Technica*, 28 June <http://arstechnica.com/gaming/news/2011/06/capcom-crushes-replay-value-of-new-game-by-making-saved-games-permanent.ars>

Lee, J. (2008a) 'Andrew Eades: Pre-owned Market Needs Reform', *GamesIndustry.biz*, 24 September <http://www.gamesindustry.biz/articles/andrew-eades-pre-owned-market-needs-reform>

——(2008b) 'Pre-owned Games Market "Damaging" Single-player Games – Braben', *GamesIndustry.biz*, 11 September <http://www.gamesindustry.biz/articles/pre-owned-games-market-damaging-single-player-games-braben>

Leichter, J. (2011) 'Investigating the Accumulation of Plastic Debris in the North Pacific Gyre', in K. Omori, X. Guo, N. Yoshie, N. Fujii, I. C. Handoh, A. Isobe and S. Tanabe (eds) *Interdisciplinary Studies on Environmental Chemistry – Marine Environmental Modeling and Analysis*, Ehime University, Japan: Center for Marine Environmental Studies, pp. 251–59.

Libby, J. (2003) 'NOTE: The Best Games in Life Are Free?: Videogame Emulation in a Copyrighted World', *Suffolk University Law Review*, 36, pp. 843–57.

Livingstone, I. and Hope, A. (2011) *Next Gen. Transforming the UK into the World's Leading Talent Hub for the Video Games and Visual Effects Industries*, London: NESTA <http://www.nesta.org.uk/library/documents/NextGenv32.pdf>

Loguidice, B. and Barton, M. (2009) *Vintage Games: An Insider Look at the History of Grand Theft Auto, Super Mario, and the Most Influential Games of All Time*, Burlington, MA: Focal Press.

Lowood, H. (2004) 'Playing History with Games: Steps towards Historical Archives of Computer Gaming', *Annual Meeting of the American Institute for Conservation of Historic and Artistic Works (Electronic Media Group)*, Portland, OR, 14 June.

——(2005) 'Real-time performance: Machinima and game studies', *iDMAa Journal*, 2(1), pp. 10–17.

——(2006) 'A Brief Biography of Computer Games', in S. Egenfeldt-Nielsen, J. Heide Smith and S. Tosca (eds) *Understanding Video Games: The Essential Introduction*, New York: Routledge pp.27–47.

——(2007) 'High-performance Play: The Making of Machinima', in A. Clarke and G. Mitchell (eds) *Videogames and Art*, Bristol: Intellect Books, pp. 59–79.

——(2009a) (ed.) *Before It's Too Late: A Digital Game Preservation White Paper* <http://www. igda.org/wiki/images/8/83/IGDA_Game_Preservation_SIG–Before_It%27s_Too_Late–A_ Digital_Game_Preservation_White_Paper.pdf>

——(2009b) 'Introduction', in H. Lowood (ed.) *Before It's Too Late: A Digital Game Preservation White Paper* <http://www.igda.org/wiki/images/8/83/IGDA_Game_Preservation_ SIG–Before_It%27s_Too_Late–A_Digital_Game_Preservation_White_Paper.pdf> p.1

Lowood, H., Spector, W., Grant, C., Bittanti, M. and Meretzky, S. (2007) 'Ten Games You Need to Play: The Digital Game Canon', *Game Developers Conference 2007*, Moscone Center, San Francisco, CA, 5–9 March.

Lowood, H., Armstrong, A., Monnens, D., Vowell, Z., Ruggill, J., McAllister, K., Donahue, R. and Pinchbeck, D. (2009) 'Before It's Too Late: Preserving Games Across the Industry/Academia Divide', *Proceedings of DiGRA 2009*, Brunel University, London <http://wiki.igda.org/images/4/43/State_of_Play_Before_Its_Too_Late.pdf>

Main, B. (2011) 'The Mysteries of the Bin', *The Escapist*, 12 April <http://www.esca pistmagazine.com/articles/view/issues/issue_301/8772-The-Mysteries-of-the-Bin>

Marino, P. (2004) *3D Game-Based Filmmaking: The Art of Machinima*, Scottsdale, AZ: Paraglyph Press.

Martin, B. (2007) 'Should Videogames be Viewed as Art?', in A. Clarke and G. Mitchell (eds) *Videogames and Art*, Bristol: Intellect Books, pp. 201–10.

Martin, M. (2010) 'GameStop: Without Second Hand Sales We Wouldn't Be Here', *GamesIndustry.biz*, 13 July <http://www.gamesindustry.biz/articles/gamestop-without-second-hand-sales-we-wouldnt-be-here>

Marvin, C. (1988) *When Old Technologies Were New: Thinking about Electric Communication in the Late Nineteenth Century*, Oxford: Oxford University Press.

Masahuri Sakurai Q&A (2010) 'Q&A: Masahiro Sakurai – One of Ninty's 3D Wizards Speaks', *GamesMaster*, September, p. 49.

Maslow, A. (1966) *The Psychology of Science*, Chicago, IL: Henry Regnery.

Master Kirby (2007) 'Replace the Battery in Your Game Cartridge! Can Your Pokemon Game Still Hold a Save?', *PokéMasters Forums*, 30 January <http://www.pokemasters.net/ forums/showthread.php?t=15464>

McCalmont, J. (2010) 'The Video Game Canon and The Age of Forgetfulness', *Futurismic*, 10 June <http://futurismic.com/2010/10/06/the-video-game-canon-and-the-age-of-forgetfulness/>

McDonald, T.L. (1999) 'You Will Be Emulated', *Maximum PC*, September, p. 41.

McDonough, J. and Olendorf, R. (2011) 'Saving Second Life: Issues in Archiving a Complex, Multi-User Virtual World', *The International Journal of Digital Curation*, 6(2) <http://www.ijdc.net/index.php/ijdc/article/view/185/252>

McDonough, J., Olendorf, R., Kirschenbaum, M., Kraus, K., Reside, D., Donahue, R., Phelps, A., Egert, C., Lowood, H. and Rojo, S. (2010) *Preserving Virtual Worlds Final Report*. Available via the University of Illinois IDEALS Repository at <http://hdl.handle. net/2142/17097>

McFarlane, K. (2011) 'Unplugging the Affective Domain: Can "Slow Spaces" Really Improve the Value of Cultural Literacy?', *Transformations*, 20.

McFerran, D. (2011) 'Nintendo 3DS Review: Part 5 – The Bundled Games', *Pocket Gamer*, 7 March <http://www.pocketgamer.co.uk/r/3DS/Nintendo+3DS/feature.asp? c=28139>

McGuigan, J. (2010) *Cultural Analysis*, London: Sage.

McQuiddy, M. (1983) 'City to Atari: "E.T." Trash Go Home', *Alamogordo Daily News*, 27 September, 89(231).

McWhertor, M. (2011) 'Crysis 2's Ultra Upgrade Explained In Pretty Images and Even Prettier Video', *Kotaku*, 27 June <http://kotaku.com/5815971/crysis-2s-ultra-upgrade-explained-in-pretty-images-and-even-prettier-video/>

MegaDrive Collection (n.d.) Sega MegaDrive Ultimate Collection Official UK Website, Sega.co.uk <http://www.sega.co.uk/games/?g=592>

Mehta, R. (2008) 'Exploring Non-destructive Techniques to Conserve Plastic Artefacts', *Materials World Magazine*, 1 March <http://www.iom3.org/news/exploring-non-destructive-techniques-conserve-plastic-artefacts>

Mensah, G. (2010) 'Canon 2.0', *Gamasutra*, 12 November <http://www.gamasutra.com/blogs/GarethMensah/20101112/6426/Canon_20.php>

Miller, D. (2000) 'Introduction: The Birth of Value', in P. Jackson, M. Lowe, D. Miller and F. Mort (eds) *Commercial Cultures: Economies, Practices, Spaces*, Oxford: Berg, pp. 77–83.

Minkley, J. (2011) 'Rein-PC gaming has "shot by" consoles News', *Eurogamer*, 9 July <http://www.eurogamer.net/articles/2011-07-08-rein-pc-gaming-has-shot-by-consoles>

Minter, J. (2004) 'Unity – an announcement', *YakYak*, 10 December <http://www.yakyak.org/viewtopic.php?t=28896>

Miyamoto, S. (2010) 'Super Mario Bros. 25th Anniversary' (interview with Shigesato Itoi), *Nintendo.co.uk*, 13 September <http://www.nintendo.co.uk/NOE/en_GB/news/iwata/super_mario_bros_25th_anniversary_19226_19227.html>

Mogensen, N. (2009) 'Wtf, Only 40 Games?', *Amazon.co.uk* (Customer Reviews, SEGA Mega Drive: Ultimate Collection), 14 February <http://www.amazon.co.uk/product-reviews/B001P5HX0Y/ref=dp_top_cm_cr_acr_txt?ie=UTF8&showViewpoints=1>

Molleindustria (2011a) 'About Phone Story', *Phone Story.org*, <http://phonestory.org>

——(2011b) 'Banned from the App Store', *Phone Story.org*, <http://phonestory.org/banned.html>

Monnens, D. (2009) 'Losing Digital Game History: Bit by Bit' and 'Why are Games Worth Preserving?', in H. Lowood (ed.) *Before It's Too Late: A Digital Game Preservation White Paper*, (IGDA Games Preservation Special Interest Group White Paper) <http://www.igda.org/wiki/images/8/83/IGDA_Game_Preservation_SIG–Before_It's_Too_Late–A_Digital_Game_Preservation_White_Paper.pdf>

monokoma (2008) 'Project Zelda 3D: The Development of Zelda 64', *Unseen 64*, 16 April <http://www.unseen64.net/articles/zelda64-project-development/>

Montfort, N. (2007) 'Video Game Preservation and the Canon', *Grand Text Auto*, 12 March <http://grandtextauto.org/2007/03/12/video-game-preservation-and-the-canon/>

Montfort, N. and Bogost, I. (2009) *Racing the Beam: The Atari Video Computer System*, Cambridge, MA: MIT Press.

Moore, C. (2009) 'Digital Games Distribution: The Presence of the Past and the Future of Obsolescence', *M/C Journal*, 12(3) <http://journal.media-culture.org.au/index.php/mcjournal/article/viewArticle/166>

Moore, G. (1965) 'Cramming More Components onto Integrated Circuits', *Electronics Magazine*, 38(8), 19 April.

Morgan, D. (2011) 'The Legend of Zelda: Ocarina of Time FAQ/Walkthrough' (version 1.25), *GameFAQs*, last updated 21 June 2011 <http://db.gamefaqs.com/console/n64/file/zelda_64.txt>

Morris, S. (2003) 'WADs, Bots and Mods: Multiplayer: FPS Games as Co-creative Media', in M. Copier and J. Raessens (eds) *Level Up: Digital Games Research Conference Proceedings*, University of Utrecht (CD-ROM).

Moulthrop, S. (2004) 'From Work to Play: Molecular Culture in the Time of Deadly Games', in N. Wardrip-Fruin and N. Harrigan (eds) *First Person: New Media as Story Performance, and Game*, Cambridge, MA: MIT Press, pp. 56–70.

Nader, M. (2004) 'The Secret of MissingNo', *Team Rocket's Rockin* <http://www.trsrockin.com/missingno_fic.html>

Neville, B. and Villeneuve, J. (2002) (eds) *Waste-Site Stories: The Recycling of Memory*, New York: State University of New York Press.

Newman, J. (2002) 'In Search of the Videogame Player: The Lives of Mario', *New Media and Society*, 4(3), pp. 407–25.

——(2004) *Videogames*, London: Routledge.

——(2005) 'Playing (with) Videogames', *Convergence: The International Journal of Research into New Media Technologies*, 11(1) pp. 48–67.

——(2008) *Playing with Videogames*, Abingdon: Routledge.

——(2009) 'On Emulation', *The National Videogame Archive blog*, 6 April <http://natio-nalvideogamearchive.org/archives/61>

——(2011) '(Not) Playing Games: Player-Produced Walkthroughs as Archival Documents of Digital Gameplay', *The International Journal of Digital Curation*, 6(2) <http://www.ijdc.net/index.php/ijdc/article/view/186/266>

Newman, J. and Oram, B. (2006) *Teaching Videogames*, London: BFI Publishing.

Newman, J. and Woolley, T. (2009) 'Make Videogames History: Game Preservation and The National Videogame Archive', *Proceedings of DiGRA 2009*, Brunel University, London <http://wiki.igda.org/images/d/d5/State_of_Play_National_Videogame_Archive.pdf>

NGamer LoZ3D Preview (2010) 'The Legend of Zelda: Ocarina of Time 3D – Hands On!', *Ngamer: Nintendo Magazine*, Bath: Future Publishing, p. 23.

NGamer Pokémon Review (2011) 'Pokémon Black/White', *Ngamer: Nintendo Magazine*, Bath: Future Publishing, pp. 56–59.

Nintendo (2003) *The Legend of Zelda: Ocarina of Time: GameCube Collector's Edition*, instruction manual.

Nintendo Legal Information (2011) 'Legal Information (Copyrights, Emulators, ROMs, etc.)', *Nintendo.com* <http://www.nintendo.com/corp/legal.jsp>

Nintendo Network @ E3 (2011) 'Wii U Demonstration [E3 demonstration video]', Nintendo corporate website (US), <http://e3.nintendo.com/hw/#/video/HW_demo>

Norman, D.A. (1988) *The Invisible Computer*, Cambridge, MA: MIT Press.

Nutt, C. (2008) 'He Is 8-Bit: Capcom's Hironobu Takeshita Speaks', *Gamasutra*, 4 August <http://www.gamasutra.com/view/feature/3752/>

Pacey, A. (1983) *The Culture of Technology*, Cambridge, MA: MIT Press.

Packard, V. (1960) *The Waste Makers*, New York: David McKay Company.

Pakinkis, T. (2010) 'News – Pre-owned "Cheats Developers" – THQ', *Computer-AndVideoGames.com*, 23 August <http://www.computerandvideogames.com/261330/pre-owned-cheats-developers-thq/>

Parfitt, B. (2010) 'Pre-owned Claims 50% of GameStop Profit', *MCV* [online edition], 18 November <http://www.mcvuk.com/news/read/pre-owned-claims-50-of-gamestop-profit>

——(2011a) 'Nintendo won't abandon buttons', *MCV* [online edition], 3 May <http://www.mcvuk.com/news/read/nintendo-won-t-abandon-buttons>

——(2011b) 'GAME – "Wii successor will 'challenge conventions'"', *MCV* [online edition], 26 April <http://www.mcvuk.com/news/read/game-wii-successor-will-challenge-con-ventions>

——(2011c) 'HMV offers £200 3DS Trade-in Guarantee', *MCV* [online edition], 21 March <http://www.mcvuk.com/news/read/hmv-offers-200-3ds-trade-in-guarantee>

——(2011d) 'GAME reveals 3DS Play-Trade DEAL', *MCV* [online edition], 22 February <http://www.mcvuk.com/news/read/game-reveals-3ds-play-trade-deal>

Parikka, J. and Suominen, J. (2006) 'Victorian Snakes? Towards a Cultural History of Mobile Games and the Experience of Movement', *Game Studies*, 6(1) <http://games-tudies.org/0601/articles/parikka_suominen>

Patterson, P. (2011) 'Donkey Kong Turns 30: How this Arcade Classic Shaped Today's Video Game World', *Examiner.com*, 10 July <http://www.examiner.com/arcade-game-in-national/donkey-kong-turns-30-how-this-arcade-classic-shaped-today-s-video-game-world>

Petit, M. (2006) 'Cleaned to eBay Standards: Sex Panic, eBay, and the Moral Economy of Underwear', in K. Hillis, M. Petit and Epley, M. (eds) *Everyday eBay: Culture, Collecting and Desire*, New York and London: Routledge, pp. 267–81.

Pigna, K. (2008) 'TGS 08: Microsoft Holding Off on Delisting XBLA Games', *1Up.com*, 12 October <http://www.1up.com/news/tgs-08-microsoft-holding-delisting>

Pinch, T. and Trocco, F. (2002) *Analog Days*, Cambridge, MA and London: Harvard University Press.

Pinchbeck, D., Anderson, D., Delve, J., Otemu, G., Ciuffreda, A. and Lange, A. (2009) 'Emulation as a Strategy for the Preservation of Games: The KEEP Project', *Proceedings of DiGRA 2009*, Brunel University, London <http://wiki.igda.org/images/d/d7/State_of_Play_The_KEEP_project.pdf>

Pine, J. and Gilmore, J. (1999) *The Experience Economy: Work Is Theatre and Every Business Is a Stage*, Cambridge, MA: Harvard Business School Press.

Pogue, D. (2009) 'Should You Worry About Data Rot?', *New York Times* [online], 26 March <http://pogue.blogs.nytimes.com/2009/03/26/should-you-worry-about-data-rot/>

Purchese, R. (2011) 'NGP Becomes PlayStation Vita', *Eurogamer*, 7 June <http://www.eurogamer.net/articles/2011-06-07-ngp-playstation-vita-european-price>

Rauch, J. (2011) 'The Origin of Slow Media: Early Diffusion of a Cultural Innovation through Popular and Press Discourse, 2002–10', *Transformations*, 20.

RawmeatCowboy (2011) 'How to Clean Game Cartridges', *GoNintendo*, February 6 <http://gonintendo.com/viewstory.php?id=149465>

Roberts, D. (2011) 'Yarnton: Today 3D Goes Truly Mainstream', *MCV* [online edition], 25 March <http://www.mcvuk.com/news/43649/Yarnton-Today-3D-goes-truly-main-stream>

Rohde-Enslin, S. and Allen, K. (2009) *Nothing Lasts Forever*, nestor/Institute for Museum Research, Germany <http://files.d-nb.de/nestor/ratgeber/ratg01_2_en.pdf>

Ronaghan, N. (2011) 'How DS Games Look on 3DS', *Nintendo World Report*, 26 March <http://www.nintendoworldreport.com/feature/25857>

Rouse, R. (1999) 'Everything Old is New Again', *Computer Graphics*, 33(2) <http://www.siggraph.org/publications/newsletter/v33n2/columns/rouse.html>

Ruggill, J. and McAllister, K. (2009) 'What if We Do Nothing?', in Lowood, H. (ed.) *Before It's Too Late: A Digital Game Preservation White Paper*, pp. 16–19 <http://www.igda.org/wiki/images/8/83/IGDA_Game_Preservation_SIG–Before_It%27s_Too_Late–A_Digital_Game_Preservation_White_Paper.pdf>

SCE (2000a) *Sony Computer Entm't v. Connectix Corp.*, 203 F.3d 596 (9th Cir. 2000).

——(2000b) *Sony Computer Entm't v. Bleem, LLC*, 214 F.3d 1022 (9th Cir. 2000).

Sega Enterprises (1995) *Virtua Fighter 2 Instruction Manual* (Sega Saturn).

Sega Ultimate Collection (2009) *Sega MegaDrive Ultimate Collection*, back cover, PlayStation 3 packaging.

Serrels, M. (2011) 'Mods vs Lockers: Region Coding and the Legal Dilemma', *Kotaku*, 16 February <http://www.kotaku.com.au/2011/02/mods-vs-lockers-region-coding-and-the-legal-dilemma/>

Shabtai, J. (2011) 'It's a Dark Time for the Rebellion', *Shabtallica*, 28 March <http://joshshabtai.squarespace.com/journal/2011/3/28/it-is-a-dark-time-for-the-rebellion.html>

Sheff, D. (1993) *Game Over: Nintendo's Battle to Dominate an Industry*, London: Hodder and Stoughton.

Silwinski, A. (2011) 'Alice: Madness Returns "Online Pass" grants you Alice 1 (it's $10 otherwise)', *Joystiq*, 20 April <http://www.joystiq.com/2011/04/20/alice-madness-returns-online-pass-grants-you-alice-1-10-ot/>

Simpsons, The (2000) 'Lisa the Treehugger' (Series 12, Episode 4), first aired 19 November 2000, Fox.

Siwek, S. (2007) 'Video Games in the 21st Century: Economic Contributions of the U.S. Entertainment Software Industry', *Entertainment Software Association* <http://www.theesa.com/newsroom/2007_eireport.pdf>

——(2010) 'Video Games in the 21st Century: The 2010 Report', *Entertainment Software Association* <http://www.theesa.com/facts/pdfs/VideoGames21stCentury_2010.pdf>

Skågeby, J. (2011) 'Slow and Fast Music Media: Comparing Values of Cassettes and Playlists', *Transformations*, 20.

Slade, G. (2006) *Made to Break: Technology and Obsolescence in America*, Cambridge, MA: Harvard University Press.

Slater, D. (2000) 'Consumption with Scarcity: Exchange and Normativity in an Internet Setting', in P. Jackson, M. Lowe, D. Miller and F. Mort (eds) *Consumer Cultures: Economies, Practices, Space*, Oxford: Berg.

Smart, B. (2010) *Consumer Society: Critical Issues and Environmental Consequences*, London: Sage.

Software Preservation Society (2009) 'Bit Rot', Software Preservation Society, 7 May <http://www.softpres.org/glossary:bit_rot>

Somers, D. (2011) 'Nintendo 3DS and DS Games: The Truth', *Jalada*, 27 March <http://jalada.co.uk/2011/03/27/nintendo-3ds-and-ds-games-the-truth.html>

SonicAD (n.d.) 'Different Versions of Sonic 1', *GameFAQs* (Sonic Mega Collection Cheats) <http://www.gamefaqs.com/gamecube/561899-sonic-mega-collection/cheats>

Sonic Retro (2010) 'Spike Damage Behavior', *Sonic Retro*, 9 April <http://info.sonicretro.org/Spike_damage_behavior>

Sony Computer Entertainment (2011) 'Sony Computer Entertainment Announces "PlayStation®Vita" as the Official Name for Next Generation Portable Entertainment System', Corporate Press Release, 6 June, Tokyo <http://www.prnewswire.com/news-releases/sony-computer-entertainment-announces-playstationvita-as-the-official-name-for-next-generation-portable-entertainment-system-123288538.html>

Sony Computer Entertainment America (2011) 'Can I Play PlayStation (or PS one) and PlayStation 2 Software Titles on the PlayStation 3 Computer Entertainment System?', *PlayStation.com* [US] <http://us.playstation.com/support/answer/index.htm?a_id=232>

Sony Computer Entertainment Europe (2007) *PlayStation 3*, marketing materials.

——(2008) 'How Do I Check the Compatibility of PlayStation and PlayStation 2 Format Software Titles for Use on the PLAYSTATION 3 System?', *PlayStation.com* (Europe) <http://faq.en.playstation.com/app/answers/detail/a_id/161>

Steppe (n.d.) *How to Rip SID Music for Dummies* <www.hvsc.c64.org/download/files/docs/Ripping_For_Dummies.zip>

Sterling, B. (1995) 'The Dead Media Project: A Modest Proposal and a Public Appeal', *Dead Media Project* <http://www.deadmedia.org/modest-proposal.html>

——(2011) 'Dead Media Beat: Federico Giordano, "Almost the Same Game"', *Wired*, 21 April <http://www.wired.com/beyond_the_beyond/2011/04/dead-media-beat-federico-giordano-almost-the-same-game/>

Sterne, J. (2007) 'Out With the Trash: On the Future of New Technologies', in C. Acland (ed.) *Residual Media*, Minneapolis, MN: University of Minnesota Press, pp. 16–31.

Stone of Agony (n.d.) 'Stone of Agony', *Zeldapedia* <http://zelda.wikia.com/wiki/Stone_of_Agony>

Strasser, S. (1999) *Waste and Want: A Social History of Trash*, New York: Henry Holt and Company.

Straw, W. (2000) 'Exhausted Commodities: The Material Culture of Music', *Canadian Journal of Communication*, 25(1) <http://cjc-online.ca/index.php/journal/article/view/1148/1067>

——(2007) 'Embedded Memories', in C. Acland (2007) (ed.) *Residual Media*, Minneapolis, MN: University of Minnesota Press, pp.3–15.

Stuart, K. (2011) 'Sony to Launch PSP Follow-up This Year', *Guardian Games Blog*, 27 January <http://www.guardian.co.uk/technology/gamesblog/2011/jan/27/sony-announces-psp-sequel-ngp>

Surman, D. (2010) 'Everyday Hacks: Why Cheating Matters', in R. Catlow, Garret, M. and C. Morgana (eds) *Artists Re:Thinking Games*, Liverpool: Liverpool University Press, pp. 74–7.

Svensson, C. (2011a) 'Stuff You Want to Know About SSFIV-AE for PC', *Capcom-Unity.com*, 25 May <http://www.capcom-unity.com/sven/blog/2011/05/25/stuff_you_ want_to_know_about_ssfiv:ae_for_pc>

——(2011b) 'SSFIV: AE PC – DRM: We Had It Wrong', *Capcom-Unity.com*, 2 June <http://www.capcom-unity.com/sven/blog/2011/06/02/ssfiv:_ae_pc–drm:_we_had_it_wrong>

Svensson, P. (2004) 'CDs and DVDs not So Immortal After All', *USA Today*, 5 May.

Swalwell, M. (2007) 'The Remembering and the Forgetting of Early Digital Games: From Novelty to Detritus and Back Again', *Journal of Visual Culture*, 6(2), pp. 255–73.

——(2009) 'Towards the Preservation of Local Computer Game Software: Challenges, Strategies, Reflections', *Convergence: The International Journal of Research into New Media Technologies*, 15(3), pp. 263–79.

swbruni (2011) 'Gears of War 3 Epic Edition Whats in it ?', *Epic Games Community Forum* (posted 20 March 2011) <http://forums.epicgames.com/threads/769663-Gears-of-War-3-Epic-Edition-Whats-in-it>.

Sweeney, M. (2003) 'TBWA Uses Humorous Tone in Its New Sony PlayStation Campaign', *Brand Republic*, 18 July <http://www.brandrepublic.com/News/185775/TBWA-uses-humorous-tone-its-new-Sony-PlayStation-campaign/>

taku (2011) 'Nintendo 3DS European Launch' p. 27 [untitled post to thread], NeoGAF, 27 March <http://www.neogaf.com/forum/showthread.php?s=84ba5b39d6 dbd1051da08-ca52fcc9e95&p=26743219#post26743219>

Taub, E. (2004) 'In Video Games, Sequels Are Winners', *New York Times*, 20 September <http://www.nytimes.com/2004/09/20/technology/20game.html?_r=1>

Taylor, A. (1982) 'Pac-Man Finally Meets His Match', *Time Magazine*, 20 December <http://www.time.com/time/printout/0,8816,923197,00.html>

Taylor, T.L. (2003) 'Multiple Pleasures: Women and Online Gaming', *Convergence: The International Journal of Research into New Media Technologies*, 9(1), pp. 21–46.

therat123 (2010) 'Sonic the Hedgehog iPhone 1.2.6 review', iTunes App Store, 22 August.

Thomas, L. (2006) 'Donkey Kong Virtual Console Review', *IGN*, 1 December <http://uk.wii.ign.com/articles/748/748752p1.html>

Thompson, J., McAllister, K. and Ruggill, J. (2009) 'Onward Through the Fog: Computer Game Collection and the Play of Obsolescence', *M/C Journal*, 12(3) <http://journal.media-culture.org.au/index.php/mcjournal/article/viewArticle/155>

Thompson, M. (1979) *Rubbish Theory: The Creation and Destruction of Value*, Oxford: Oxford University Press.

Totilo, S. (2010) 'In Search of History's Best Video Games: Canon Fodder, Season One', *Kotaku*, 29 March <http://kotaku.com/5504403/in-search-of-historys-best-video-games-canon-fodder-season-one>

Toy Story (1995) dir: John Lassiter.

Trautman, E.S. (2004) *The Art of Halo: Creating a Virtual World*, New York: Del Rey.

Trina (2010) 'Buy Play Trade-Pre-owned Games now at more than 200 Asda Stores', *Your Asda*, 10 October <http://your.asda.com/2010/10/10/buy-and-trade-in-your-old-games-at-asda>

Vail, M. (2000) *Vintage Synthesizers*, San Francisco, CA: Miller Freeman.

Valve (2004) *Half-Life 2: Raising the Bar*, Roseville, CA: Prima Games.

Van den Eynden, V., Corti, L., Woollard, M. and Bishop, L. (2009) 'Managing and Sharing Data: A Best Practice Guide for Researchers [second edition]', Colchester: UK Data Archive <http://www.data-archive.ac.uk/media/2894/managingsharing.pdf>

van Lente, H. and Rip, A. (1998) 'Expectations in Technological Developments: An Example of Prospective Structures to be Filled in by Agency', in C. Disco and B. van de Meulen (eds) *Getting New Technologies Together*, Berlin: Walter de Gruyter, pp. 195–220.

Vowell, Z. (2009) 'What Constitutes History?' in H. Lowood (ed.) *Before It's Too Late: A Digital Game Preservation White Paper* <http://www.igda.org/wiki/images/8/83/IGDA_Game_Preservation_SIG–Before_It%27s_Too_Late–A_Digital_Game_Preservation_White_Paper.pdf>

Walker, W. (2003) 'Sonic the Hedgehog', *GameFAQs*, last updated 22 June 2003 <http://www.gamefaqs.com/genesis/454495-sonic-the-hedgehog/faqs/9357>

Watkins, E. (1993) *Throwaways: Work Culture and Consumer Education*, Stanford, CA: Stanford University Press.

Watson, J. (1999) *Literature and Material Culture from Balzac to Proust: The Collection and Consumption of Curiosities*, Cambridge: Cambridge University Press.

Watts, S. (2010) 'THQ Has Little Sympathy for Pre-Owned Buyers', *1Up.com*, 24 August <http://www.1up.com/news/thq-sympathy-pre-owned-buyers>

Welcome to MAME ... (n.d.) *MAME – The Official Site of the MAME Development Team* <http://mamedev.org>

Welsh, O. (2011) 'Game of the Week: Ico and Shadow of the Colossus Collection – Article', *Eurogamer*, 30 September 2011 <http://www.eurogamer.net/articles/2011-09-30-game-of-the-week-ico-and-shadow-of-the-colossus-collection-article>

Wheeler, B. (2003) 'Sony's Dancing Robot Hits the Mark', BBC News [online], 9 December <http://news.bbc.co.uk/1/hi/magazine/3301551.stm>

Which? (2010) 'Video Games Lose Value Faster than Used Cars', *Which?*, 26 December <http://www.which.co.uk/news/2010/12/video-games-lose-value-faster-than-used-cars-240675/>

White, M. (2006) 'My Queer eBay: "Gay Interest" Photographs and the Visual Culture of Buying', in K. Hillis, M. Petit and Epley, M. (eds) *Everyday eBay: Culture, Collecting and Desire*, New York and London: Routledge, pp. 245–65.

Whittaker, J. (2004) *The Cyberspace Handbook*, London: Routledge.

Wilonsky, R. (2002) 'Joystick Cinema: It's Man vs. Machinima when Video Games Become, Ahem, Movies', *Screen Entertainment Weekly*, 14 August.

Wilson, A. (2010) 'Online Pass Questions Answered', *EA Sports.com*, 10 May <http://www.easports.com/news/item/file/Online_Pass_Questions_Answered>

Wilson, J. and Jacobs, J. (2009) 'Obsolete', *M/C Journal*, 12(3) <http://journal.media-culture.org.au/index.php/mcjournal/article/viewArticle/170>

Woodward, S. (2006) Keynote presentation, BAFTA Video Games Awards, London.

World of Spectrum (2011a) 'Distribution Permissions – Individual Programmers – Artist', *World of Spectrum.org* <http://www.worldofspectrum.org/permits/individuals.html>

——(2011b) 'Distribution Permissions – Individual Software Houses', *World of Spectrum.org* <http://www.worldofspectrum.org/permits/publishers.html>

Yin-Poole, W. (2010) 'THQ-We Won't Punish Used Game Buyers', *Eurogamer.net*, 24 August <http://www.eurogamer.net/articles/2010-08-24-thq-we-wont-punish-used-game-buyers>

Zaitchik, A. (2007) 'Soviet-Era Arcade Games Crawl out of Their Cold War Graves', *Wired*, 7 June <http://www.wired.com/gaming/hardware/news/2007/06/soviet_games>

zGreeNArroWz (2011) 'Gears Of War 3 Epic Edition', *Epic Games Community Forum* (posted 21 March 2011) <http://forums.epicgames.com/threads/769834-Gears-Of-War-3-Epic-Edition>

INDEX